John Ha

Genesis 15

John Ha

Genesis 15

A Theological Compendium of
Pentateuchal History

Walter de Gruyter · Berlin · New York
1989

Beiheft zur Zeitschrift für die alttestamentliche Wissenschaft

Herausgegeben von Otto Kaiser

181

Printed on acid free paper
(ageing resistent — pH 7, neutral)

Library of Congress Cataloging-in-Publication Data

Ha, John, 1947—
    Genesis 15 : a theological compendium of pentateuchal history /
John Ha.
    p.   cm.   Beiheft zur Zeitschrift für die altestamentli-
che Wissenschaft, ISSN 0934 2575 ; 181)
    Revision of the author's thesis (doctoral—Pontifical Biblical
Institute, 1986)
    Bibliography: p.
    Includes indexes.
    ISBN 0-89925-291-5 (U.S. : alk. paper)
    1. Bible. O. T. Genesis XV—Criticism, interpretation, etc. I.
Title. II. Title: Genesis fifteen. III. Series: Beihefte zur
Zeitschrift für die alttestamentliche Wissenschaft ; 181.
BS410.Z6 vol. 181
[BS1235.2]
221.6 s—dc20
[222.1106]   89—12080
                                                               CIP

Deutsche Bibliothek Cataloguing in Publication Data

Ha, John:
[Genesis fifteen]
Genesis 15 : a theological compendium of Pentateuchal history /
John Ha. — Berlin ; New York : de Gruyter, 1989
    (Beiheft zur Zeitschrift für die alttestamentliche Wissenschaft ;
    181)
    Zugl.: Rom, Päpstl. Bibelinst., Diss., 1986
    ISBN 3-11-011206-X
NE: Zeitschrift für die alttestamentliche Wissenschaft / Beiheft

ISSN: 0934-2575

Gratefully dedicated to

My Father and Mother,
    my first teachers of God's Word;

Frs. J. L'Hour, MEP, and A. Cody, OSB,
    my first teachers of biblical
    exegesis

PREFACE

This work is a slightly revised edition of my doctoral dissertation defended at the Pontifical Biblical Institute, Rome, on June 2nd, 1986.

The dissertation was written under the competent direction of Professor J. Alberto Soggin. I am deeply grateful to him for his scholarly advice and friendly encouragement. My sincere thanks also go to R.P. Horacio Simian-Yofre, SJ, the second reader of my dissertation. His suggestion and sharp observations proved to be invaluable for my work. I would like to record a word of thanks to R.P. Aelred Cody, OSB, who guided my studies during my doctoral year. I am deeply indebted to Professor Otto Kaiser for graciously accepting this work for the series, Beihefte zur Zeitschrift für die alttestamentliche Wissenschaft.

Without the financial support of the Congregation for the Evangelization of Peoples, Rome, it would have been impossible for me to pursue my studies at the Pontifical Biblical Institute. My heartfelt thanks therefore go to the Cardinal Prefect and Secretary General of the Congregation for the scholarship they awarded me. At this juncture I would also like to thank my local Ordinary, Archbishop Peter Chung, for his kind approval of my study leave.

Finally, I would like to assure my many relatives and friends of my ever profound gratitude to them for their unfailing support and encouragement throughout the years of my work.

I deem it useful to note that due to lack of access to adequate library facilities, I have been unable to update my bibliography.

Kuching (Malaysia), February, 1989   John Ha

TABLE OF CONTENTS

INTRODUCTION

"Gen. 15 does not belong to the old material of the
Abraham tradition. Rather, at one time - before precedence
was given to the Hebrew stories that were linked to the figure of Abraham at a late stage - it was placed before the
Abraham story or probably even before the whole
'patriarchal' narrative as an introduction. This was done
in order to let the true basic motif of the 'patriarchal'
narrative - namely, the promise of descendants and the promise of arable land for the descendants - sound out immediately in an especially solemn way with the first appea-
rance of Abraham....even at that time the formulation
envisaged the grand unity of the Pentateuchal narrative,
which was already completed in its basic structure."

These are among the very few remarks about Gen. 15 that
the renowned Pentateuchal exegate, Martin Noth, has left us
with in his classic work, A History of Pentateuchal Traditions[1]. Complementing them is a statement he made in footnote 544: "According to the scanty E material preserved, in
E.... there is presented a programmatic summary of the entire Pentateuchal narrative in the form of the brief divine
prediction (vss 13-16)."

While we may question Noth's hypothesis about the original position of Gen. 15 and the presence of E in the chapter, his basic thesis about its summary nature seems to be
very well founded. It may well be the key to the understanding of the rather problematic chapter. Yet, G.W. Coats'
lament about Gen. 15:14, "The relationship between the unit
and the Exodus traditions in Ex. 5-13 has not yet been
adequately defined"[2], holds true also for the entire

---

1 Cf. pages 200f.
2 G.W. Coats VT, 18 (1968), 450, footnote 2.

chapter in respect of the entire Pentateuch.

The present work is an attempt to take up Coats' observation on a broader basis and elaborate on the relationship
in question in the direction of Noth's view about the literary character of Gen. 15. For this we are confronted with
a choice between at least two alternatives. The first is to
toe the line taken by Noth in his analysis of the composition of the Pentateuch. Noth's literary and traditio-
historical criticism would involve showing how the various
themes and perhaps brackettings strained out by Noth are
recapitulated in Gen. 15. Apart from its rather complex
intricacies, Noth's analysis makes certain connections
which do not seem to stand up to objections raised by a
few scholars like R.M. Polzin[3]. For this reason, I have op-
ted for the second alternative which is inspired by what
is called the 'new Pentateuchal criticism", although even
at the present time this approach has yet to offer a clear
and stable direction in Pentateuchal studies. Precisely because of its lack of clarity, it would be important for us
at this juncture to sketch the new approach briefly and
take a stand in respect of it. For the very same reason,
our presentation of it has to be restricted to the theories of individual studies. For our purpose, it suffices to
consider two major representatives of our school, namely,
John Van Seters and Rolf Rendtorff.

Restricting his study to the Abraham tradition,
Van Seters[4] undertakes an extensive critique of the external evidence for a datation of this tradition in the second
millennium B.C. All evidence seems rather to point to the
fact that the episodes making up this tradition "were
written from the historical and cultural perspective of
a later day"[5]. Van Seters ventures to support his stand

---

3 R.M Polzin, Biblical Structuralism, 174-201.
4 J. Van Seters, Abraham in History and Tradition.
5 Id, 121. The stories about the migatory movements of the patriarchs
  "recognize the spread of settlement in upper Mesopotamia and even
  lower Mesopotamia". The patriarchs' use of camels and tents and
  their contact with the established "Philistines" in the border re-
  region seem to fit in well with the mid-first millennium B.C. "The

through an extensive form and tradition analysis of the
traditions. In his attempt, he consciously and consistently
controls his source and traditio-historical analysis with
form criticism and structural analysis.

On the basis of his literary analysis of the patriarchal
tradition, especially Gen. 15[6], Van Seters concludes that
the Yahwistic version of the patriarchal history, considered as the earliest source, is to be dated in the exilic
period. For, it is closely connected with the Deuteronomic-
Deuteronomistic tradition. Consequently, the priestly
version which was a subsequent addition to the earlier
traditions must be later and post-exilic. The author questions the "whole existence of an extensive E source in the
Pentateuch"[7] while he maintains that "the Abraham corpus
does contain important examples of what have been characterized as Deuteronomistic redaction"[8]. However, Van Seters
does not give an explicit treatment of this redaction.

Van Seters' study is a success in so far as it "seeks to
raise more basic questions about the present method of evaluating the traditions about early Israel"[9]. Though "the
Abraham tradition is a most suitable unit for this purpose"[10] its scope is too restricted to allow conclusions to
be drawn about the literary sources of the rest of the
Pentateuch. Van Seters himself is well aware of this[11]. Thus,
his positions about the sources need to be tested for their
validity for the rest of the Pentateuch. This goes beyond

---

reference to Ur of the Chaldeans and its association with Haran
and a route to the West reflect the political circumstances of
the neo-Babylonian period." The invasion of Palestine by an eastern
coalition in Gen. 14 would have been impossible before the first
millennium B.C.

6 Van Seters maintains that "the heart of the problem of dating, as
well as the understanding of the Yahwist's 'message', lies in one's
evaluation of the promises to the fathers. The question of dating
can only be taken up after the literary, form-critical and
traditio-historical treatment of these promises, and especially
Genesis 15, has been finished" (153).
7 Id, 311.
8 Id, 131.
9 Id, 4.
10 Id, 4.
11 Id, 3.

the scope of the present dissertation. While leaving the door
open for the J and E strands, because they have been great-
ly disputed, it is quite commonly accepted that Dtr and P
were exilic schools. Van Seters' post-exilic datation of P
is to a great extent forced by his exilic datation of J.

   Pointing out the uncertainties of the "newer documentary
hypothesis" established under the influence of
J. Wellhausen, R. Rendtorff[12] proposes a new approach to
Pentateuchal criticism. The exegete is urged to take into
account the "larger units" out of which the Pentateuch has
been composed, namely, primeval history, patriarchal history, exodus narrative, Sinai pericope, tradition of
Israel's wandering through the wilderness, and narrative
about Israel's conquest of the land[13].

   Each of the larger units is made up of smaller narrative
traditions and shaped by certain perspectives and leading
theological ideas[14]. Thus, in the patriarchal history, the
two cycles (Abraham and Jacob) and the various stories
(Isaac and Joseph) find their distinctive mark in YHWH's
promise to the patriarchs. The focal point of the exodus
narrative is the exodus interpreted by faith. The larger
unit of the Sinai tradition highlights the special position
of Moses and connects it with the law. Israel's wandering
in the wilderness is marked by the people's "murmuring"
against YHWH and His servant Moses[15]. The Pentateuch ends
with Israel at the threshold of the promised land. That
part of the pre-settlement story places the people in
contact with the powers-that-be they had to reckon with as

---

12 R. Rendtorff, Das uberlief. Problem, 80-146. One point where there
   is such uncertainty concerns the E source. For quite a long time it
   was thought that the beginning of this source lay in Gen. 15. However, in the wake of more arguments for a Dtr character of the
   chapter, the E source has been given a new beginning - in Gen. 20.
   Another point of contention among source analysts revolves around the
   question as to whether later sources were independent of earlier
   ones and later combined with them, or whether they were later sup-
   plements or even new editions of the earlier ones.
13 Id, 29-79.
14 R. Rendtorff, The Old Testament, 161.
15 R. Rendtorff, Das uberlief. Problem, 73.

they made their entry into the land. It recalls the "credo"
formula (cf. Num. 20:15,16a)[16].

These larger units bear a certain continuity that holds
them together as one single history. Amongst the elements
fostering this unity, especially from Exodus to Numbers and
Deuteronomy, the figure of Moses stands out. But a greater
bond of unity is furnished by the theme of YHWH's oath to
the patriarchs. Indeed, the entire history of Israel presented in the Pentateuch is clearly a working out of YHWH's
promise[17].

Despite his position regarding the earlier sources of the
Pentateuch, Rendtorff accepts Dtr and P. However, like Van
Seters, he maintains that P is not an independent tradition
but rather a priestly revision of earlier sources[18]. Of the
two theological schools, Dtr seems to have exerted a much
greater influence on the redaction of the Pentateuch. The
literary relationship between the two schools in the Pentateuch is largely unclear.

Rendtorff's approach towards Pentateuchal criticism is
sound. For one thing, it is more objective and less specu-
lative than the documentary hypothesis which is often
guilty of an a-prioristic analysis of a text[19]. Moreover,
Rendtorff's analysis allows the critic to come to grips
with the relationship among the component passages of each
larger unit as well as among the larger units themselves.
This is important as it leads to a deeper understanding of
the theology of both the larger units and the Pentateuch as
a whole. A serious weakness of the documentary hypothesis
is that it concentrates almost all attention on small units
so that the analyst is lost in a forest of such units. And
yet, these small units are there to enhance the theology of
the larger unit.

---

16 Das überlief. Problem, 74.
17 Id, 147.
18 Id, 112-142.
19 A good illustration of such a-prioristic analysis is the attribution
   of a text to P on the basis of a precise chronology. Cf. Rendtorff's
   handling of this criterion in Das überlief. Problem, 131-136.

The present study has benefitted from Rendtorff's
approach. His conclusion about the important role played by
the theme of YHWH's promise to the patriarchs in the theological redaction of the Pentateuch increases the present
author's confidence in tracing the suspected relationship
between Gen. 15 and the Pentateuch. The "larger units"
highlighted by Rendtorff have provided an insight into how
the various parts of Gen. 15 recapitulate the different
major historical sections of the Pentateuch: patriarchal
history, the journey to and sojourn in Egypt, the exodus
tradition, the Sinai pericope, and the journey to the promised land. This has naturally saved the present study the
ordeal of a very complicated analysis of the chapter from
the standpoint of literary and tradition criticisms. The
two latter approaches have yielded very different
results[20]. If this is true of just one chapter, how much
truer would it be for the entire Pentateuch.

Gen. 15, even on first reading, strikes one as a theological composition. Thus, it is not to be taken as a mere
compendium of Pentateuchal history but a theological one.
The theology reflects the basic theological thrust of the
Pentateuch itself, although where necessary the author of
Gen. 15 seems to have taken the liberty to introduce his
own reinterpretation.

Gen. 15 is not the only theological compendium in the OT.
At least three others have been detected: Jos. 11:16-12:24;
23; and Jdg. 2:6-3:6[21]. Without subjecting themselves to
any fixed literary form, these compendia serve either to
introduce or conclude a particular book or section thereof.
The two pericopes from Joshua are examples of the latter.

---

20 Cf. table between pages 30 and 31, and schema on pages 31-33 of the
   present thesis.
21 R. Rendtorff The Old Testament, 184. Two other possible Dtr compendia are 2 K 17:7-20 and 22f (cf. Id, 184, 186). The former provides
   a theological explanation for the fall of the Northern Kingdom in
   the hands of the Assyrians and the exile of its citizens: Israel's
   apostasy and persistent disregard for the repeated warnings given
   her. The latter, according to Rendtorff, is "the real conclusion" to

Jos. 11:16-12:24 reviews the subject matter of Jos. 1:1-11:
15 (i.e. the conquest of the land) in 11:16-23 and lists
out the kings conquered in the east of the Jordan (12:1-6)
as well as in the west (12:7-24). Similarly, Jos. 23 concludes the Deuteronomic edition of the narrative of the
conquest[22] by taking up concrete passages like 21:43-45 and
22:1-6 and even having v. 16 continued in 24:28[23]. It needs
to be pointed out that the resumes are not merely historical. Their theological character is marked by their intention to impress upon the readers that the whole conquest of
the land is YHWH's doing. This is clear from the theological interpretation in 11:20,23. The past is presented as a
theological motive for an appeal to a steadfast fidelity to
YHWH (23:6,11-12,15-16).

Jdg. 2:6-3:6[24] serves not only to introduce but also set
the tone for what is to come in the chapters following it
in the Book of Judges. It resumes Jos. 24:18-31[25] in 2:6-10
and summarizes the standard pattern followed by each narrative about Israel's judges[26]: Israel's sin of apostasy and
idolatry (vv. 11-13) - YHWH's anger and judgement by giving

---

the Dtr history as it "represents the concluding summary of the cult
in Israel and Judah" (186).

22 Thus A.J. Soggin, Joshua, 217.

23 Id. K. Baltzer, The Covenant Formulary, 61-65, detects the structure
of the covenant formula behind the composition of Jos. 23. Soggin,
Id, thinks that the reason for this is that Jos. 23 "was perhaps intended to replace ch. 24, because it was not possible to reedit it
fully without emptying it of its original content." For the covenantal formula underlying the structure of Jos. 23, cf. J.L'Hour,
RB, 69 (1962), 5-36, 161-184, 350-368; and L. Perlitt, Bunderstheo-
logie, 239-284.

24 There is no literary unity in this text. Cf. J.A. Soggin, Judges,
41-42.

25 Strictly speaking, it is only vv.7 and 10 that logically follow after Jos. 24:28-30. Vv. 6 and 8-9 were most probably late additions;
cf. Soggin, Id.

26 The pattern is followed regardless of whether the narrative is about
"judges" in the strict sense or about "judges" who are in fact "saviours". W. Richter makes a distinction between the two senses and
maintains that the "Retterbuch" (i.e. "the Book of Saviours") is the
original core of the Book of Judges. This core was enlarged by a later author and further expanded by two "Deuteronomic" redactors. Cf.
W. Richter's two important works, Traditionsgeschichtliche Untersu-
uchungen zum Richterbuch and Die Bearbeitungen "Retterbuches".

His people over to their enemies (vv. 14-15) - Israel's cry
of distress (v. 18bB) - YHWH's appointment of judges to
serve them (vv. 16-18bA) - Israel's relapse into sin on the
death of each judge (v. 19) leading to a repetition of the
cycle for the next judge. The pattern itself, though having
to deal with history, is clearly theological in character[27]. As an introduction, it is programmatic in function.

A common denominator among these compendia is their theological interpretation of historical events which they seek
to summarize. History, therefore, becomes the locus of Israel's experience of YHWH and relationship with Him. On this
ground, the past does have a bearing on the present and
holds out hope for the future. This is precisely what the
author of Gen. 15 set out to do in his masterly composition:
to present Israel's history in the Pentateuch as a 'type'of
that of his own generation and assure the latter, on the
basis of YHWH's oath to Abraham, that they would experience
YHWH's intervention as their forefathers did.

Certain traits of prophetic influence are apparent in the
chapter. They have led me to believe that this influence is
not merely a general one but has come from particular prophets like Isaiah and Jeremiah. Thus, another major concern
of this thesis is to demonstrate the influence of these prophets on the chapter.

Finally, two questions that deserve full attention, if
Gen. 15 is taken as a compendium, are: (i) is the chapter a
literary unity? and (ii) why is it found where it is and
not, as would normally be expected, before Gen. 12? A logical procedure requires the first question to be treated at
the very outset. The second question, however, would seem
to be best dealt with at the end of the thesis as certain
elements for consideration would have to presuppose one or
another section of the rest of the thesis.

A word must now be said about the methodology adopted in
this work. First of all, with regard to the literary unity

---

27 Cf. W. Richter, Die Bearbeitungen "Retterbuches", 87ff.

of the chapter, an analysis is made of the relationship -
literary, grammatical, thematic and functional - among all
the verses of the chapter. This is followed by a study of
how these verses and their relationships are organized into
a coherent whole.

Then there is the relationship that Gen. 15 bears to each
of the larger units of the Pentateuch. As the title of the
thesis suggests, our task is to trace this relationship in
terms of recapitulation and theology. Convenience dictates
that we consider the element of theology first. By theology, in respect of the relationship under study, is meant
very strictly the two theologoumena: YHWH's oath to the patriarchs (comprising all or part of His promises of
blessing, guidance, son, descendants and land); and the patriarch's response of faith supported by signs. These
theologoumena, which must be distinguished from "themes",
play a dominant role in Gen. 15 as well as in the Pentateuch.

Our demonstration of this focuses on the strategic positions the theologoumena occupy in the patriarchal traditions
and their role as the vital force as well as the goal of
Israel's history in the other larger units. YHWH's oath to
the patriarchs and the response of faith to it "co-shaped"
Israel's history in the Pentateuch.

The recapitulation aspect of the relationship between
Gen. 15 and each of the larger units is traced mainly
through an analysis of the vocabulary and, if need be, the
themes as well as their arrangement in both the texts under
study. This approach also applies to the prophetic texts
believed to have exerted a certain influence on Gen. 15.
With regard to vocabulary, affirmation of relationship is
made only when it has been shown that a certain word used
in Gen. 15 and its parallel has, apart from its general
meaning, the same specific sense in both texts. Thus, for
example, the word "Shield", when used metaphorically of
YHWH, has the general sense of "protector" in all the texts
where it occurs. But in Gen. 15:1 and Dt. 33:29, it takes
on a special sense: that of YHWH's relationship to Israel

as her protector through the gradual working out of His oath
to the patriarchs. It is this special sense that founds a
relationship between the two texts. Or, if two different
words are used in Gen. 15 and another text believed to be
its parallel, their relationship is maintained only after
proving that the two words are synonymous and refer to the
same event in both texts. A case in point is dān in Gen.
15:14aB and špṭ in Ex. 6:2-8 and 7:1-5. Both words have the
same sense of judgement unleashed by YHWH through the ten
plagues prior to the exodus.

At the level of themes, contacts between Gen. 15 and
other OT texts are less readily maintained "sui iuris" than
those based on vocabulary, except in cases where there is
support from the latter. It is on the basis of the existence of a number of similar themes in a similar context
and at times with a similar arrangement of the themes that
relationship between two texts is maintained. For example,
the Balaam story in Num. 22-24 is of interest to the author
of Gen. 15 because of its dominant theme of blessing (cf.
Num. 22:12; 23:8,20; 24:1,9) which encompasses the vital
contents of YHWH's oath to Abraham, namely, posterity (Num.
23:10; 24:7a) and land (Num. 24:18f). For, the recurrence
in both Gen. 15 and Num. 22-24 of the theme together with
that of maḥăzeh (Num. 24:4,16; Gen. 15:1) in the context of
the conquest of Israel's enemies (Num. 21:21-35) generi-
cally represented by the Amorites (Gen, 15:16) could hardly
be fortuitous.

The above exposition of the methodology touches on the
more commonly applied approaches in the thesis. The "odd"
ones (e.g. the similar pattern in which the materials of
Gen. 15 and Is. 7:1-17 are organized) have to be left to
sections where they are discussed.

To close our introduction, a remark must be made on the
principle whereby the thesis affirms the dependence of
Gen. 15 on the historical corpus of the Pentateuch as well
as certain parts of prophetic literature. The points of contact between the chapter and all these other areas of OT
traditions are too many and too close to be merely a matter

of coincidence. There must therefore be a certain relationship of dependence between them. The very intricate network
Gen. 15 builds up with these traditions does not allow for
the possibility of the chapter being a blueprint for an expansion into Pentateuchal history. Likewise, the fact that
the prophetic literature rarely alludes to patriarchal traditions makes it highly improbable that Jer. 34:18-20 and
Is. 7:1-17 would have drawn on Gen. 15. Positively, we must
affirm that Gen. 15 was composed as a theological compendium of Pentateuchal history and its prophetic flavour came
from the prophetic schools in general and Jeremiah and
Isaiah in particular.

PART ONE

GENESIS 15: UNITY AND PROPHETIC INFLUENCE

CHAPTER 1

TEXT, PROBLEMS AND SOLUTIONS

1. Text

Since not everything about the sense of Gen. 15 has met
the unanimous agreement of exegetes, it would be useful to
provide a translation of the text with comments to explain
the option made in this work. For ease of reference later
on, the presentation of the translated text divides the
verses into their component stichs followed throughout the
present work.

1. Translation and Division

```
1aA: After these things,
 aB: YHWH's word came to Abram
 aC: in a vision to this effect:
 bA: "Fear not, Abram!
 bB: I am your Shield.
 bC: Your reward (will be) very great!"
2aA: Whereupon Abram said,
 aB: "Adonay YHWH, what will You give me,
 bA: whilst I am going (to my death) childless
 bB: and the usurper of my house - he is a Damascene - is Eliezer?"
3aA: And Abram said,
 aB: "Behold, to me You have not given any offspring,
 bA: and so, here is this steward of mine
 bB: (ever-ready) to succeed me."
4aA: There therefore came this word of YHWH's to him:
 aB: "This (one) will not succeed you;
 bA: rather the one to issue from your own flesh-and-blood
 bB: he indeed will succeed you."
5aA: Then He took him outside
```

```
aB: and said, "Look toward the sky and count the stars,
bA: if indeed you can count them."
bB: Then He said to him, "Thus will your descendants be!"
6a : He kept his faith in YHWH
 b : while He reckoned it to him as righteousness.
7aA: And then He said to him,
 aB: "I am YHWH who brought you out
 bA: from Ur of the Chaldaeans
 bB: to give you this land to possess."
8a : Whereupon he said,
 b : "Adonay YHWH, how am I to know that I shall possess it?"
9aA: He said to him,
 aB: "Bring Me a three-year-old heifer,
 bA: a three-year-old she-goat and a three-year-old ram,
 bB: and a turtledove and a young pigeon."
10aA: And he brought Him all these;
 aB: then, he cut them into halves,
 bA: and placed each part against the other;
 bB: but the birds he did not cut.
11a : Then there descended birds to prey on the carcasses
 b : and Abram drove them away.
12aA: As the sun was just about to set,
 aB: a deep sleep fell upon Abram
 bA: and at the same time fear
 bB: of a great darkness
 bC: fell upon him.
13aA: Then (YHWH) said to Abram, "Know for sure
 aB: that your descendants shall be foreigners
 aC: in a land not their own
 bA: and will be slaves to those
 bB: who will oppress them
 bC: for four hundred years.
14aA: But indeed the nation which they will be serving
 aB: I Myself will judge,
 bA: after which they will come out
 bB: with great wealth.
15a : As for yourself, however, you will go to your fathers in peace;
 b : you will be buried in a good old age.
16a : Four generations afterwards they will return here
 b : since the iniquity of the Amorites is not yet complete."
17aA: When the sun had set
 aB: and darkness fallen,
 bA: there appeared a smoking fire-pot
 bB: and a flaming torch
 bC: which passed between these parts.
18a : On that day, YHWH swore an oath to Abram saying:
 b : "To your descendants I have decided to give this land,
 c : from the River of Egypt to the Great River, the River Euphrates,
19  : the land of the Kenites, the Kenizzites, the Kadmonites,
20  : the Hittites, the Perizzites, the Rephaim,
21  : the Amorites, the Canaanites, the Girgashites and the Jebusites."
```

2. Comments

V. 1bB

From the widespread application in the OT, especially in
the Psalms[1], of *māgēn* in its metaphorical sense to YHWH, we
do not see any need to revocalize the Hebrew root at all[2].
Neither do we agree with the opinion that "shield" just
does not fit in with the present context[3] since it refers
to YHWH.

---

1 Cf. Dt. 33:29; 2 Sam. 22:3,31,36; Prov. 2:7; 30:5; Pss. 3:4; 7:11;
  18:31,36; 28:7; 33:20; 35:2; 59:12; 84:10,12; 89:19; 115:9,10,11;
  119:114.
2 In his article in VT, 14 (1964), 494-497, M. Kessler maintains that
  'ānōkî is an emphatic form of *'ănî* and *māgēn* being "a new element in
  the clause", is also emphatic. On the ground that one emphatic immediately following another is "a highly unlikely situation", he proposes a revocalization of *mgn* to *mōgēn*, its *qal* participle. He maintains that *mgn* is a poetic motif-word for "to give" and is one of the
  key words recurring in Gen. 14 (cf. v. 20) and 15. "Then the oracle
  in XV 1 may be seen as a spiritual 'heightening' of XIV 20: it is important that God should 'give' Abraham's enemies into his hand, but
  far superior is the 'very great reward' which God is about to give
  Abraham by virtue of the covenant" (496). To support the grammatical
  construction of *'ānōkî* + a *qal* participle, he cites Gen. 15:2; 16:2;
  Jer. 32:42. We do not deny the correctness of this grammatical construction. But it seems doubtful to us that (i) there is any ground
  for taking *mgn* in the poetic sense of "to give" or "to deliver"; and
  (ii) *'ānōkî* is the emphatic form of *'ănî*. Moreover, Kessler's proposal gives rise to an objection which he fails to provide an answer
  to, namely, "On the other hand, Yahweh's designation as *māgēn*
  (shield) is well attested in the Psalms" (496). Another difficulty
  has to do with the appeal to *mgn* in Gen. 14:20 for support for the
  poetic sense of the root in Gen. 15:1. It must be noted that in Gen.
  14:20 *mgn* occurs in its *piel* conjugation while in our text Kessler
  proposes a *qal* participle for the root.
3 In interpreting *mgn*, we cannot ignore the view of a renowned Ugaritic
  scholar, the late M. Dahood. In his article in Bib, 55 (1974), 76-82,
  he saw an incongruity between "shield" and "great reward". Thus, he
  felt the need to repoint *māgēn* (=shield) to *māgān* (=suzerain), arguing that the question *mah titten lî* is "more properly addressed to a
  sovereign than to a shield" (cf. 78). We take issue with Dahood here
  because his problem of incongruity results from his strictly literal
  understanding of "shield" while its usage in not a few Psalms (cf.
  e.g. 3:4; 18:3,31; 28:7; etc.) seems to be metaphorical depicting God

V. 2bA

The word ʿărîrî is found only four times in the Hebrew OT:
twice in the singular in Gen. 15:2 and Jer. 22:30 and twice
in the plural in Lev. 20:20,21. Its Hebrew root is clear,
that is, ʿrr meaning "to be stripped" or "to strip oneself"[4]. Situated within the context of Gen. 15:2-4, which
talks about a blood-heir, ʿărîrî quite obviously takes on
an extended meaning, that is, "childless" (="stripped of"
children)[5]. This, in fact, is the meaning intended in
Jer. 22:30 and Lev. 20:20,21.

---

as Protector. On this point, cf. C. Westermann, Genesis 12-36, 258-
259. To YHWH as "Shield" the question *mah titten lî* could be properly
addressed in our text as much as in Pss. 59:12 and 84:10. O. Loretz's
rendering of *mgn* as "Geschenk" (cf. UF, 6 (1975), 492) is doubtful
because of the difficulties involved. For, quite apart from the lack
of OT evidence of YHWH being personally presented as man's "reward",
the parallelism he traces between *mgn* and *śkr* would have either
(i) omitted the pronominal suffix of *śkr* so that *lk* serves as the indirect object for both *mgn* and *śkr* or (ii) repeated *lk* for *śkr* in
place of the pronominal suffix.

4 Cf. BDB, ad loc.. H. Cazelles' interpretation of the word, as proposed in RB, 69 (1962), 321-349, deserves a discussion here. First of
all, he thinks that "la traduction de ʿaryry par 'sans enfant' dans
ce passage est beaucoup moins sûre qu'il n'apparaît a première vue.
Le mot est rare et ne se trouve qu'en Jér., xxii,30 et Lév., xx,20-21.
.. On est obligé de se poser la question, car l'étymologie du terme
est loin d'être claire" (329). He therefore appeals to the Ugaritic
ʿwr or ʿrr for clarification of the sense of ʿarîrî. The meaning thus
obtained is "stirred up" or "aroused" which, on the basis of YHWH being the "arouser" of war in Is. 41:2, he claims to be in line with
the military context he has traced in the preceding verse. Moreover,
for him the word *hôlēk*, in the light of Gen. 32:7 and Dt. 1:30, bears
the meaning of "to go ahead to meet (an enemy)". The "question" that
"on est obligé de poser" is "si Abram, au lieu d'affirmer ici qu'il
est sur le point de mourir sans enfant, n'affirme pas au contraire
qu'il part en guerre 'suscité' par Yahvé comme le Cyrus d'Is., xli,
2 ou le Mot d'Ugarit" (id). Cazelles' explanation is not surprising
in view of his attempt to situate the whole of Gen. 15 within the
context of war. But it seems a little far-fetched. In fact, his appeal to the Ugaritic root of ʿărîrî does not seem warranted because
the word does have a semantically clear root in Hebrew.

5 R.E. Clements, Abraham and David, maintains rather strongly this traditional interpretation of ʿărîrî: "Since...the question of an heir
for Abraham is vital to the section as a whole, the traditional interpretation of ʿarîrî cannot be dispensed with" (18, fn. 2). N. Lohfink, Die Landverheissung als Eid, 39, also subscribes to this meaning of ʿarîrî and regards it as an old and hardly intelligible word.

Again in the context of a desire for a blood-heir, the
verb *hōlēk* very likely assumes the idea of death in the very same vein as the expression *hinnēh 'ānōkî hōlēk lāmût*
(Gen. 25:32)[6], which is given in connection with the motif
of *b^ekōrāh* - a motif that includes the status of the first-
born as the rightful heir. If this interpretation is right,
Abraham was preoccupied with his death that was going to
leave him childless.

V. 2bB

The real crux of the problem in v. 2 is *ûben-mešeq*[7] *bêtî*
whose middle word bears "a most unreassuring resemblance to
dmśq, only three words further on"[8] and whose remaining two
words appear as a compound of their own in v. 3. Of the
proposals made so far, L.A. Snijders'[9] which, on the basis
of Is. 33:4 where the verb *maššaq* (from the root *šqq,* Meaning "to attack") describes "the activity of locusts attack-
ing the crops"[10], interprets *ben-mešeq* as "the attacker,
the man who forces himself upon a person"[11], seems to be
the most acceptable as (i) it fits in very well with the
sense of vv. 2-3; (ii) it leaves the consonantal text in-
tact; and (iii) it has found its justification within the
OT itself. It is therefore not surprising that it has been

M.Anbar, JBL,101 (1982), 42, also accepts the above meaning of the
word but maintains, "This word also appears in Lev. 20:20-21; Jer.
22:30 and in Ben-Sira, and thus seems to be late."

6 Cf. also Ps. 39:14; O. Procksch, Die Genesis,295; and W.B. Smaltz,
JBL, 71 (1952), 211f, notwithstanding B. Panknin's reply in ZAW, 70
(1958), 256.

7 BHK proposes reading with Targum (Pentateuch): *ûben-mōšēl,* meaning
"son of the one governing" (my house). It would be quite unlikely
that Abraham who was himself the *mōšēl* of his own house would refer
to anyone else therein by that word.

8 Cf. H.L. Ginsberg, BASOR, 200 (1970), 31.

9 L.A. Snijders, in B. Gemser et elii, Studies on the Book of Genesis,
261-267.

10 Id, 270.

11 Id. To justify his interpretation of *ben,* Snijders in fn. 20 calls
attention to two references: *ben-mari,* a recalcitrant one (Num 17:
25), and *ben-'ōn,* a miserable man (Prov. 31:5).

well received by some scholars[12]. Thus, *ben-meśeq bêtî*
would refer to some kind of a "usurper-to-be" of Abraham's
house. The author identifies this threatening figure thus:
hû *dammeśeq* *elî'ezer*[13]. This identification is hardly
surprising in view of the long-standing enmity between
Abraham's descendants and Damascus.

The hostile character of Eliezer may be a problem vis-à-
vis Gen. 24:2. There we are introduced to Abraham's servant
as "the oldest of his house, who had charge of all that he
had". Though not explicitly done in the text, there may be
an easy tendency to identify this servant with Eliezer. For,
it seems reasonable to presume that Eliezer's special position in Abraham's household was such that Abraham had to put
him in charge of all that he had as well as take him for his
heir in the event of his childlessness. But far from har-
bouring any hostile attitude, that servant - in the story in
Gen. 24 - proved to be helpful to his master.

The problem may be resolved in two ways. First of all, if
the text does not identify the servant with Eliezer, there
is no reason for us to do so. Therefore the problem in respect of Gen. 24 does not arise. Secondly, even if as a servant in Abraham's household, Eliezer should be helpful, that
was only to be expected of him as of any other servant and
more so since he was the heir apparent to his master. For
the patriarch, however, he was an alien and his position as
heir apparent would pose a serious threat to Abraham's future. In other words, he was imposing on the patriarch his
claim to succession and in that sense, he was a "hostile"
figure.

A brief review of each of the major solutions proposed for the problematic v. 2b may be in order to explain our reason for not accepting
them. A. Schulz[14] suggests an elimination of *dmśq* and a reconstruction

---

12 E.g. H. Gazelles, RB, 69 (1962), 330; and T.L. Thompson, The Historicity of the Patriarchal Narratives, 230.
13 Both BHK and BHS propose a deletion of *hû* *dammeśeq* as a gloss. BHK
   further suggests inserting *yôreš* *ōtî* after *elî'ezer*. The suggested
   deletion lacks documentary support and the later reconstruction
   would leave the reading of v. 3b problematic.
14 A. Schulz, ZAW, 52 (1934), 274-279.

of *'ly'zr* into *lō' zar'î*. He thus translates v. 2b as "und der Sohn
meines Hausmeisters ist nicht mein Nachkomme." The elimination of *dmśq*
as secondary seems to be a matter of convenience. The transposition of
the component letters in the name "Eliezer" disrupts the text far too
much to be acceptable.

Taking up from W.F. Albright's unpublished comments on Gen. 15:2f,
M.F. Unger[15] attempts to restore the original reading. Assuming both a
haplography and a transposition, Albright proposes the following reading: *û-ben bêtî (ben) mešeq* - "and the son of my house is the son of
Meseq". Unger, however, sees the transposition as unnecessary and reads
the text thus: *û-ben mešeq (ben) bêtî* - "and the son of Meseq is the son
of my house". He argues that "by homoiarkton it would be easy for one
ben to fall out, which, however, occurred some time before the third
century BC." He regards *hû' dammešeq 'ĕlî'ezer* as having been "applied
at an early date to explain the peculiar idioms." Unger's reconstruction
creates another difficulty: who was Meseq and how was his son to succeed
Abraham?

H. Seebass[16], "unter Annahme einer Dittographie und einer Buchstaben-
umstellung", proposes the following reading: *ûben-mešeq (ben-)bêtî hû'*
lî zera' - "der Sohn Meseqs ('der Meseqaner'), mein Haussklave, wird mir
Nachkomme sein." Apart from disrupting the text, Seebass' proposal fails
to take into account the rather restrictive sense of *zera'* which can
only refer to one of physical descent.

F. Vattioni[17], on the basis of the LXX reading, follows C.H. Gordon's
proposal[18] of a *hiphil* participle for *mšq*, from the root *šqh* meaning,
"il figlio di chi fa bere" and translates it thus: "figlio della coppa".
The reference is "non.... di un coppiere, ma di uno che versava l'acqua
sulla tomba dei morti". The *hiphil* participle should be *mšqh*. What,
then, has become of the final *h*?

H.L. Ginberg's "minimum emendation"[19] includes "the omission of *mšq*
as a variant of *dmšq* and the correction of *dmšq* itself to *y(y)ršnw*, i.e.
yîrāšennû" with the transposition of *'ly'zr* to the beginning, so that
the text reads, *w'ly'zr bn byty hw' y(y)ršnw*. This so-claimed "minimum
emendation" has given an almost totally new reading to the text and this
is hardly acceptable.

Zeph. 2:9bA may be proposed as a possible solution to Gen. 15:2bB in
view of its *mimšaq*. But this word itself is a "hapax" whose sense is not
clear[20]. Attempts to clarify it include one that appeals to Gen. 15:2
for support[21]. How is it possible then to take it to explain our text?

---

15 M.F. Unger, JBL, 72 (1953), 49-50
16 H. Seebass, ZAW, 75 (1963), 317-319.
17 F. Vattioni, RStOr, 40 (1965), 9-12.
18 C.H. Gordon, Ugaritic Textbook, 439, entry no. 1565.
19 H.L. Ginsberg, BASOR 200 (1970),31
20 BHS proposes an emendation of the word to *môraš*. The Vulgate renders
   it as "siccitas spinorum" while the LXX offers Damaskos eklelimmene.
   BDB, ad locum, suggests that *mimšaq* means "possession" or "place of
   possession", but remarks that this is "wholly dubious".
21 Thus G. Gerleman, Zephanja, 37. J.C. Greenfield, in S.R. Brunswick,
   FS Leon Nemoy, 79-82, maintains that *mimšaq ḥarûl* means "a place for
   harvesting nettles" and argues from the Targum *mšmṭ mlwḥyq wmḥpwryn*
   dmlḥ. But his explanation of *mimšaq* from *mšmṭ* is too complex not to
   cast doubts about its reliability. First of all, it appeals to the
   rare meaning of *šmṭ* (= "picking"; "removing"). Then, it conjectures

Finally, it must be noted that some scholars have merely dismissed
ben-mešeq, if not the entire v. 2b, as incomprehensible[22].

V. 3b

The compound noun *ben-bêtî* bears some similarity and at
the same time a striking difference from the *ben-mešeq bêtî*
of v. 2bB. H.L. Ginsberg's translation of the expression
with "steward", which he claims to be "a well established
meaning of *bn byt* in Roman Hebrew"[23], fits in very well with
the whole thrust of vv. 2-3.

The imminent threat posed by this steward is expressed
through the use of $w^e hinn\bar{e}h$[24] + active participle *(yôrēš)*[25].
The effect produced by this construction is the assertion of
the claim of succession by the steward and corroborates the
concept of *ben-mešeq*. It can be adequately expressed only by
a translation such as this: "and so here is this steward of
mine (ever-ready) to succeed me."

V. 4bA

The word $m\bar{e}$ʿ*îm* (plural of $m\bar{e}$ʿ*eh*) is taken to refer to the
"seat of life's origin"[26] and may thus be used not only of

---

how *š* becomes *ś* and *ś* in turn becomes *s* in order to explain its deri-
vation from the root *msq* which in Mishnaic Hebrew means "to pluck /
pull olives". It must be noted that in Heb. the confusion between *š*
and *ś* is not easy to make and much less between *ś* and *s*.

22 So N. Lohfink, Die Landverheissung als Eid, 39 and J. Van Seters,
   Abraham in History and Tradition, 255.

23 H.L. Ginsberg, BASOR, 200 (1970), 31, fn. 1. He observes further that
   "the idea that a slave is homeborn is expressed not by *bn byt* but by
   by ylyd byt, e.g. in Gen. 17:12,23."

24 T.O. Lambdin, Introduction to Biblical Hebrew, par. 135, makes a very
   strong remark about the traditional rendition of *hinnēh* as "behold".
   It merely "points up the translators' refusal to come to grips with
   the meaning and syntactic functions of *hinnēh* in terms of modern
   English correspondents." The meaning of *hinnēh* depends to a large extent on its context. This explains the different renditions we make
   of the five recurrences of *hēn/hinnēh* in our translation of Gen. 15.

25 Cf. Ges.-K., par. 116f.

26 This is an expression from C. Westermann, Genesis 12-36, 262: *"mʿyn*
   gelten als Sitz der Entstehung des Lebens".

a woman as in Gen. 25:23 and Ruth 1:11, but also of a man as
in 2 Sam. 7:12[27] and 16:11. The one to issue from Abraham's
$mē^{c}îm$ is the son of "his own flesh-and-blood".

V. 6

The *waw*-perfect in v. 6a breaks the continuity of the narrative in order to express a continuous state of mind rather
than a single act.

Turning to v. 6b, we encounter a serious problem. What is
the subject of $ḥšb$, since both Abraham and YHWH seem to qualify equally well as subject? Quite apart from the equality
of strength of a chiastic structure to a "parallelismus membrorum"[28], two reasons favour "YHWH" as the subject of the
verb. Firstly, the pronominal suffix $hā$ necessarily refers

---

27 This text contains exactly the same relative clause as Gen. 15:4.
28 Generally, scholars take YHWH as the subject of the verb $ḥšb$; cf.
   B. Johnson, Svensk Exegetisk Årsbok, 51-52 (1986-87), 108-115. But in
   very recent times two authors call this into question. One of them,
   Lloyd Gaston, Horiz. BT, 2 (1980), 39-68, accuses the YHWH-proponents
   of being prejudiced by the "displacement theory" which misinterprets
   Paul as "deliberately and provocatively contradicting the theology
   of the synagogue" (39). Cautioning that we should "refrain from a
   change of subject unless this should be indicated or necessary" and
   respecting "the phenomenon of Hebrew parallelism" (41), he maintains
   that "Abraham" is the subject of the verb. The other scholar is
   M. Oeming, ZAW, 95 (1983), 182-197. After an analysis of some of the
   recurrences of the verb $ḥšb$ in the OT, he quite rightly states his
   disagreement with G. von Rad's conclusion "dass der traditionsgeschichtliche Hintergrund von Gen. 15:6 die priesterliche Kultpraxis
   sein soll" (198). On the ground "dass an den beiden Qal-Stellen, an
   denen $ḥšb$ 'anrechnen' bedeutet, einmal Jahweh Subjekt ist (Ps. 32:2),
   einmal ein Mensch (II Sam 19:20)," and that "die Satzstruktur eines
   synthetischen parallelismus membrorum entspricht der Sprachstruktur
   des Hebräischen wesentlich besser als ein abrupter" (191), he has no
   doubt that Abraham is the subject of $ḥšb$ in Gen. 15:6, which he considers as "ein syntaktisches Hapaxlegomenon".
   With regard to the argument based on Hebrew parallelism, there is an
   equally typically Hebrew literary feature namely, the chiastic
   structure of which Gen. 15:6 qualifies as a fine example. While
   Oeming is right in his observation about 2 Sam. 19:20, he fails to
   add that the human subject in this text refers to David, a superior
   party in respect of Shimei. This superiority of David's is an important point to note in connection with the use of $ḥšb$.
   For a further evaluation of Oeming's view, cf. B. Johnson, art. cit..

to the verbal idea of $w^eh e'\v{e}min$ in v. 6a [29] and not the whole
preceding unit, vv. 1-5, as M. Oeming maintains[30]. Secondly, of the 258 occurences of $\dot{h}\check{s}b$[31] in the OT, apart from
our text, only three others have a moralistic overtone –
one used with $\dot{s}dqh$, viz. Ps. 106:31 and two with $\dot{}\bar{a}w\bar{o}n$,
viz. 2 Sam. 19:20 and Ps. 32:2. Thus, only these three
texts can throw light on the point under consideration about
Gen. 15:6b.

Ps. 32:2 clearly has YHWH for the subject of $\dot{h}\check{s}b$: $l\bar{o}'$
$yah\dot{s}\bar{o}b\ yhwh\ l\hat{o}\ \dot{}\bar{a}w\bar{o}n$. 2 Sam. 19:20 reports Shimei's appeal
for David's clemency: $'al-yah\v{a}\check{s}\bar{o}b-l\hat{\imath}\ '\v{a}d\bar{o}n\hat{\imath}\ \dot{}\bar{a}w\bar{o}n$. David
could exercise the clemency requested by Shimei, only be-
cause he was the latter's superior (King). From these two
texts, it is clear that $\dot{h}\check{s}b$ in a moral sense is the imputation of a certain judgement by a superior to a subject.

What about Ps. 106:31 which, of all the three texts, bears
the closest affinity with Gen. 15:6b: $watt\bar{e}\dot{h}\bar{a}\check{s}eb\ l\bar{o}$
$li\dot{s}^ed\bar{a}q\bar{a}h$? The verb recurs in its niphal conjugation so that
it has a passive force with the meaning "and it was rec-
koned". There seems to be a switching around of the pronominal object $h\bar{a}$ to become the implied subject, since the passive verb used is in the 3rd fem. sing. The righteousness
accorded to Phinehas was thus for what v. 30 reports him to
have done: $wayya\dot{}\v{a}m\bar{o}d...\ way^epall\bar{e}l$. In acknowledgement of
his righteousness, "the plague was stopped". Since it was
YHWH who had unleashed the plague on His people for their
idolatrous practices[32], it must have been He who stopped it.
Therefore, it must have been YHWH who acknowledged Phinehas'
righteousness.

---

29 Ges.-K., par. 135p (also par. 112q), explains that "the suffix of the
   third person singular feminine sometimes refers in a general sense to
   the verbal idea contained in a preceding sentence" and cites Gen. 15:
   6 as an example. Other examples are: Num. 23:19; 1 Sam. 11:2; 1 K 11:
   12; Is. 30:8; Am. 8:10.
30 Cf. M. Oeming, ZAW, 95 (1983), 192.
31 Id, 189.
32 Ps. 106:30 does not give the precise intervention made by Phinehas as
   presented in Num. 25:6-8. This has no bearing on the point we want
   to demonstrate here.

From the above considerations the more likely subject of
ḥšb would be YHWH.

V. 12b

The participle *nōpelet* appears in the feminine singular
though there are two nouns of the feminine gender. To drop
ḥašêkāh as a gloss[33] begs two questions: (i) how is it that
the glossator, whose aim was to smoothen or explain a text
through his gloss, made the text more difficult by not linking the two nouns with the conjunction *waw* and converting
the participle into its plural form? and (ii) if, as M. Anbar maintains[34], *ḥašêkāh* is redundant, why did the glossator
have to add it? Thus, not withstanding a lack of documentary
evidence to this effect, we maintain the entire expression
as original and propose that *'êmāh* be emended to its construct form of *'êmat*, of which the ending *t* was probably
miscopied as *ḥ* that begins the next word. Our proposal
would thus read, "the fear of a great darkness fell upon
him"[35].

V. 18c

BHS proposes an emendation of the name, *minn^e har miṣrayim*,
which is not found anywhere else in the OT, to the more commonly attested *minnaḥal miṣrayim*[36] and suggests that *n^e har-
p^e rat* is perhaps a gloss, probably because, in view of the
preceding reference to the Euphrates, it is redundant.

33 In their "apparatus critici", both BHK and BHS raise the question as
   to whether *ḥašêkāh* is a gloss. M. Anbar, JBL, 101 (1987), 47, thinks
   it is probably so, since "the verb *nōpelet* refers to *'êmāh*" and since
   he maintains that *ḥašêkāh* is redundant. C. Westermann, Genesis 12-36,
   268, dismisses the whole clause as unncessary.
34 M. Anbar, JBL, 101 (1982), 47.
35 Fear often overtakes an individual or a people when confronted with
   an intervention by YHWH, which could take the form of an invasion by
   an enemy as in Dt. 32:25 and Hab. 1:7 or a personified being as in
   Ps. 88:16 and Job 9:34. The *tardēmāh* that befell Abraham was in intervention by the Lord and it is not surprising therefore that he
   should experience a great fear.
36 E.g. Num. 34:5; Jos. 15:4,44; 1 K. 8:65 = 2 Chr. 7:8; Is. 27:12.

To this second suggestion, it must be objected that the full designation of the Euphrates as given in Gen. 15:18 is also found in Dt. 1:7 and Jos. 1:4. This means that it was in all likelihood one of the stereotyped designations for the River.

With regard to the first emendation, the fact that there is a lack of textual support for one reading and many recurrences of the other cannot by itself be taken as sufficient reason for dropping the former in favour of the latter. Moreover, in our text, $n^e har\ misrayim$ seems to have been intentionally used as the south-western counterpart of the north-eastern $n^e har-p^e rat$. It is true that the Nile with its large Delta could hardly have served as a satisfactory boundary. But there is no indication of the author's intention to maintain any strict geographical accuracy here.

II. Problems

Gen. 15 betrays a strange and complex state of affairs
with regard to its contents as well as its literary character. On first reading it appears to be very much of a narrative, marked by verbs in their *wayyiqtol* form[37]. Yet, on
closer analysis, we find that of its twenty-one verses,
sixteen contain direct speech[38], giving the chapter the character of a dialogue report, which includes discourses as
well. Moreover, there are only two personages involved in
the entire chapter, namely, YHWH and Abraham - hardly enough
to constitute a narrative.

A more serious problem that calls the chapter as a narrative to question is its apparent lack of thematic unity and
narrative plot. Indeed, the themes that go in to make up the
chapter are so varied that many seem to be unrelated to one
another: for example, YHWH's self-introduction as "Shield",
promise of a great reward (v.1), Abraham's complaint about
his childlessness (v. 2), followed by promises of an heir
(v. 4) and countless descendants (v. 5), assertion of Abraham's faith (v. 6) followed by a promise of land (vv. 7, 18)
and a rite (vv. 9-10, 17) as well as a covenant (v. 18) to
confirm it, with an interruption by the descent of birds of
prey (v.11) and prophetic utterances about the destiny of
Abraham (v. 15) and his descendants (vv. 13-14, 16).

The lack of unity seems apparent also from the doublets
and discrepancies in the chapter. Thus, for example, there
are two "word advent" formulae in vv. 1 and 4 and two successive uses of *wayyō'mer* to introduce Abraham's speech in
vv. 2 and 3 and YHWH's in v. 5. The two discrepancies of the

---

37 Cf. vv. 2,3,5b,7,8,9,13 (*wayyō'mer*), 5a (*wayyôṣē'*), 6b (*wayyaḥšebehā*),
   10 (*wayyiqaḥ*), 11a (*wayyēred*), 11b (*wayyašeb*), 12a, 17a (*wayhî*) and
   12b, 17b (*wᵉhinnēh*).
38 Cf. vv. 1,2,3,4,5,7,8,9,13-16,18,19-21.

chapter involve (i) the time of the "event": vv. 5 and 17
present it as a night scene whilst v. 12 as a sunset scene;
and (ii) the time of the exodus of Abraham's descendants
from the land of oppression: v. 13 has "four hundred years"
and v. 16 "four generations afterwards".

To aggravate the issue, Gen. 15 gives some a very strong
impression of being composed of many literary forms[39], according to which it may be segmented into the following
units: a prophetic advent of God's word followed by an oracle of salvation (vv. 1,4), a lament form (vv. 2-3), a metaphor for a great multitude (v. 5), a cultic declaration of
worthiness for a liturgical celebration (v. 6), a quasi-
Exodus formula (v. 7), a request for a sign (v. 8) followed
by the granting of it (vv. 9-12, 17), a prophetic discourse
(vv. 13-16), a "terminus technicus" for the sealing of a
covenant (v. 18a) together with a formula for the grant of
land (v. 18b) and two different descriptions of the land
(vv. 18c, 19-21).

The lack of literary unity for the chapter has been further argued for on the ground of the existence of the so-
claimed archaic elements[40] like $\cdot\check{e}l\hat{i}\,\dot{}ezer$ (v. 2), the ancient rite of passing between the pieces of the animals (vv.
9-10, 17), alongside relatively late elements like the deuteronomistic metaphor for a countless multitude (v. 5) and
the gentilic list (vv. 19-21)[41].

From all this, there arises the problem about the tradition history as well as the literary sources of the chapter.
Worded in another way, the problem consists of a series of

---

39 Two important works that make an extensive use of form-criticism to
   control their analyses of the chapter are: N. Lohfink, Die Landverheissung als Eid; and J. Van Seters, Abraham in History and Tradition, 249-278. O. Kaiser, ZAW, 70 (1958), 107-126, and M. Anbar, JBL,
   101 (1982), 39-55, have to some extent gone into a form-critical analysis of the chapter.
40 H. Cazelles, RB, 69 (1962), 347.
41 The deuteronomistic authorship of these two literary elements is more
   widely accepted by recent scholars. Cf. J. Skinner, Genesis, 279,
   283f; O. Kaiser, ZAW, 70 (1958), 117 and 124; L. Perlitt, Bundestheologie im Alten Testament, 68-77; J. Van Seters, Abraham in History
   and Tradition; H.H.Schmid, Der sogennante Jahwist, 119-153; C. Westermann, Genesis 12-36, 263 and 271; M. Anbar, JBL, 101 (1982) 43 and 53.

related issues: have any original traditions been preserved?
If so, which? How did it/they evolve to form the chapter?
Who was/were responsible for the formation of the chapter?
When and for what purpose was the chapter composed?

There are scholars who, convinced that every patriarchal
tradition must be connected with a sanctuary, have been dis-
turbed by the absence of an "Ortsgebundheit" from the chapter[42].

---

42 For example, A. Jepsen, in G. Mayer (Ed), FS Albrecht Alt, 139-155,
   esp. 152-153, proposes Mamre-Hebron as the sanctuary. His proposal
   is supported by R.E. Clements, Abraham and David, 40-46. O. Kaiser,
   ZAW, 70 (1958), 121-122, argues for Shechem, while N. Lohfink, Die
   Landverheissung als Eid, 85-88, maintains that the locus was originally Hebron-Mamre but later shifted to Jerusalem.

III. Solutions

Confronted with this enigmatic character of Gen. 15, a
good number of scholars have investigated the chapter.

1. Literary and Redactional Analysis

Many have carried out a literary-critical and redactional
analysis of the chapter to solve the enigma. The following
table assembles the literary source divisions proposed by
major works from H. Gunkel[43] onwards. They argue for Gen. 15
as a composition of at least two sources undertaken by a
redactor who has left some vestiges of his work in the
chapter.

Practically all the above authors agree that Gen. 15 consists of two main parts: vv. 1-6 and 7-21. Apart from that,
however, as the table shows, there are only very few verses
about whose literary sources source-analysts have reached a
general consensus. The remaining verses have been attributed
by different analysts to different sources[44].

---

43 The following works are those cited in the table on the following two
   supplementary pages minus those that have already been referred to in
   the foregoing footnotes. H. Gunkel, Genesis, 177-184; 264-272;
   R. Smend, Die Erzählung des Hexateuch, 44f; 64f; 284-290; P. Volz and
   W. Rudolph, Der Elohist als Erzähler, 25-34; C.A. Simpson, The Early
   Traditions of Israel, 73-75; G. Hölscher, Geschichtsschreibung in
   Israel, 278-290; G. von Rad, Genesis, 181-190; A. Caquot, Sem., 12
   (1962), 51-66; R. Killian, Die vorpriesterlichen Abrahamsüberlieferungen, 36-73; A. de Pury, Promesse divine et légende cultuelle, 295-
   327; W. Zimmerli, 1 Mose 12-25: Abraham, 48-59.
44 J. Van Seters, Abraham in History and Tradition, 250, observes thus:
   "... some verses, such as vv. 3,5,6,7,13-16 and 18-21, are assigned
   to a redactor who would be merely supplementing the previous account.
   It is noteworthy that the same verses can often be ascribed by one
   author to a variant version, for example E, and by another to a redactor, even though two entirely different processes are involved."

Source-critical analysis chart (Genesis 15), by verse (columns 1–21, with sub-divisions aA aB aC bA bB bC …). Best-effort reading of a rotated tabular chart.

```
        1     2     3     4     5     6     7     8     9    10    11    12    13    14    15    16    17    18   19  20  21
        aA aB aC  bA bB bC  aA aB aB  bA bB bC   a  b   a   aA aB  bA bB bC  a  b  c
```

Source assignments and notes by scholar

GUNKEL (1910)
Codes: J J E E E J ? ? E E E J E J G E E E E E G G … J J J J G G G / (lower) D D D D R R R
Notes: Redactor had J as basic text. 7bB = Dtr; 14bB + 15b = P expressions.

SKINNER (1910)
Codes: J J E J D J J J J J J J J E J G G E E G G E D D D J D … (lower) D D D D D (P) R R R R R
Notes: 14bB+ 15b = P expressions.

SMEND (1912)
Codes: --- J2 + E ---- -- J2 -- J1 [box] | --------- J2 + E --------- --- E --- J G J2 ------- | E [box] E | ------ J2 -------
Notes: Eliezer in 2bA = J1. 13bC & 14bB = not E. YHWH in 1,4,6=Yahwistic.

PROCKSCH (1913)
Codes: J J J J E E E J E E E E E E E E E D D J J J J E J G D D / R R R D D / R R
Notes: —

VOLZ & RUDOLPH (1933)
".............. Independent Narrative 1 .... Independent Narrative 2 ....Independent Narrative 2."
"-------- J combined two totally independent and different narratives --------"
"======= Redactional Expansion ======="

SIMPSON (1948)
"-------- A late material throughout – the result of one or more elaboration of a much simpler story --------"
"============ Elaboration except ============   .... Original nucleus is found here, with the subtraction of: ...."
"======= Elaboration except ======="
G* G G G G G G G G
Inter-polation | Further Expansion
Notes: 2bB: G* = "he is a Damascene". 14bA: G*="after which". Interpolation to connect new material with original.

NOTH (1948)
Codes: J J E E ? ? E E J J J J J J J J E E E E E E E E E J J J J D D / R R R
Notes: Assignment of E cannot be demonstrated on the basis of Gen 15 but is probable in view of what is generally found in Pent.

HÖLSCHER (1952)
Codes: E E E E E E E G G G E E E E E E E E E ---Rp--- ------- E2 ------- Rp -- E2 -- Rp E2 Rp ------- E2 ------- D D / R R
Notes: Rp = Priestly Redactor. E2 = Later reworking in the same line as E. 2bB: Gloss= "he is a D"

JEPSEN (1953-4)
"-------- Basic material received by J to which J inserted his passage about the history of Abraham's descendants --------   ...... Insertion by J ...."

VON RAD (1956)
"-------- In part Elohistic --------   E E E E J J J J J J J J J J ----- Insertion: from E? -----   J J J J J J J"

KAISER (1958)
"-- Original Kernel re-worked by J --   E E E E J J J J J J J J   Original Kernel reworked by J"
"...... Secondary Hand under deuteronomistic influence......   D D D / R R   .... Secondary Hand ....   D Secondary / R Hand"
"Sec. Hand | Sec. Hand"   G*   G G
Notes: Original Kernel = oral tradition in 2 strata - connected with Abraham's people at Hebron; . merged with federated tribal covenant at Shechem. Ortsgebundheit= dropped by Secondary Hand.

CAQUOT (1962)
"-------- A fictitive composition by a cleric out of existing traditions about Abraham in the form of a Midrash with two parts: --------"
".............. Part A .... Part B ...."
G* Possible Gloss | =Parenthesis= T T T T / M M M M | G | T T T T / M M M M
Notes: G* = Double gloss: "He is a Damascene"; . "He is Eliezer". V. 3 = to explain 2bB. TM = drawing on Traditional Material.
```
```

Source-critical comparison chart (Genesis 15), with verse columns 1–21 across the top.

	1	2	3	4	5	6	7	8	9	10	11	12	13	14	15	16	17	18	19	20	21
(verse sub-units)	aA	aB aC	bA bB bC	aA aB	bA bB	aB	a b	aA aB	bA bB	aA aB	bA bB	bB	a b	c b	aA-bA	bB	a b	c b	aA	bA	bB bC a b c

CAZELLES (1962) — E "Battle Text"; J "Posterity Text" & less conserved. 2bB: Gloss = "He is a Damascene". 18b-c: E = beyond Eup.; J = from Egypt to Eup.

SEEBASS (1963) — R ... JE ...

KILIAN (1966) — J ... Pe (Pe = pre-elohistic), R (Redactor), E, G*, Grundschicht, G.
- PeR = Post-elohistic Redactor.
- 7bB: PeR = "to possess it".
- 16: E* = hennāh = R.

LOHFINK (1967) — Pre-J reformulation of old traditions already established in the form of oracles — organized into two parallel parts. Part 1 ... Part 2 ... Basic Text ===== =Addition=
- Pre-J reformulation = received into the narrative of J.

CLEMENTS (1967) — Oldest Material in Chapt. — J? ... Oldest Mat. in ch. ... R
- J = originally independent tradition incorporated into J.

PERLITT (1969) — ===== Secondary insertion with an elohistic base but on the way towards Dt. ===== D D D R R R
- Thematic and temporal closeness between E and Dt gives rise to intertweaving of layers.

DE PURY (1975) — -- Pre-literary narrative with promise of land. C C C Compiler ..... Compiler
- A blending of traditions: either E or post-Jehowistic. Addition: Either by E or under his influence.
- E or post-Jehowistic; Proto Dt; D D D R R R.
- 7aB,bA = transferred from initial promise of pre-literary narrative by Compiler (C).

ZIMMERLI (1976) — A young account about Promise of Son and Abraham's Faith. Old Independent Tradition (OIT). Dtr Hand ... OIT? ... Dtr Hand.

ANBAR (1982) — A Conflation of two independent Deuteronomic Compositions drawing their inspiration from earlier sources — thus, late work (perhaps Exilic). Ancient Promises of Son and Innumerable Offspring. Ancient Promise of Land.

R = Redactor.
G = Gloss.

More dissensions emerge as we extend the survey to traditio-historical criticism. Upon A. Alt's suggestion that Gen. 15 contains the oldest patriarchal tradition dating back to pre-Israelite times[45], traditio-historical studies have tried to unearth this oldest tradition. Those who claim to have found it hold rather varied views about it. Below is a schematic presentation of the main positions regarding the tradition history behind Gen. 15[46].

O. Kaiser

Oldest Tradition - Sanctuary:	Hebron-Mamre.
Content:	An oral tradition about the Covenant of the God of Abraham with Abraham's people (the southern tribe) promising land to them.
Growth towards Gen. 15	Merged with federated tribal covenant at Shechem. A later redaction following Dtr[47] style.
Purpose:	Of merger: to legitimatize the Davidic Kingdom whose confines correspond to the boundaries of the land described in Gen. 15. Of redaction: to "make old history a present reality".

H. Cazelles

Oldest Tradition - Sanctuary:	Probably Mamre.
Content:	Two ancient traditions: "Battle text" (E) - in line with the Hittite and Semitic treaties of the second millennium B.C. "Posterity text" (J) - familial and dynastic expectations of the Phoenician texts of Ras Shamra.
Growth towards Gen. 15:	Composition from the two sources with the minimum of interventions.
Purpose:	To strengthen the union of the tribes of Israel, all of whom were heirs to the Covenant between God and Abraham.

---

45 A. Alt, Der Gott der Väter, 1-78, maintains that his ancient cultic legend told how the God of Abraham had first revealed himself and later on came to be known as the "Shield of Abraham". In the course of time, he was identified with YHWH, the national God.
46 The works selected here are found in the table on the supplementary pages above.
47 "Deuteronomistic" redaction here is to be understood "im Sinne des 'Deuteronomischen Geschichwerks'" aiming at "eine Aktualiesierung der alten Geschichte" (O. Kaiser, ZAW, 70 (1958), 124).

R. Kilian

Oldest Tradition - Sanctuary: (Not given)
                   Contents: Tradition about Abraham preparing for the
                              sealing of the covenant by getting the
                              animals ready, the deep sleep and fear
                              befalling him, YHWH's theophany, the ac-
                              tual sealing of the covenant and the pro-
                              mise of land (="Grundschicht").
Growth towards Gen. 15:   Expanded by E and a new stress given by
                              J's sketch of history through the rework-
                              ing of the promise of land coupled with
                              the sealing of the covenant.
Purpose: To legitimatize David's Kingdom.

R.E. Clements

Oldest Tradition - Sanctuary: Mamre.
                   Contents: El-deity of Mamre made an oath to Abraham
                              entitling him and his descendants to
                              dwell in the land.
Growth towards Gen. 15:   Fused with Calebites' tradition about the
                              promise of Moses giving the land to Caleb
                              as a reward for his courage as a spy.
                              Substitution of YHWH for El-deity.
                              J. wove this tradition into his presenta-
                              tion of the patriarchal era as an age of
                              promise.
Purpose: As a presage of the rise of Israel and
                              David - thus, to lend support to the
                              Davidic dynasty.

N. Lohfink

Oldest Tradition - Sanctuary: Shechem.
                   Content: Tradition about Abraham's incubation by
                              the tree of oracles in the Canaanite
                              sanctuary. The divinity gave Abraham the
                              confirmation he sought for of the promise
                              of land through a human ceremony of oath.
Growth towards Gen. 15:   Recasting and reinterpretation of the
                              tradition in established linguistic forms
                              (e.g. oracles).
Purpose: To offset the tendency after the occupa-
                              tion of the land to value YHWH's oath as
                              a secondary matter vis-à-vis Israel's
                              covenant.
                              Also, to link the reality of David's
                              reign to the patriarch Abraham.

A. de Pury

Oldest Tradition - Sanctuary:	Mamre.
Content:	The initial promise in v. 1, but with land for its object (v. 7), to answer Abraham's need as a nomad to sojourn in his place of arrival. Abraham's faith (v. 6) and request for a sign (v. 8). Response: imprecatory rite (vv. 9-12,17) and its interpretation (v. 18abA).
Growth towards Gen. 15:	Expansion by compiler (cf. table between pages 29 and 30).
Purpose:	(Not given).

2. Studies treating Gen. 15 as a Literary Unity

Not satisfied with the results of the above literary-critical, redactional and traditio-historical analyses, some scholars[48] - relatively few in number - prefer to treat Gen. 15 as a literary unity[49]. Below we present in a nutshell the results of their work.

P. Heinisch (1930)[50]

Heinisch argues for the literary unity of the chapter by pointing out the literary connections between those sections customarily held as containing discrepancies[51] and the rest of the chapter. V. 12 is required by v. 17 whilst v. 18

---

48 J. Van Seters, Abraham in History and Tradition, 250, hits out very strongly against these analyses of Gen. 15.

49 Even N. Lohfink, Die Landverheissung als Eid, 47-49 and 114, who argues for the chapter as a composition of a narrative base and secondary elements, admits that there is a literary unity in it, though in view of his thesis, he qualifies that this unity is "formal", meaning to say, the structure of the second part (vv. 7-21) is natural, while that of the first (vv. 1-6) is constructed on the model of the first.

50 P. Heinisch, Das Buch Genesis, 229-234.

51 P. Heinisch singles out Gunkel's and Eissfeldt's analyses to point out these apparent discrepancies as well as the difficulties arising from the attempts to attribute these discrepancies to the traditional sources: cf. 233.

makes no sense without v. 8 which is itself connected to v.
7. YHWH sealed the covenant in v. 18 with the ceremony in
v. 17, "wie er später auf dem Sinai mit dem Volker durch
Moses einen Bund schloss"[52]. The divine speech in vv. 13-16,
which is "die unbedingt notwendige Erklärung der Vogelszene
v. 11"[53], serves to fill in the time lapse between vv. 12
and 17. Since v. 11 cannot be separated from v. 10, vv. 10,
11, 13-16 must be taken together as connected to vv. 12, 17-
18. For his stand against attributing vv. 19-20 to a redactor, Heinisch merely refers to the work of Smend and
Eissfeldt. Thus, vv. 7-21 constitute a literary unity[54]. It
must be noted that Heinisch does not explain how vv. 1-6,
"ein in sich selbständiges Stuck", forms a unity with vv.
7-21.

J. Hoftijzer (1956)[55]

The chapter shows a complete literary unity and serves as
the central narrative to one group of promise texts[56], which
are consequently designated as the Gen. 15-group. The contents of Gen. 15 are to be tied together thus: in a noctur-
nal apparition, YHWH promised Abraham not only a son but also an innumerable posterity. Abraham believed this, although
it sounded quite incredible. As a reward, YHWH made him a
promise of land as well. On Abraham's request, this last
promise was confirmed by YHWH Himself by means of covenant. The chapter also ties Israel's exodus and legal traditions with the patriarchal promise[57], in that the exodus becomes the historical example of the fulfillment of the

---

52 P. Heinisch, Das Buch Genesis, 232.
53 Id, 234.
54 P. Heinisch does not make any explicit remark about v. 9. Since this
   verse records YHWH's command carried out by Abraham in v. 10, it may
   be presumed that Heinisch takes it as being implied in v. 10 and thus
   as being part of the literary unity.
55 J. Hoftijzer, Die Verheissung, 17-55.
56 The texts are: Gen. 12:2f,7f; 13:14ff; 15; 18:18ff; 22:15ff; 24:7;
   26:2ff,24; 28:13ff; 32:10ff. The other group is called the El-Shaddai
   group and comprises Gen. 17:1ff; 28:3f; 35:11ff; 48:3f.
57 Historically, the traditions about the exodus and the law were earlier than the promise tradition.

promise while the promise guarantees that Israel as a people
will not be annihilated in spite of their infidelity to the
law[58].

L.A. Snijders (1958)[59]

For Snijders, the literary unity of Gen. 15 is supported
by the logical coherence between "land" and "people" and
thus between the promise of a multitudinous posterity and
that of land. "The promise of posterity and the multiplica-
tion into a people calls up the question about the way of
existence and the dwelling place."[60] Another unifying factor is the "literary resemblance" consisting in the "parallelism of word and answer"[61] and the frequent use of the
term $yrš$[62]. The covenant sealing recorded in v. 18 summarizes the whole event of Abraham's meeting with YHWH, in which
Abraham's future was talked about.

J. Van Seters (1975)[63]

The two parts of Gen. 15, namely, vv. 1-6 and 7-21, are
unified by the theme of inheritance as well as by v. 6.
Their parallel structures are made to sustain the varied
"genres" drawn from the royal court, prophetic narrative
conventions and legal spheres. The chapter is most likely
a Deuteronomistic work.

H.H. Schmid (1976)[64]

Gen. 15 was composed at a time when a great threat hung

---

58 J. Hoftijzer, Die Verheissung, 49-55.
59 L.A. Snijders, in B. Gemser et alii, Studies on the Book of Genesis,
   261-279.
60 Id, 266.
61 The questions in vv. 2 and 8 are introduced by the same vocative
   'ǎdōnāy yhwh. Cf. id, 267.
62 Id, 267.
63 J. Van Seters, Abraham in History and Tradition, 249-278.
64 H.H. Schmid, Der sogennante Jahwist, 119-143.

over the land and people to provide a "Heilsorakel" (vv.1-6)
and an overview of history, especially the exodus, covenant
and golden era of the Solomonic kingship (vv. 7-21). The
dominant Deuteronomistic language betrays the author.

R. Rendtorff (1980)[65]

Gen. 15 is the result of several stages of development. In
its final stage, it achieves its literary unity through the
use of two key words: $yr\check{s}$ and $zera^c$. In a very skilful way,
the final redactor poses two concerns of Abraham. The first
is about his childlessness (vv. 2-3) which, put in the form
of a question, reads to this effect: who will be my heir-
a stranger or a blood-descendant? The second is Abraham's
concern about land possession: "How shall I know I will possess it (i.e the land)?" (v. 8).

Rendtorff reformulates these two concerns together in one
"Doppelfrage": "Who will possess the land?"[66] The answer is
given in v. 18: "To thy sees ($l^e zar^c \bar{a}k\bar{a}$) I shall give this
land"[67]. In this way, the two promise themes are unified.
V. 6 records Abraham's faith in this "Doppelverheissung"[68].
The whole chapter thus takes on the character of a theological interpretation of patriarchal history.

C. Westermann (1981)[69]

Gen. 15 is a composition made in a late monarchical period. Its two component parts treat the promises made to
Abraham in his "Nachgeschichte"[70] and stress their uncondi-
tionality, so important at the current time of threat and of
a serious crisis of faith. In this chapter Abraham is idea-
lized as "Vater des Glaubens" with whom God has sealed a
covenant[71].

65 R. Rendtorff, in R. Albertz et alii, FS. C. Westermann, 74-81.
66 Id, 75, 79.
67 Id, 78.
68 R. Rendtorff, in R. Albertz et alii, FS. C. Westermann, 81.
69 C. Westermann, Genesis 12-36, 250-275.
70 Id, 274.
71 Id, 275.

3. Theological Approach - H. Gross (1977)

H. Gross[72] devotes his study to a theological analysis of
Gen. 15. It is clear, however, that he cannot avoid taking
the structure of the chapter into account. For this he seems
to adopt'N. Lohfink's observation that v. 6 serves to hinge
vv. 1-5 and 7-21 together. Gross finds himself compelled to
take a stand, albeit in a very brief and general manner,
regarding the literary strata in the composition of the
chapter: there are at least two strata - the older being
vv. 7-21 and the redactor's work. It would seem that Gross
does not subscribe to the literary unity of the chapter.

Briefly, Gross' reconstruction of the theology of Gen. 15
highlights the theologoumenon of faith and that of the covenant. The first theologoumenon, being presented in vv. 1-6,
serves as the irrevocable basis for the second narrated in
vv. 7-21. Since the declaration about Abraham's faith in
v. 6 in response to the promise of innumerable descendants
in v. 5, reflects Abraham's call and his acceptance of it in
12:1-4, the relationship between vv. 1-6 and vv. 7-21 may be
taken as reflecting a fundamental biblical structure found
in Ex. 19 and 24: election (of the people of Israel) and
covenant. In Gen. 15 the covenant founded on Abraham's faith
and response and affected by the animal rite carried out by
YHWH but prepared for and witnessed to by Abraham can hardly
be considered a unilateral oath. It establishes a permanent
relationship between YHWH and Abraham to be lived in the
land which God promised to give to Abraham's descendants and
as such comes very close to the "everlasting covenant" in
Gen. 17:7.

Gross' position about the stratified composition of Gen.
15 has evidently to reckon with the same criticisms levelled
against others of the same school of thought. His theology
stemming as it does from this literary view of his needs

---

72 H. Gross, in G. Braulik, FS W. Kornfeld, 25-35.

also to be assessed in the light of the above criticisms.
His suggestion about Abraham's faith being the patriarch's
acceptance of the promise of innumerable descendants (v. 5)
and the irrevocable basis for the covenant inclusive of the
promise of land tied to it (v. 18) does not seem to comply
with his acceptance of N. Lohfink's view about the "Gelenkfunktion" of v. 6 as this "Gelenkfunktion" would qualify
Abraham's faith as a simultaneous response to the promises
in vv. 1-5 and vv. 7-21. This would weaken the base on
which he builds his idea about $b^e r\hat{\imath} t$ as a bilateral covenant.

   It is not by accident that the consensus reached among the
latter scholars is greater than among the literary-critical,
redactional and traditio-historical analysts. Gen. 15 in
reality does have a coherence and unity both literarily and
thematically. However, there are further major arguments for
the unity of the chapter that have not been treated by the
above studies. It is to these that attention is now turned.

CHAPTER 2

UNITY AND ORGANIZATION OF GENESIS 15

We have already pointed out that the literary unity of
Gen. 15 has been called into question on account of the many
repetitions, discrepancies, antitheses and breaks of continuity that seem to characterize the chapter. It is our present concern to attempt to demonstrate that:
1. the repetitions are not mere repetitions but do in fact
contain a certain progression of thought from one to the
other - thus the term "progressive doublets";
2. there are in fact no discrepancies in the chapter;
3. its antitheses are not contradictions but, as in the case
of the progressive doublets, are marked by a progression
from thesis to antithesis; and
4. there is no real break of continuity but, on the contrary, an unbroken thread ties up all the verses and themes
into a neat whole.

Because of the frequent recurrence of their interplay in
many verses, an individual treatment of the above literary
characteristics cannot help hopping back and forth between
certain verses. Thus, a better organized analysis would be
to treat these characteristics as they appear in the chapter
verse by verse. This approach has the advantage of facilita-
ting the tracing of the unbroken thread running through it.

I. Literary Characteristics

Before proceeding to an analysis of the chapter, it is important to identify every single recurrence of the above-listed literary characteristics.

1. Progressive Doublets

A. The two "word advent" formulae in vv. 1 and 4.

B. The two successive uses of *wayyō'mer 'abrām* to introduce the same idea of childlessness in vv. 2 and 3.

C. The two recurrences of *wayyō'mer* to introduce YHWH's apparently single utterance in v. 5.

D. The two promises of land donation in vv. 7 and 18.

E. The two notices about Abraham's numinous experience bearing a similar grammatical pattern and introduced by almost the same temporal formula: *wayhî haššemeš lābô' (bā'āh)* + *wᵉ* + noun + perfect + *wᵉhinnēh*.

F. The double description about Abraham's descendants being foreigners in v. 13: *gēr* and *bᵉ'reṣ lō' lāhem*.

G. The double affirmation of their slavery: *waʿabādûm* (v. 13) and *yaʿăbōdû*.

H. The two clauses in v. 15 about Abraham's death.

I. The two descriptions of the land in v. 18b and vv. 19-21.

2. Apparent Discrepancies

The two discrepancies in the chapter have already been pointed out[1].

---

1 Cf. pages 27-28 above.

3. Antitheses

A. Promise of a great reward (v. 1) - Abraham's apparent lack of interest in it because of his preoccupation with his childlessness and therefore lack of blood-heir (v. 2).

B. *zeh* (referring to *ben bêtî*, thus a "non-son" of Abraham, vv. 3b,4a) - *hû'* (referring to *'ăšer yēṣē' mimmē'eykā*, Abraham's son, v. 4b).

C. *lō' yirāšᵉkā* (v. 4a) - *yîrāšᵉkā* (v. 4b).

D. Childlessness (v. 3) - innumerable descendants (v. 5).

E. Departure from Ur of the Chaldaeans (v. 7a) - gift of "this land" (v. 7b).

F. *lātēt lᵉkā* (v. 7b) - *lᵉzar'ăkā nāttatî* (v. 18b).

G. Preparation of the animals for ritual (vv. 9f) - descent of the birds of prey to consume them (v. 11).

H. Descent of the birds of prey to prevent rite (v. 11) - passing between the parts as accomplishment of rite (v.17b).

I. Abraham's peace (v. 15) - oppression of his seed (v. 13).

J. Abraham *bᵉšālôm* (v. 15) - Amorites' guilt *lō' šālēm* (v. 16).

K. Abraham's seed in slavery in a foreign land (v. 13a) - Abraham's seed being liberated *birᵉkuš gādôl* (v. 14b).

L. Oppressors of Abraham's seed (v. 13) - stand under God's judgement (v. 14a).

4. Apparent Discontinuity

In a number of places, the narrative thread seems to be badly broken by the non-use of the consecutive *waw* or by the insertion of an apparently disconnected idea.

Instances of the First Case

A. V. 6 starts off with $w^e he$'$\check{e}min$ ($hi.$ pf.) when a waw-consecutive is expected.

B. Vv. 14-16 seem to avoid the use of waw-perfect to maintain a continuity of the prophecy begun in v. 13, while in this latter verse alone there are two recurrences of the waw-perfect: $wa\,$'$\check{a}b\bar{a}d\hat{u}m$ and $w^e\,$'$inn\hat{u}$.

C. V. 18 totally dispenses with the use of waw in its opening temporal phrase: $bayy\hat{o}m\ hah\hat{u}$'.

Instances of the Second Case

A. The most striking tension in the chapter is that between the promise of son-descendants in vv. 1-6 and the promise of land in vv. 7-21.

B. YHWH's abrupt taking of Abraham "outside" without any indication of "inside' in v. 5.

C. Abraham's question in v. 8 seems to contradict the affirmation of his faith in v. 6.

D. The descent of the birds of prey seems to be uncalled for. In fact, its notice cuts the preparation of the rite in vv. 9-10 from its accomplishment in v. 17.

E. The entire block constituted by vv. 12-16 distracts the reader's attention from the rite in vv. 9-10,17.

F. Even within the divine speech in vv. 13-16, there seems to be a disharmony of ideas: v. 15 talks about Abraham's death when all the rest of the divine speech focuses attention on the plight of his descendants.

G. The entire gentilic list in vv. 19-21 seems to be a "misfit" in the chapter.

II. Literary Unity

1. V. 1

The adverbial phrase *bammaḥăzeh* seems to break the prophetic formula of the advent of the divine word and has therefore been considered as a secondary insertion[2]. On the basis
of several texts, especially in Jeremiah[3], which have either
a word or even a whole clause before *lē'mōr*, there is no
reason to take *bammaḥăzeh* as secondary.

YHWH's oracle in v. 1 seems to have an elastic character
as it is in a general "Heilswort" with no specific application. His self-identification, "I am your Shield", qualifies
Him as Abraham's protector in a general sense, applicable
thus to any situation of danger. As for the reward promised
to Abraham, not only is its form unclear but there is also
no clear indication of what it is for. This was why Abraham
had still to ask, "What will you give me?" (v. 2aB). The reward could not be for Abraham's service narrated in chapter
14 because (i) the payers of the *śākār* in such a case would
naturally have been the beneficiaries of the patriarch's
service, that is, the five local kings and Lot; and (ii)
Abraham even refused for himself the offer made to him by
the king of Sodom (vv. 21-24).

The entire thrust in v. 1 seems to present a rather elastic "Heilswort" to allow for a wide range of possibilities
for specification.

---

2 H.F. Fuhs, Sehen und Schauen, 241, calls attention to this without,
   however, taking a stand on it: "Das Gotteswort in 1b wird einegeleitet
   mit der Wortgeschehensformel.... Die Formel ist hier unterbrochen
   durch *b-mḥzh*. Ob dies sekundär mit Blick auf v. 12 geschehen ist, oder
   ursprünglich so konzipiert wurde, lasst sich kaum entscheiden; jenden-
   falls ist dieser Verbindung einzig."
3 Jer. 1:13 and 13:3 have *šenît* before *lē'mōr*; 28:12; 33:1 and 36:27
   have a whole temporal clause before it; cf. also 34:12 and 43:8.

2. Vv. 2-3 and 4

Even if C. Westermann is correct in suggesting that the
author of Gen. 15 had at his disposal two versions of what
he thinks to be Abraham's lament[4] - as the double *wayyō'mer*
'abrām at the beginning of the two verses would seem to indicate - the inclusion of both shows that v. 3 is not a mere
repetition of v. 2 but marks a real progression of thought
from it. For, while there is a common denominator between
them, viz. lack of blood-heir, there is also a real difference: v. 2 signals the presence of an obvious foreign heir
while v. 3 states his position in Abraham's household thereby grounding his claim to succeed his childless master. By
virtue of this progression from v. 2 to v. 3 there is a coherent thematic unity between them. However, the literary
unity between the double *wayyō'mer* *'abrām* still needs to be
considered and it cannot be done without taking v. 4 into
account.

V. 4 is clearly YHWH's promise of a blood heir to Abraham[5]. It is highlighted by means of an antithesis between
lō' yîrāš^{e}kā zeh (v. 4aB) and *hû' yirāšekā* (v. 4bB). This
promise resolves the tension between YHWH's promise of a
great reward in v. 1bC and Abraham's childlessness in vv.
2-3. Vv. 1-4 are therefore held together by the theme of the
promise of a blood-heir.

Stylistically, the author presents this theme in the form
of a dialogue between YHWH and Abraham. Abraham's question
in v. 2 is the patriarch's reaction to YHWH's word in v. 1.
By it, the patriarch is calling for a specification of
YHWH's promise of a great reward and implying the uselessness of such a promise without a blood-heir[6]. V. 3 with its

---

4 Cf. C. Westermann, Genesis 12-36, 259. For the reason given immediately below, we do not agree that vv. 2-3 constitute a lament.
5 On v. 4, C. Westermann, The Promise to the Fathers, writes, "This is
  actually not formulated as a promise; the formulation derives rather
  from the statement of Abraham's grievance (v.3)" (17).
6 C. Westermann, Genesis 12-36, 261, affirms, "Keinen Sohn haben, be-

explicit statement about Abraham's preoccupation paves the
way for v. 4 in which that preoccupation is given a solution. Therefore the double dialogue between YHWH and Abraham is set on the pattern: YHWH speaks - Abraham responds;
Abraham speaks - YHWH responds. Thus, the double introduction for each speaker: *hāyāh dᵉbar-yhwh 'el-'abrām* (v. 1)
and its variant in v. 4 for YHWH, and *wayyō'mer 'abrām* (vv.
2 and 3) for Abraham.

Given the literary and thematic unity of vv. 1-4, it may
be said that v. 4 provides the specific content for the
vague utterance in the opening verse which v. 2 is looking
for. In promising Abraham a blood-heir, YHWH "protects"
Abraham's future from passing into the hands of a foreign
heir and thereby serves as Abraham's "Shield"[7]. He also cla-
rifies the sense of the "great reward". As a result, the
assurance *'al-tîrā'* is also given its foundation.

In terms of literary function, Abraham's question in v. 2
appears to be his way of requesting a sign from YHWH to confirm the promise in v. 1 by assuring its long-term value for
him[8]. V. 4 is as much a sign as a concrete proposal.

3. V. 5

The opening clause of v. 5 is somewhat strange since there
is no indication of YHWH and Abraham being "inside" any
place. The strangeness may be ironed out by pointing out
that there is no place intended in the clause under consideration. It is significant that the root *yṣ'* is used in the
hiphil conjugation. For, in the first place, it expresses

---

deutet nicht keinen Erben haben, sondern keine Zukunft haben."

7 The metaphorical meaning of "Shield" as a title for YHWH allows for
a wide range of usages.

8 Paraphrased, Abraham's request may read something like this: "Adonay
YHWH, it's all very well that You will give me a reward. But, short
of a blood-heir - and currently I don't have a single one - whatever
You will give me will not bring me a long-term benefit and will thereby cease to be a great reward. Please, therefore, give me a sign to
assure that the promised reward will not pass into the hands of Eliezer who, being the steward of mine, will be my legal heir."

YHWH's initiative which is undoubtedly a central concern of
the chapter. In the same vein, the same word in the *hiphil*
conjugation is found in v. 7. Secondly, v. 5aB records YHWH
asking the patriarch to "look toward the sky and count the
stars". The stars in the sky constituted a cosmic sign of
YHWH's power[9]. That means YHWH took Abraham outside to manifest His power to him. This coincides with the meaning of
yṣ'-hiphil as "manifesting" or "making known" as used in
Ps. 37:5-6; Jer. 51:10 and Is. 42:1b[10]. It must be noted
that this meaning of *yṣ'-hiphil* is only implied in v. 5 because its direct object is not "YHWH's power" but "him"
(i.e. Abraham).

If *wayyôṣē'* in our text has a theological sense, then the
adverb *haḥûṣāh* that goes with it must also be theologically
understood. Evidence of an "a-local" sense of *ḥûṣāh* is furnished by Is. 42:2[11]. Abraham's inability to count the stars
reflected his helplessness in the face of YHWH's power[12].
YHWH's intention of taking Abraham "outside" and showing him
His power was most probably to broaden the patriarch's out-
look - to look "outside" of himself into all that YHWH could
offer and get out of his narrow preoccupation with a blood-
heir as well as plunge himself into the vast future of a
large posterity which He had in store for him: "thus will
your descendants be." A second *wayyō'mer* introduces this
promise so as to distinguish it from the sign that precedes
it.

The cosmic sign presented in v. 5aB-bA complements the
verbal sign offered in the form of a promise in v. 4b and at
the same time provides the metaphorical terms for the next

---

9 The reference to "stars" as a cosmic sign of YHWH's wisdom and power
   is found in Job 9:7-10 and Ps. 147:4; cf. also Job 22:12; 31:35; and
   Is. 40:26.
10 H. Simian-Yofre, in Simposio Biblico Español, 309-323, especially
   311-314, argues for this sense of *yṣ'-hiphil*.
11 Id, 318-320, on the basis of Prov. 24:27 and Hos. 7:1, maintains,
   "No es, pues, possible simplimente excluir 'a priori' para *baḥûṣ* en
   Is 42,2 una significión diferente de la meramente local. El servidor
   no se espresa, exteriormente."
12 For a similar contrast between God's almighty power signalled by
   cosmic entities and man's smallness and helplessness, cf. Ps. 8:4-5.

promise in v. 5bB.

Innumerability implies greatness. In this way, v. 5bB
gives a concrete specification to the promise made in v. 1
and links itself with it.

4. V. 6

V. 6, with its *waw*-perfect, is meant as a theological
declaration[13] which comes in very fittingly after Abraham is
reported to have seen the cosmic sign of God's power. To
that is added a declaration about YHWH's positive reaction
to his faith (v. 6b). As such the entire v. 6 provides the
reader a chance to look back over all the preceding promises
right till v. 1 and forms a fitting conclusion to all that
has been said[14]. At the same time, the permanence of
Abraham's faith disposed him to accept the future with equal

---

13 This does not mean that *he'ĕmîn* here is taken in a declarative sense.
   A. Jepsen, in TDOT, I, 309, maintains, "One hardly does justice to
   the meaning of *he'ĕmîn* by taking the hi. causatively or declara-
   tively."
14 J. Van Seters, Abraham in History and Tradition, 256, writes, "So he
   believed Yahweh....' This is a most appropriate conclusion, form-
   critically, to a unit that contains a salvation oracle and a lament
   and confirms the connection of vv. 5-6 with vv. 1-4." M.G, Kline,
   WThJ, 31 (1968), 1-11, takes *h'myn* as "another of these delocutive
   verbs" drawn attention to by D. Hillers, JBL, 86 (1967), 320-324.
   Kline claims that "its delocutive origin is discernible in Gen. 15:6
   (and elsewhere). This verse will then state not (explicitly) that
   Abram's inner attitude was one of faith but that Abram voiced his
   "Amen" (*'āmēn*) in audible response to the word of God." He then adds,
   "Genesis 15 is the account of a solemn covenant ritual and an "Amen"
   response by the covenant vassal in such ceremonies is attested in the
   records of both biblical and extra-biblical covenants." The obvious
   question that Kline has to reckon with is why the "Amen" is given
   here and not after the covenant in v. 18. Foreseeing this objection,
   he replies, ".... it is possible that in this chapter, as often in
   Genesis and in other biblical narratives, the arrangement of the
   materials is not simply chronological" (id, 8). This answer is hardly
   satisfactory as a suzerainty covenantal form, if its existence is
   maintained - at least implicitly - by Kline, is not "simply a chronological arrangement" but a conventional procedure, whose form would
   be fairly strictly maintained. A more radical objection to Kline's
   hypothesis concerns its presumption of the existence of a suzerainty
   covenant behind Gen. 15. Does this chapter contain such a covenant at
   all? Hardly.

openness. In this way, the verse also thrusts the reader's
attention into the promises to be made in the next section
of the chapter.

5. V. 7

V. 7, with its introduction of a new theme, quite clearly
begins a new section in the chapter. But it is not uncon-
nected with the first section.

Literarily its presentation of YHWH's self-identification
recalls that found in v. 1 and gives it its specification.
YHWH was Abraham's "Shield" in that He had safely led him
from Ur of the Chaldaeans to "this land", according him all
the protection he needed in this perilous journey of his.

YHWH's self-identification is expressed through the use of
the traditional confessional exodus formula, except for the
change of the place of departure which is necessitated by
its application to Abraham. Quite apart from the very likely
intention of providing a theological link with the tradition
about Israel's exodus[15], the $h\hat{o}\d{s}\bar{e}$'$t\hat{i}k\bar{a}$ could also well have
been intended to continue the theological line followed by
v. 5 through its use of the verb $y\d{s}$' in its $hiphil$ conjugation. If so, an important theological point that this formula underlines is that YHWH had led Abraham out of his own
small world, represented by his home in Ur of the Chaldaeans, to a whole bright future marked by the promise of
"this land". The prospects "this land" was offering are
subtly implied in the fact that "this land" was a gift of
the God of power depicted in v. 5aB-bA by the presence of
countless stars in the heavens. But this, once again, was
matter of faith - thus, its connection with v. 6.

The promise of land is expressed in terms of $l\bar{a}t\bar{e}t$ and
$l^{e}ri\check{s}t\bar{a}h$ (v. 7b). Again, the two verbs ntn and $yr\check{s}$, while

---

15 Cf. Ex. 6:6; 7:4,5; 12:17,51; 16:6; 18:1; 20:2; Lev. 19:36; 25:38,
   42,55; 26:13,45; Num. 15:41.

found in the traditional land donation formula[16], also cast
a retrospective glance at vv. 1-4. Abraham's question in v.
2, "What will you give me?", is given a direct answer: "this
land". YHWH's answer here also gives a further specification
to His promise of the great reward in v. 1. The land would
be given $l^e ri\check{s}t\bar{a}h$ for it would not fall out of Abraham's
hands in view of the promise of a blood-heir in v. 4bB.

6. V. 8

Abraham's question here seems to create a tension with the
declaration about his faith in v. 6[17]. The tension is real
if Abraham's question is taken as an expression of doubt[18].
But does v. 8 really contain a doubt?

The formula b^e + pronoun or interrogative particle + yd^c
in the imperfect + $k\hat{i}$ is employed to introduce a confirmative sign[19]. Thus, although the word $\dot{o}t$[20] is not used, the

---

16 Dt. 9:6; 12:1; 15:4; 19:2,14; 21:1; 25:19; Jos. 1:11.
17 Cf. H. Gunkel, Genesis, 177.
18 R. Rendtorff, in R. Albertz et alii, FS C. Westermann, 75, maintains
   that v. 8 "signalisiert.... worum es in Gen. 15 eigentlich geht: um
   eine Auseinandersetzung mit der zweifelnden Frage nach der Gültigkeit
   der Verheissung. Man kann diese Frage zusammenfassend so formulieren:
   Wer wird das Land bestizen?" Rendtorff's jump from the question as
   formulated in v. 8 to this formulation is difficult to understand.
19 In Gen. 24:14 the sign is to confirm YHWH's steadfast love to Abraham; 42:33 to confirm the honesty of Joseph's brothers; Ex. 7:17 to
   confirm YHWH's identity; and Ex. 33:16 to confirm YHWH's pleasure
   with Moses and His people.
20 In his classnotes, Messianic Hope, 61-64, H. Simian-Yofre analyses
   the uses of $\dot{o}t$ in the OT and distinguishes four fundamental meanings
   of the word: (a) an anticipatory sign which "is a symbolic act (except Dt. 28:46, a thing; Is. 20:3; Ezk. 4:3, an action; Ezk. 14:8, a
   person) which in some way contains the reality represented or announced". It occurs in Ex. 8:19; Dt. 28:46; 1 Sam. 2:23; 2 K. 19:29;
   Is. 7:14; 19:20; 20:3; 37:30; 55:13; 66:19; Jer. 44:29; Ezk. 4:3;
   14:8; (b) a memorial or mnemonic sign "which must be commemorated in
   the future, as a memorial of the covenant, or salvation, or of a special intervention of YHWH"; it occurs in Gen. 9:12,13,17; Ex. 13:9,
   16; 31:13,17; Num. 17:3,25; Dt. 6:8; 11:18; Jos. 4:6; Ezk. 20:12,20;
   (c) a distinctive sign which consists of a "mark or object given to
   someone in mortal peril, meant for others to see so that it protects
   the bearer of the sign from violent death" as in Gen. 4:15; Ex. 12:13
   and Jos. 2:26; and (d) a confirmative sign which "is an event, extra-
   ordinary in itself or by reason of its circumstances in which YHWH or

recurrence of the formula in our verse does not favour the
verse as an expression of doubt but rather as a request for
a sign. As such, it is directly tied to v. 7 whose promise
it seeks to confirm. As a question raised by Abraham to
Adonay YHWH it manifests some correspondence to v. 2.

7. Vv. 9-10

Since these two verses report Abraham's preparation of the
animals and birds, it is best to treat them together.

From the *wayyōʾmer ʾēlâw* in v. 9, it would appear that the
rite was intended as an answer to Abraham's request. While
the relationship between v. 9 and v. 10 is clearly that of
command and execution, it is a little strange that the latter seems to go beyond the former's prescription. The omission in v. 9 of Abraham's "further action"[21] could have been
due to the author's presumption that his addressees knew
this rite well[22]. At the same time, it has the advantage of
avoiding a sheer repetition without affecting any progression at all.

8. V. 11

A theological intention links the present verse with vv.
2-4 of the chapter. In the context of the ritual prepared
for in vv. 9-10 and accomplished in v. 17, birds of prey
constituted a foreign element that posed a threat to

---

his representative assures someone that a transmitted message or an
entrusted mission comes from YHWH. Thus, the receiver is led from a
state of fear, worry or indecision to one of security and decision."
The texts using *ʾôt* in this last sense are: Ex. 3:12; 4:8a,b; Dt. 13:
2,3; Jdg. 6:7; 1 Sam. 14:10; 2 K. 20:8,9; Is. 7:11; 38:7,22; Ps. 86:
17.
21 The "further action" comprised the bisecting of only the animals and
not the birds and lining them up in two rows so as to form a passage
in between them.
22 Cf. O. Kaiser, ZAW, 70 (1958), 120.

Abraham[23]. Alternatively to the consumption of the carcasses[24], these birds of prey might have been intended to
pass between the parts in place of the smoking fire-pot and
the flaming torch in v. 17. If this had happened, they would
have foiled the entire purpose of the ritual Abraham was
preparing for. It is precisely this that allows for a correspondence between v. 11 and vv. 2-4, where the presence of
Eliezer, a foreigner, also posed a threat to Abraham.

9. V. 12

At face value, there is a discrepancy between the opening
temporal clause, "As the sun was just about to set", and the
night scene reported in v. 5. But if we bear in mind the
Hebrew way of reckoning the day from sunset to sunset, then
there is no difficulty in seeing the event reported in v. 12
as marking the end of the day that began with the sundown
just before the event in v. 5. This interpretation finds
support in Abraham's slaughtering of the animals described
in vv. 9-10. It is hardly conceivable that this was done in
the darkness of the night. It must have been carried out in
broad daylight.

Moreover, there were three animals to be slaughtered. The
patriarch would naturally need a good bit of time to accom-
plish YHWH's command. The two nights would ensure one full
day for Abraham to carry out his task.

There is therefore no discrepancy between v. 12 and v. 5.

At the close of the day, a *tardēmāh* befell Abraham. In the
OT, *tardēmāh* practically always heralds a special interven-

---

23 On this ground, R. Kilian, Die vorpriesterlichen Abrahamsüberliefe-
   rung, 48, maintains the secondary nature of v. 11.
24 A very common interpretation of the first part of the verse sees it
   as signalling an ill-omen. Cf. J. Skinner, Genesis, 281; P. Heinisch,
   Das Buch Genesis, 231; G. von Rad, Genesis, 182; J. Van Seters,
   Abraham in History and Tradition, 258; M. Anbar, JBL, 101 (1982), 47.
   As such it points to the servitude described in vv. 13-16. This interpretation fails to take into account the context of the animal
   rite, according to which the purpose of the birds of prey swooping
   down on the carcasses was to eat them up.

tion by the Lord[25]. In our text the *tardēmāh* is given in
view of the prophecy to follow immediately in vv. 13-16 and
the passing of the smoking fire-pot and the flaming torch
between the parts of the cut animals in v. 17. It must
therefore refer to some kind of visionary sleep here. There
is thus a double vision in Gen. 15: the first extending from
v. 1 to v. 5 and the second from v. 12 to v. 17.

As fear (*'ēmāh*) was common experience in the face of a
special intervention by YHWH[26], its occurrence here in Abraham's vision would seem to be quite ordinary.

10. Vv. 13-16

The Lord's long prophetic utterance began with *yādō*[c]*a*
tēda[c], thereby signalling an intention to answer Abraham's
bammāh *'ēdāh* in v. 8. If, as we have noted, v. 8 expresses
Abraham's request for a confirmative sign, then vv. 13-16
must be some sort of confirmation of the promise of land.

The prophecy being about the fate of Abraham's *zera*[c] maintains a certain link with the promise of a multitudinous
zera[c] in v. 5. It is the same *zera*[c] promised there who are
here prophesied to go through oppression and later be liberated.

The prophecy apparently intends to set an antithesis between Abraham and his descendants. There is, first of all,
a reversal of Abraham's exodus for his descendants: Abraham's exodus was from his homeland to a foreign land while
that of his descendants' would be from *hā'āreṣ lō' lāhem*
where they were considered as *gēr* (v. 13) to their homeland,
insofar as it was the land given to their father Abraham.
The verb used, *yāšûbû* (v. 16), is one that indicates a return - corroborating thereby the idea of home as the place

---

25 Cf. Gen. 2:21; 1 Sam. 26:12; Is. 29:10; Dan. 8:18; 10:9; Job 4:13;
   33:15. Prov. 19:15 seems to be the only exception.
26 For examples of an *'ēmāh* arising from YHWH's intervention, cf. Ex.
   15:15; 23:27; Dt. 32:25; Jos. 2:9 (here, the men of Jericho feared
   the Israelites because YHWH had given the latter the land); Job 13:21;
   20:25f.

of arrival. Secondly, the terrible oppression of Abraham's
descendants (v. 13) contrasts with the notice about Abraham's
peaceful death (v. 15).

But the thesis and antithesis find their synthesis in the
first case precisely in the *hā'āreṣ hazzō't* promised to Abraham for a heritage (v. 7), referred to here as *hēnnāh* and
promised as a gift to the descendants (v. 18). This undoubtedly ties the prophetic utterance as a whole to the rest of
the chapter. In the second case, the synthesis lies in the
idea of blessing. To die at a ripe old age is, in the OT
thinking, a great blessing[27] for Abraham. The exodus of his
descendants *bir^{e}kuš gādôl* (v. 14) certainly rings forth as a
blessing as well. Hence, the prophetic utterance sets in
bold relief the gift of land and bestowal of blessing as the
bond between Abraham's future and that of his descendants'.

The double blessing underlined here figures as a twofold
antithesis to the double curse of which vv. 2-3 smack: dying
without an offspring which, as we have seen, also implies
the uselessness of the promise of a great reward for Abraham. It seems likely that the *r^{e}kuš gādôl* (v. 14) refers
back to the promise in v. 1, thus giving it a further specification. In view of the unity between v. 1 and vv. 2-3, the
link of vv. 14-16 with v. 1 also stretches to vv. 2-3, so
that the double antithesis marks a literary unity rather
than a literary division.

Another difficulty in vv. 13-16 concerns a discrepancy
that seems to exist between the descendants' "four hundred
years" of oppression (v. 13bB) before their exodus and the
"four generations" (v. 16a) before their return "hither".
A. Caquot[28] provides a good solution to the problem[29]. There
are two different periods involved. The "four hundred years"

---

27 Old age is considered as a sign of God's favour (cf. Dt. 30:19-20;
   Prov. 16:31; 20:29). Gideon (Jdg. 8:32) and David (1 Chr. 29:28)
   were blessed with death at a good old age. Cf. also Job 42:17;
   Is. 65:20.
28 A. Caquot, Sem., 12 (1962), 63.
29 Another possible solution to the problem is to assume that the author
   of Gen. 15 drew his information from two different traditions - one
   attesting to "400 years" and the other to "four generations" - with-

refers to the sojourn in Egypt and the "four generations" to
the period after the exodus during which the "return" would
be effected. Not only is there no discrepancy between the
two chronological data in vv. 13 and 16, but positively they
tie in very well together. V. 16, while prophesying the return *hennāh,* clearly focuses on its delay - its length and
reason. In this way, it serves to explain the reason for the
long sojourn of Abraham's descendants in the land of slavery
announced in v. 13bB and the further four generations after
the exodus in v. 16a.

Finally, there appear to be a number of repetitions within
the unit. But these are not mere repetitions as they serve
to emphasize different aspects of the situations they pre-
dict. V. 13aB seems to repeat the information about Abraham's descendants being strangers:*gēr yihyeh zarʿăkā bᵉʾereṣ
lōʾ lāhem.* The apparent repetition is, in fact, a subtle affirmation of two different aspects that tie the verse to
two different parts of the chapter. The word *gēr* stresses
the aspect of Abraham's descendants, thereby connecting the
verse to v. 5, while *lōʾ lāhem* emphasizes that of the land
and thus looks ahead to the exodus (v. 16) and the gift of
the land in v. 18. Next, we have the use of *ʿabādû* in v.
13bA and v. 14aA. The first recurrence once again expresses
the standpoint of Abraham's descendants and the second that
of their oppressors. Finally, Abraham's death is foretold in
two parts in v. 15. At first sight, the two parts seem to be
synonymous, in which case the verse may be taken to contain
a repetition and thereby interpreted as an evidence of dis-
unity in the text. But it must be stressed that to die in
peace is not quite the same as to be buried at a ripe old
age. The first expresses the atmosphere or manner in which
the patriarch would die while the second prophesies in a
general way the time in which he would be buried. The OT
considers both as blessings. Therefore, the two stichs of

---

out harmonizing these data. But this solution poses two difficulties:
(i) it has to prove the existence of these two traditions for which
so far there is no evidence; and (ii) it goes against the literary
unity of the chapter.

v. 15 may be said to give a double reason for considering
Abraham's death a blessing.

11. V. 17

V. 17 opens with a grammatical construction parallel to
that in v. 12: *wayhî haššemeš bā'āh* (*lābô* in v. 12) followed
by *wᵉ* + noun with its verb in the perfect and then by
wᵉhinnēh. However, the time difference between the two
verses must be noted: v. 12 sets the time at sunset while
v. 17 brings the reader to a night environment. This latter
ambience seems to be necessitated by the author's desire to
present a deep impression Abraham was to have of what he was
about to see, as fire contrasts sharply with darkness. The
author's desire is betrayed by the recurrence of *ʿălāṭāh*
which, though tautological vis-à-vis the opening time indication of v. 17, he still uses. Viewed from the perspective
of this desire, his going beyond the limit of the full day
(from sundown to sundown) as expressed by *bayyôm hahû'* in
v. 18a is understandable.

The final expression *haggᵉzārîm hā'ēlleh* in v. 17 obviously refers to the parts of the animals prepared by Abraham.
Thus, the passing between the parts of the animals brought
to completion the entire ceremony begun in vv. 9-10. The
ceremony as such reflects very closely the character of the
sign that Gideon asked YHWH for to confirm his commission to
deliver the Israelites from the Midianites' oppression in
Jdg. 6:11-24[30]. It seems most probable, therefore, that the
rite of passing between the parts functioned as a sign. If
so, v. 17 ties in very well with vv. 13-16.

---

30 We note the following similar characteristics in Jdg. 6:11-24:
   (i) there was an apparition of the angel of the Lord (v. 11);
   (ii) after being commissioned, Gideon asked, *bammāh 'ôšîᶜᵃ 'et-
   yiśrā'el* (v. 15) which is explained as a request for confirmation
   through a sign *wᵉᶜāśîtā lî 'ôt* (v. 17); (iii) the sign to be given
   involved a preparation consisting of a command and the execution of
   the command (v. 20) and an action carried out by the angel of the
   Lord on what had been prepared by Gideon (v. 21).

The bond between v. 17 and vv. 13-16 exists not only at
the level of literary function but also at the level of contents. For this consideration, the use of the smoking fire-
pot *(tannûr ʿāšān)* and the flaming torch *(lappîd ʾēš)* in v.
17 is significant.

In the OT, by virtue of its power to consume, fire and
smoke that naturally accompanies it become not only symbols
but also means of punishment whereby God's anger breaks
forth against His enemies (cf. Gen. 19:24; Dt. 29:19; Pss.
18:9; 89:47; Is. 30:27; Jer. 4:4; 15:14; 21:10; Lam. 1:13;
2:3; Ezk. 22:31). The salvific aspect of fire derives from
its power to purify (cf. Is. 43:2; Zech. 13:9; Mal. 3:2).

Both these aspects are portrayed in the use of *lappîd (ʾēš)*
or *tannûr*. The former is found in Is. 62:1 and Zech. 12:6
where it expresses the salvation of Jerusalem (and Judah) as
well as the destruction of her enemies. Mal. 3:19f employs
the latter to depict the burning on the Lord's day that results in the destruction of the evildoers and the liberation
of those who fear YHWH.

In the OT, fire and smoke are also known to be elements
accompanying a vision or divine theophany. Thus, for example, in Isaiah's vision of YHWH, the temple was filled with
smoke (Is. 6:3-4) while a flaming torch *(lappîd)* was a cons-
tituent element of Ezekiel's vision (Ezk. 1:13) as well as
Daniel's (Dan. 10:6). If fire and smoke signal God's presence, Is. 31:9 is perfectly justified in depicting YHWH's
presence in Jerusalem in terms of *tannûr*.

In Gen. 15:17, the destructive-salvific qualities of the
smoking fire-pot and the flaming torch undoubtedly fit the
prediction in vv. 13-16 about the liberation of Abraham's
descendants resulting from YHWH's judgement on their oppressors. The connection of the implements with a vision or divine theophany[31] ties in well with the context of Abraham's
vision in vv. 12-17.

---

30 The smoking fire-pot and the flaming torch were most likely instru-
   ments used by Israel to produce smoke in a cultic theophany, Cf.
   O. Kaiser, ZAW, 70 (1958), 121; J. Van Seters, Abraham in History
   and Tradition, 258.

12. Vv. 18, 19-21

Dispensing with the use of *waw* altogether, v. 18 gives the impression of its being cut off from the rest of the chapter. Yet, its record of YHWH's promise to Abraham to give the land to his descendants can hardly be said to ignore all that has been said before. In fact, *zarʿăkā* must necessarily refer back to v. 5 and vv. 13-16 for all these verses talk about Abraham's *zeraʿ*. So too must "this land" refer back to the land promised in v. 7 and alluded to in v. 16.

In the light of the above, v. 18 is not an altogether new promise. Neither is it just a recapitulation of all the previous promises. It contains an element of both newness and recapitulation. The impression resulting from this is that v. 18 brings to bloom all the previous promises which thus build up to it as their climax.

The impression finds its confirmation in the use of *kārat bᵉrît*, the "terminus technicus" for the Sinaitic covenant[32], although there was no "covenant" in its technical sense involved here. The *bᵉrît* "cut" here added a great solemnity and seriousness to the promise: the land given to Abraham for the heritage would become heritage for his own son and descendants.

Of this land there are two definitions: one is a general geographical description (v. 18c)[33] and the other a gentilic one[34]. There is thus a progression of thought from the first to the second delineation.

---

32 In the entire Pentateuch, Gen. 15:18 is the only text which uses this technical term with the patriarchal promises as its object. Extra-Pentateuchal texts containing a similar usage of the expression are: Ps. 105:10-12 // 1 Chr. 16:16-18 and Neh. 9:8.

33 In Dt. 11:24, the formula appears without the adjective *haggādôl* and in 2 K. 23:29; 24:7 and Jer. 46:2,6,10 only the name *nᵉhar-pᵉrāt* is given.

34 Some exegetes view vv. 19-21 as an addition: cf. G. von Rad, *Genesis*, 267; C. Westermann, *Genesis 12-36*, 273. Westermann offers the following reasons for his stand; (i) while v. 18 is clearly rhythmic, vv. 19-21 are prosaic; and (ii) the list in vv. 19-21 is "eine Doppelung"

Since the boundaries delineated correspond to the ideal
confines of the Israelite kingdom in the Davidic-Solomonic
period[35], the land is seemingly depicted as "great" and thus
intended to add the final specification of the "great reward" promised in v. 1. Moreover, this land would be the
heritage of Abraham's descendants whose innumerability was
also considered "great".

The progression from v. 1 to vv. 18,19-21 is also found in
the sharpening of the concept of YHWH's self-identification
in v. 1. To serve as Abraham's "Shield", that is, "Protector", YHWH ought to possess power. Indeed, He had power, manifested by its cosmic sign indicated by the stars. In addition, He exercised it in His protection of Abraham from the
latter's exodus to his safe arrival in the Promised Land. He
would grant the same protection to Abraham's descendants by
liberating them from oppression and accompanying them all
the way from their exodus from the land of slavery to "this
land" to ensure their safe arrival there. It is not without
significance that all these manifestations of YHWH's power
and protection are presented in those sub-sections of the
chapter that, as we have traced, play the role of a sign.
This leads to the suspicion that ʾānōkî māgēn is intended to
signal these "sign subsections".

Along with the sharpening of focus of the above two stichs
of YHWH's "word" to Abraham in v. 1, the ground for the assurance ʾal-tîrāʾ becomes correspondingly clearer as well.

Thus, at both levels of theme and literary composition,
Gen. 15 is a coherent and closely-knit whole, whose unity
has been remarkably worked out by its author.

---

in respect of v. 18b: "Die geographische (v. 18b) wurde durch eine
politische Gebietsangabe erganzt." However, the rhythmic style of
v. 18 is not at all clear; in fact, it is even questionable. There
seems to be an incongruity in Westermann's second reason, since the
function of vv. 19-21 as an "Ergänzung durch eine politische Gebietsangabe" means it supplies a new element - in which case vv. 19-21
cannot be "eine Doppelung".

35 Cf. also 1 K. 4:21.

II. Literary Organization

1. Analysis based on the two Personages of the Chapter

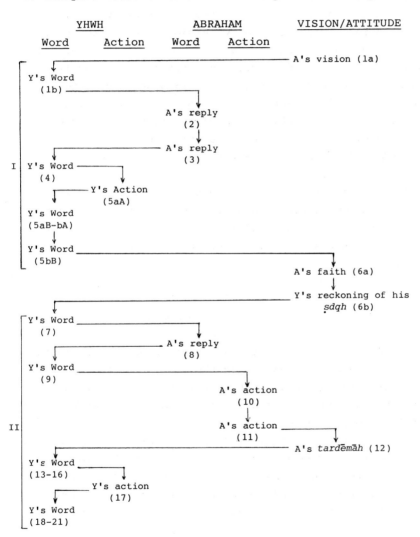

Since Gen. 15 revolves around only two personages, namely,
YHWH and Abraham, the simplest point of departure for an
analysis of its literary composition is constituted by individual units of their utterances introduced by the verb *'mr*
and their actions and attitudes/experiences. The above schema shows this personage-based literary organization of the
chapter. From the schema it stands out clearly that YHWH
made eight oral interventions and performed two actions,
while Abraham was accorded two visions, made three responses
and performed two actions. V. 6 divides all these elements
attributed to the two personages more or less equally between vv. 1-5 and vv. 7-21. Thus, YHWH has four utterances
and one action in each section. Abraham's two visions are
found in both the sections. However, of his three replies
two are distributed in the first section and one in the
second while both of his actions are reported only in the
second section.

These observations further corroborate the overall two-
part literary composition of the chapter traced by several
authors: vv. 1-5 and vv. 7-21, clamped together by v. 6. We
are now in a position to analyse the details of this composition.

2. Analysis of Details

The details of the literary organization of the chapter
may be unearthed by analysing the chapter on the basis of
the literary functions that contribute to its literary unity
that we have considered and the general organization based
on its two personages.

The foremost result yielded by this analysis is the parallelism between the subsections of which the two main sections of the chapter have been composed. Bearing in mind the
elements of correspondence we have traced between these main
sections, we may outline their parallel subsections as
follows:

I Vv. 1-5	II Vv. 7-17

Circumstantial note (1aA)

Abraham's vision (1aBC) ┤ Abraham's vision (12)

YHWH's promise accompanied by sign (v. 1 // v. 7)
. YHWH's word (1b) ┤ YHWH's word (7)
  + "Fear not" (1bA)
  + Self-identification (1bB)┤ + Self-identification (7a)
  + Promise ($ś\bar{a}k\bar{a}r$, 1bC) ┤ + Promise (of land, 7b)

Abraham's request for a sign (vv. 2-3 // v. 8)
. Abraham's word (2-3) ┤ Abraham's word (8)
  + Adonay YHWH (2aB) ┤ + Adonay YHWH
  + Question (2aB) ┤ + Question (Request for a
                                       sign)

  + Death in childlessness
    (2bA)
  + Usurper (= foreign ele- ┤ + Self-imposition of a
    ment, 2bB-3)   foreign element (11a)

Dispelling of Foreign Element (v. 4aB // v. 11)
. YHWH's word disqualifying ┤ Abraham's action (10-11)
  foreign element (4aB)   driving away foreign ele-
                       ment (11)

YHWH's verbal confirmation of promise (v. 4b // vv. 13-16)
. Blessing in the form of ┤ Blessing in the form of
  promise of heir (4b)   prophecy about Abraham's
                     death and his descendants'
                     exodus with great wealth
                     (13-16)

YHWH's action serving as visual sign (v. 5bA // v. 17)
. Led Abraham outside ┤ Passed between the parts
YHWH's word (5aB-bA)

YHWH's Promise specifying the "great reward" (v. 5bB //
                                     vv. 18-21)

. Promise of innumerable ┤ Promise of land-donation to
  descendants   descendants (18b)
                     Definition of land (18c-21)

Theological Declaration:
Abraham's faith and
YHWH's reckoning of righteousness (v. 6)

In both main sections, the central concern does not lie
with the person of Abraham as such but rather with his descendants - thus, in v. 5bB and v. 18b. Paradoxically
enough, in each case, the centrality of concern is set in

relief, not by a long statement about these descendants but rather by a short but forceful utterance[36]. In this way, the author gives the impression of purposely doing the unexpected to draw greater attention from his audience to the present utterance. In taking them by surprise through his abruptness, he apparently wants to leave his audience to wonder about the present utterance and somehow forget all that has gone before. If the impression we get is correct, the author has successfully achieved his aim.

Given the pattern, promise-sign-promise, in the literary organization of the chapter and the centrality of the second promise in each main section, we may safely maintain that while not unrelated to the first, the sign is primarily directed towards the second promise. It is probably for this reason that the sign in either part is sandwiched between the two promises[37]. The initial promise serves to announce the second and as such, is intentionally kept vague in v. 1 and incomplete in v. 7[38]. In turn, therefore, the second promise gives precision to the first.

This relationship between the first and the second promises at the level of the parts is also applicable to the two second promises at the level of the chapter. The promise of innumerable descendants necessarily calls for that of the gift of land, as a multitude without land could hardly survive. Thus, the second promise of the second part has $zera^c$ as one of its essential component terms and brings its corresponding promise to completion. It is precisely through this interplay between the two main parts of the chapter that its literary unity is strengthened.

----

36 The core of the second utterance is the one presented in v. 18b.
37 It would be a logical sequence to have the sign follow on the promise or assurance which it serves to confirm. Cf. Jdg. 6:11-24.
38 The promise has for its content the gift of land to Abraham alone: $l^ek\bar{a}$. In a context where innumerable descendants have been promised, their exclusion from the promise of land would be surprising.

CHAPTER 3

PROPHETIC INFLUENCE

    Despite its concern with patriarchal and, therefore, his-
torically pre-prophetic times, Gen. 15 contains certain
phrases as well as literary-stylistic elements and a mode of
organization that betray an extensive prophetic influence
on it. By "prophetic influence" here is meant the bearing
the relevant canonical prophetic writings have on Gen. 15,
regardless of whether such writings have themselves been
touched upon by the Deuteronomist or not. Generally, the
more recent trends tend to see a Deuteronomistic hand in the
final edition of much of the prophetic literature[1]. The
presence of the Deuteronomist in the prophetic literature is
inferred from the close affinity between the theological
concerns of both. There is, for example, "hardly any doubt
that Jeremiah agreed with the intentions of Deuteronomy and
Josiah's reform, since the central place given to criticism
of the Canaanite cult is a common factor between the two"[2].
    Debatable, however, is the extent to which the prophetic
literature owes its extant edition to the Deuteronomist.
Thus even at the level of just one book, namely, Jeremiah,
scholars find it difficult to reach a consensus[3]. What

---

1 R. Rendtorff, The Old Testament, 185, affirms, "Recently it has become
   increasingly clear that 'Deuteronomistic' revisions can also be recog-
   nized in many other areas of Old Testament literature. This holds not
   only for the Pentateuch, but also for the prophetic books, psalms and
   so on. Evidently this 'school' (or 'movement') worked widely in col-
   lecting, editing and reshaping the religious traditions of Israel."
2 Id, 207. Jer. 25:1-13 displays clear connections with 2 K. 17.
   E.W. Nicholson, Preaching to the Exiles, maintains that the sayings of
   Jeremiah in the prose tradition of the book were transmitted by the
   Deuteronomistic circle as they reflected the same theological issues
   facing this circle (cf. pages 12-13; 122-123; 131-133).
3 Cf. the major theories summarized by R.P. Carroll, Jeremiah, 38-50.

R.P. Carroll affirms of Jeremiah is true of all the prophetic books which exegetes regard as having been edited by the
Deuteronomist: the interpretation of the prophetic book depends on the answers given to the structure and date of the
Deuteronomistic history and their bearing on the book in
question. These answers are varied[4].

Without pretending to have more than just scratched one
small area of the very complex problem of the relationship
between the Deuteronomist and the prophetic literature, we
merely state our position here and hasten to qualify that it
is only one possible line of thinking. The Deuteronomistic
school undoubtedly represents a very advanced stage in Israel's theological development in the sixth century B.C. But
precisely because of the same theological advancement, it
would be difficult to accept merely one theological school
even in one particular decade. One has only to think here of
the commonly accepted "Priestly" school. Therefore, it would
not be far-fetched to postulate a prophetic school alongside
the Deuteronomistic and Priestly schools. As contemporaries,
they would have faced the same theological issues and even
at times given the same answers because: (i) they had basically the same theological tradition behind them; and
(ii) they would have, to some extent, influenced each other.

Vis-à-vis the present section of our work, it would make
very little difference if and to what extent the prophetic
literature has been influenced or edited by the Deuteronomist. What matters is that there is a distinct body of literature classified as prophetic and Gen. 15 betrays a certain
influence by this corpus in general and Jer. 34:18-20 and
Is. 7:1-17 in particular.

---

4 Cf. R.P. Carroll, Jeremiah, 49.

I. Typically Prophetic Language

1. The Formula of the Advent of the Divine Word

The introduction to YHWH's address in v. 1aB and its variant nominal form in v. 4aA occurs only in Gen. 15 in the
entire Pentateuch. It is a stereotyped introduction to a report of either a divine speech or a divine revelation to a
prophet[5]. Its use here is the first and clearest evidence of
a prophetic influence on the chapter[6].

2. *bammaḥăzeh*

In the entire OT, the word *maḥăzeh* - a derivative of *ḥzh* -
occurs only in four texts, namely, Gen. 15:1; Num. 24:4,6;
and Ezk. 13:7. It is beyond the scope of our study to analyse the occurrences of the root *ḥzh* and all its derivatives
in the OT[7]. It suffices for our present purpose to consider
only the above texts.

The two texts from Numbers are situated in the context of
at least four attempts[8] made by Balak the Moabite king to
request Balaam, a pagan prophet, to curse the Israelites in
the face of a serious threat from the latter. On all these

---

5 Except for 1 K. 6:11 where Solomon is the addressee, and Hag. 1:1,3;
2:1,10 where *b^eyad* in place of *'el* or *l^e* presents the prophet not so
much as the addressee but as the agent of *d^ebar-yhwh*, the formula records God's word going to a prophet.

6 Cf. O. Kaiser, ZAW, 70 (1958), 110. In footnote 12, Kaiser points out,
"Als terminus tech. für den Offenbarungsempfang des Propheten erscheint
es zuerst bei Jeremia 1:2,4,11,13; 2:2; 13:3,8; 16:1 u.ö. Bei den äl-
teren Propheten begegnet es nur in den Überschriften, vgl. Hos. 1:1;
Mi. 1:1; Zeph. 1:1."

7 Cf. H.F. Fuhs, Sehen und Schauen, for a very detailed analysis of the
root *ḥzh* as it is used in both ANE and OT texts.

8 Cf. Num. 22:6; 22:41; 23:13-14; 23:17. In one other attempt, Balak
asked Balaam neither to curse nor bless the Israelites; cf. Num. 23:25.

occasions God worked Balaam into blessing His people.

Balaam's explanation for his utterances of blessing on the
Israelites in Num. 24:3b-4 is reiterated in 24:15b-16. Each
of these explanations opens with a triple $n^{e'}um$ followed
every time by a qualification about Balaam and introduces an
oracle, again of blessing on Israel and Jacob (= Judah). The
first qualification is clear enough. It identifies Balaam as
"son of Beor" (vv. 3bA; 15bA). The second and third qualifi-
cations (vv. 4 and 16) are problematic. The word $\check{s}^e tum$ has
been given two opposite meanings: "closed" and "opened"[9].
The grammatical function of the divine names in the third
qualification is not clear.

In an extensive study of Num. 22-24, H. Roulliard[10] has
demonstrated clearly that the triple qualification of $n^{e'}um$
in Num. 24:3b-4 and 15b-16 points back to the story about
Balaam's ass. For, the expression $n\bar{o}p\bar{e}l\ \hat{u}g^el\hat{u}y\ ^c\bar{e}n\bar{a}yim$ (vv.
4b, 16b) refers to the divine intervention in that story
causing Balaam to "fall on his face" and have his "eyes
opened" (Num. 22:31)[11]. It would appear from this latter remark that initially Balaam set out in response to Balak's
request with a hostile attitude towards the Israelites. This
would be the sense of $\check{s}^e tum$ in the second qualification as
is confirmed by the Arabic word $\check{s}atuma$ which means "to be
malicious"[12].

A comparison with 2 Sam. 23:1-13 unearths the grammatical
function of the divine names as subjective rather than objective genitives. In other words, $'imr\hat{e}-'el$ means "what God
says" while $mah\check{a}zeh\ \check{s}adday$ "what Shadday sees". If that is
so, the third qualification clearly goes back to God's words
in Num. 22:12,20,35 and 23:15,16[13] and to what He sees in
24:1: $k\hat{\imath}\ t\hat{o}b\ b^{e'}\hat{e}n\hat{e}\ yhwh\ l^eb\bar{a}r\bar{e}k\ 'et-yi\acute{s}r\bar{a}'\bar{e}l$[14]. On this

---

9 Cf. G. Vermès, Scripture and Tradition, and H. Roulliard, La Péricope
  de Balaam, 347-350.
10 H. Roulliard, Id.
11 For this reason, Roulliard maintains that the earliest stratum of
   Num. 22-24 lies in the story of Balaam's ass (cf. Id, 350-351).
12 H. Roulliard, Is, 350.
13 God's words are reflected in the oracles to follow: 23:7-10, 19-24.
14 The opposite of it was wished by Balak in Num. 22:27b.

ground Balaam became single-minded in his mission in that he
proclaimed only what he had heard from God (cf. Num. 22:18,
38; 23:12,26; 24:13) and seen from Him (cf. Num. 24:4,16).

The two oracles in Num. 24:4-9 and 16-19 are therefore
oracles of blessing. Basically, they announced YHWH's working out for Israel and Jacob His promises of posterity
(24:7)[15] and land (24:17-19). The triple n^e'um introducing
them emphasizes the intention to give them a prophetic character[16]. The two roots $šm^c$ and hzh bring to bold relief the
fact that Balaam was true to his mission by faithfully com-
municating YHWH's words and vision about Israel and Judah -
the object of the prophet's own hearing and vision. In this
sense, he was God's legitimate spokesman[17].

Passing on to the next text, we find that the utterance
of Ezk. 13:7 came as a reaction against the activities of
Israel's false prophets. These latter claimed to have
$mahăzeh$ to make believe that their utterances were n^e'um
YHWH because it was common knowledge that prophetic oracles
came from God in a $mahăzeh$. Through a rhetorical question,
Ezekiel declared their $mahăzeh$ delusive and their divination
false because 'ănî lō' dibbartî. In other words, the false
prophets had not uttered what YHWH had uttered. In fact,
YHWH had simply not spoken to them at all. By implication,
YHWH too had not appeared to them to show them what He had
seen. Therefore, their "vision" was delusive. On these two
grounds, they had no authority or authorization to speak on
YHWH's behalf, that is, to function as His prophets. Once
again, we are confronted with the prophetic connotation of
$mahăzeh$.

---

15 On Num. 24:7a, H. Simian-Yofre, Messianic Hope, 30, points out that
   $mayim$ in the OT "can biologically signify human seed, and as a consequence, ancestry" (cf. Is. 48:1), nzl "does not mean only to overflow....but also to flow smoothly" (cf. Dt. 32:2; Jer. 19:17; Song
   4:16), and the dual form of $d^e li/doli$, derived from dly II (= dll II:
   "to make to descend, to let hang, to suspend, to balance oneself")
   refers to a man's reproductive organ. Thus, Num. 24:7a does allude
   to posterity.
16 H. Roulliard, La Péricope de Balaam, 353, considers n^e'um as "du mo-
   dèle du discours proprement prophètique."
17 Cf. H.F. Fuhs, Sehen und Schauen, 178.

As we have seen, the formula of the advent of the divine
word in Gen. 15:1 is clearly prophetic. As such, it is the
equivalent of n^e'um yhwh found in prophetic oracles. If
maḥāzeh is used with it, there is every reason to take Gen.
15:1 as intending to bring out the double dimension of a
prophetic oracle: audition and vision[18]. What was communicated to Abraham was precisely what YHWH was uttering and
seeing. That is to say, Abraham was made to hear what YHWH
was uttering and see what He was seeing about the patriarch's posterity and their inheriting a land. The
patriarch's acceptance of the entirety of this vision and
audition is expressed by his faith in YHWH (Gen. 15:6).
Thus, Abraham was made to enjoy the prophetic qualification
given to Balaam but denied to the false prophets of
Ezekiel's time.

Yet, Abraham is not presented as exercising a prophetic
role. He had no audience to which to communicate His message. Moreover, the message was more a promise or, to be
precise, an oath than a prophecy. Therefore, the prophetic
traits, especially the formula of the advent of YHWH's word
and maḥāzeh, strictly speaking, do not belong to Gen. 15.
The author of the chapter must have found his inspiration
from prophetic texts like Num. 24 and Ezk. 13:7.

3. 'ădōnāy yhwh

Of the four Pentateuchal texts employing this double title
of God, Gen. 15 claims two, viz., vv. 2 and 8, while the
other two are Dt. 3:24 and 9:26. It is significant that of
the other 280 occurrences of the title in the OT, 257 are
found in the prophetic literature - 216 in Ezekiel, 22 in
Isaiah, 20 in Amos, 12 in Jeremiah, and one each in four

---

18 We disagree with J. Lindblom, HUCA, 32 (1961), 95, that "the narrator
   in 1-6 wanted to say that Abraham had a vision of Yahweh in which the
   subsequent dialogue and action took place." For, d^ebar-yhwh in v. 1aB
   does not mean "word about YHWH" but rather "word spoken by YHWH".

minor prophets[19]- while the Deuteronomistic historical
book[20] have only 12 and the Psalter[21] 7. These statistics
reveal the prophetic predominance in the use of the double
title and perhaps point to its prophetic slant.

The way the double title is used by the prophets is also
significant. Many prophetic oracles are introduced with
the opening formula, $kōh$ '$āmar$ '$ădōnāy$ $yhwh$, which recurs
137 times or concluded with n^{e}'um $yhwh$ found in 89 texts.
These formulae have the force of authenticating the divine
origin of the oracles to which they are attached.

Almost all the non-prophetic texts[22] employ the title to
address YHWH either in a prayer or dialogue with Him. While
this usage differs from the normal prophetic uses of the title dealt with above, it is not unknown among the prophets.
Thus, for example, Am. 7:2,5 address YHWH as '$ădōnāy$ $yhwh$ in
a plea for forgiveness and mercy. Similarly, the use of the
title to refer to God as a third person is as much in evidence in the prophetic literature (cf. Mi. 1:2; Zech. 9:14)
as in 1 K. 2:26 and Ps. 68:9.

It is possible, as we have considered in the opening para-
graphs of this chapter, that the prophetic and non-prophetic
uses of the title emerged from their own respective ambience. But from the rather wide range of the ways the
prophets handled the title, this would seem very unlikely.
Apart from what has been presented above, two other modes in
which the prophets employ the title may be noted. Am. 4:2
and 6:8 connect the title with YHWH's oath, while Ezk. 36:4
calls attention to '$ădōnāy$ $yhwh$. If the prophetic use of the
divine title is so widespread and fluid, it would be difficult to deny altogether any kind of influence it would have
exerted on the deuteronomistic texts that use the title. In
the case of Gen. 15, especially in v. 2, in view of its prophetic setting, such an influence from the prophets seem obvious. The '$ădōnāy$ $yhwh$ placed on Abraham's lips in vv. 1

---

19 Hab. 3:19; Zech. 9:14; Ob. 1; Mi. 1:2.
20 Jos. 7:7; Jdg.6:22; 16:2; 2 Sam. 7:18,19(bis),20,22,28,29; 1 K. 2:26; 8:53.
21 Pss. 68:21; 69:7; 71:5,16; 73:28; 109:21; 141:8.
22 The exceptions are 1 K. 2:26; Pss. 68:9; 71:16(?); 73:28(?)

and 8 express his recognition of the divine origin of the
promises in vv. 1 and 7.

II. Two Specific Texts

If the above expressions and style point to some prophetic influence on the chapter in a general way, there are traces of a specific influence from Jer. 34:18-20 and Is. 7:1-17.

1. Jer. 34:18-20

A close parallel seems to exist between the rite of passing between the parts of the cut animals in Gen. 15:9-10,17 and that in Jer. 34:18-20.

The origin and significance of this rite have drawn the attention of not a few scholars[23]. Among them a good number have looked to extra-biblical documents of the second millennium B.C. for light. They see Mari and Alalakh as offering the best elements for a solution.

From Mari we have two texts that have been considered as parallels to Gen. 15:17. The first refers to the making of a treaty between "the Hana people and the people of the region of Idamaraz who both belonged to the administrative territory of Mari"[24] supervised by a representative of King Zimrilim. While the covenanting partners brought "puppy and lettuce", the royal representative in obedience to the King's order slaughtered "the foal of an ass"[25] whereby the treaty was concluded.

---

23 Apart from commentaries on Genesis and studies on Chapter 15, the following articles treat this problem extensively, if not exclusively: P.J. Henninger, Bib., 34 (1953), 344-353; M. Noth, in The Laws in the Pentateuch and Other Studies, 108-177; F. Vattioni, Biblos-Press, 6 (1965), 53-61; S.E. Loewenstamm, VT, 18 (1968), 500-507; M. Weinfeld, JAOS, 90 (1970), 184-203 and 468-469; Id, TDOT, II, 253-279; A. de Pury, Promesse divine et légende cultuelle, 312-321; G.F. Hasel, JSOT, 19 (1981), 61-78; G.J. Wenham, JSOT, 22 (1982), 134-137: K.S. Kapelrud, JSOT, 22 (1982), 138-140.
24 M. Noth, The Laws in the Pentateuch and Other Studies, 109.
25 Cf. ANET, 482, Col. b.

The second Mari text records the treaty between Naram-Sin
and the Elamites involving the sacrifice of a bull and two
doves[26].

From Alalakh, the Šurpu documents talk of "an oath taken
by holding a torch", "the oath of furnace, stove" and so
forth, as well as "the oath of the slaughtered sheep and the
touching of its wound"[27]. From these documents, M. Weinfeld
concludes that the "torch and the oven are part of the procedure of taking the oath"[28].

Another text has to do with the oath made by Abba-El involving the cutting of the neck of a lamb[29] to guarantee
Yarimlim his gift of the city of Alalakh to Yarimlim in ex-
change for the destroyed Irridi. As he carried out the ritual, Abba-El said, "(May I be cursed) if I take back what
I gave you"[30].

A text more commonly studied in connection with Gen. 15 is
the treaty between Ashurnirari V of Assyria and Matti'ilu of
Arpad[31]. Matti'ilu would become like the slaughtered lamb
involved in the treaty if he should fail to abide by it.

None of the above texts tells of a cutting of the animals
used in the ritual into two and a passing between their
parts. These two actions were essential elements in the rite

---

26 In footnote 130, M. Weinfeld, JAOS, 90 (1970), reproduces S.N. Kramer's translation of the treaty text as found in The Sumerians, 311:
   "Two doves on whose eyes he had put spices (and) on whose heads he
   had strewn cedar (?) he caused to be eaten for Enlil at Nippur (with
   the plea): 'As long as dogs exist... if the Unmaite... breaks his
   words..'"
27 For the documents in general, cf. E. Reiner, AfO Beiheft, 11 (1958).
   The specific texts that concern us here are Šurpu III:93: "curse
   caused by holding a torch and taking an oath"; Šurpu III:145: "the
   oath of furnace, grill, kiln, stove, brazier or bellows"; and Šurpu
   III:35: "an oath sworn by slaughtering a sheep and touching the wound".
28 M. Weinfeld, JAOS, 90 (1970), 196.
29 On the ground that the lamb was supplied by Yarimlim, M. Weinfeld,
   JAOS, 90 (1970), 197, sees a parallel situation to the rite in Gen.
   15:17: "the inferior party delivers the animals while the superior
   party swears the oath". But the information regarding Yarimlim sup-
   plying the lamb is obtained from another text in the same series of
   documents which is partly damaged.
30 This is D.J. Wiseman's translation of šumma ša addinukummi eleqqu;
   cf. JCS, 12 (1958), 126.
31 This treaty belongs to the 8th cent. B.C. Cf. the translation by E.
   Weidner, AfO Beiheft, 8 (1932-33), 16ff, reproduced in ANET, 532f.

described in Gen. 15:9-10,17. Thus, none of the above texts
can truly be said to contain a parallel to Gen. 15.

One text that records a passing between the parts of a cut
victim[32] is the Hittite ritual for the purification of an
army. But then, this rite had nothing to do with a promise,
an oath or a covenant. Moreover, purification does not fit
in with Gen. 15 at all. Would God need purification? If so,
from what?

Before ruling out the ANE as a possible source for the
rite in Gen. 15, one final text needs to be examined. It
contains a treaty between Barga'yah, King of KTK, and Matti-
'ilu, King of Arpad, and dates back to about the middle of
the eighth century B.C.[33]. Maledictions were given in terms
of the melting of wax, blindness of "a man of wax" and cutting up of a calf. While it is clear that the last symbolic
representation alluded to the fate of the transgressor of
the covenant, its parallelism with Gen. 15 must be rejected
since, like all the other ANE rites, it lacked the essential
passing between the parts of the cut animals.

Upon close examination, therefore, none of the ANE texts
passes as an appropriate parallel to the animal rite in Gen.
15[34]. This leaves us with just Jer. 34:18-20 to consider.
This pericope is situated within a passage denouncing the
transgressors of the $b^e r\hat{\imath} t$ proclaiming the emancipation of

---

32 Cf. O. Masson, RHR, 137 (1950), 5-25.
33 This document was written in old Aramaic. Attention has been called
   to it in connection with Gen. 15 by G.F. Hasel, JSOT, 19 (1981), 61-
   78, and in connection with Jer. 34:18-20 by D.L. Petersen, BiR, 22
   (1977), 8. The text, translated by F. Rosenthal, is reproduced in
   ANET, 660.
34 D.L. Petersen, id, attempts to demonstrate the Hittite or Mesopota-
   mian origin of the animal slaughter as a component ratification ritual and trace a shift in its significance from the second millennium texts (which include Gen. 15) to the first millennium ones (including Jer. 34). His appeal to the manipulation of blood in Ex. 24:
   3-8 - half being sprinkled on the altar and half on the people - and
   in Enuma Elish (vi, 32ff) to explain the meaning of the animal slaughter has no relevance to Gen. 15 where no blood is mentioned at all.
   Marduk's creation of the heavenly vault with one half of Tiamat's
   corpse and of the base for the earth with the other half had entirely
   nothing to do with any imaginable covenant. In fact, it had to do
   with its opposite, as it involved a fight that ended with murder.

the slaves in accordance with the Mosaic law of manumission.
The $b^e r\hat{\imath}t$ was made thus: $h\bar{a}^c\bar{e}gel\ldots k\bar{a}r^e t\hat{u}\ li\check{s}nayim$
$wayya^cabr\hat{u}\ b\hat{e}n\ b^e t\bar{a}r\bar{a}w$ (v. 18).

As far as the rite is concerned, both Gen. 15:19-10,17 and
Jer. 34:18-20 involved the cutting of an animal into two
parts, a placing of these parts opposite each other and a
passing between them. Unlike the similar Hittite rite considered above, the two cases here were connected with a $b^e r\hat{\imath}t$
whose terms coincided: the liberation of Abraham's descendants from oppression (= slavery) in Gen. 15 (cf. v. 14) and
of all slaves in Jer. 34 (cf. vv. 14-15). Moreover, the
$b^e r\hat{\imath}t$ was unilateral[35] as the obligation fell only on one
party. The liberation was to be effected by the superior
party. In Gen. 15 the superior party was YHWH who was represented by the cultic implements (v. 17). In Jer. 34, "the
princes of Judah and Jerusalem, the eunuchs, the priests and
all the people of the land"[36] were the only ones reported to
have passed between the parts (v. 19). They made this $b^e r\hat{\imath}t$
before YHWH ($l^e p\bar{a}n\bar{a}y$ in vv. 15, 18)[37]. Its terms were those
contained in YHWH's covenant with their fathers (v. 13) so
that when they failed to keep them they were considered to
have transgressed YHWH's covenant ($b^e r\hat{\imath}t\hat{\imath}$ in v. 18). Thus,
the $b^e r\hat{\imath}t$ made through the animal rite in Jer. 34:18-20 was
in reality a unilateral oath. Vis-à-vis the subjects of the
covenant, namely, the slaves to be liberated[38], those who

---

35 Some scholars maintain that the $b^e r\hat{\imath}t$ in Jer. 34:18-20 was bilateral;
    cf. e.g. A. Caquot, Sem., 12 (1962), 61; P. Kalluveetil, Declaration
    and Covenant, 14.
36 By the time of Jeremiah, "the people of the land" had become such a
    dominant power in the capital city that they were ranked among the
    national leaders; cf. Jer. 37:2; 44:21; 52:6,25. On the basis of some
    royal annals in the Books of Kings and Chronicles, T. Ishida, AJBI,
    1 (1975), 23-28, reaches the conclusion that they played such an im-
    portant role in the royal crises that they became a force to be rec-
    koned with.
37 S.E. Loewenstamm, VT, 18 (1968), 503, interprets $l^e p\bar{a}n\bar{a}y$ as expres-
    sing YHWH's role of being the divine witness to guarantee observance
    of the $b^e r\hat{\imath}t$. For support he appeals, in footnote 1, to evidence from
    Sfiré A. 11:10-13.
38 J.A. Soggin, History of Israel, 251, thinks that the emancipation of
    the slaves was probably aimed at strengthening the army.

"passed between the parts" were the superior party[39]. In this regard, their position corresponded to YHWH's in Gen. 15:17.

Granted the very close parallelism between the rites and their significance in both texts as well as the absence of any other evidence for a similar use of the animal rite in both the OT and ANE, it is reasonable to presume a literary relationship between Gen. 15:9-10,17 and Jer. 34:18-20. Further light on this relationship is shed by the use of the root *btr* in both texts. Apart from Cant. 2:17 where there are variant readings for *bāter* [40], all the other five occurrences of the root *btr* throughout the OT are clustered in our two texts[41]. It refers to the act of dissecting the animals or the resultant parts thereof. We note that the more common word for "cutting into parts" seems to be *gzr* which occurs as a noun in Gen. 15:17[42]. Despite the author's awareness of this word, he still chose to use *btr* in v. 10. What is even more significant is the triple use of that word in one verse. It would seem that there the author was not prepared to sacrifice any of these three occurrences of the word to avoid the literary clumsiness that they would unavoidably effect on the verse. There must be a reason for all this.

A plausible explanation is forthcoming if one subscribes to a literary dependence of Gen. 15:9-10,17 on Jer. 34:18-20. For, the clumsy triple use of *btr* was probably due to a situation of some constraint the author of Gen. 15 was

---

39 There is no ground for M. Weinfeld's statement, "... in Jer. xxxiv ... it is the inferior who does it" (i.e. places himself under oath); cf. JAOS, 90 (1970), 199. D.L. Petersen's statement, "...we know of no covenant in which the obviously superior party... is put under a potential curse" [BiR, 22 (1977), 9] fails to take this detail of Jer. 34 into account.
40 Cf. the variants in the lower critical apparatus of BHK.
41 The word is used as a verb twice in Gen. 15:10 and as a noun once in Gen. 15:10 and twice in Jer. 34:18f.
42 Cf. 1 K. 3:25,26; 2 K.6:4; Ps. 136:13. Its popular usage might have given rise to its derived meanings like "eating up" or "slaughtering" in war (Is. 9:19), "being separated from" (2 Chr. 26:21; Is. 53:8), "being taken away" (Lam. 3:54). The author's switching-over to the use of a popular word should not cause any surprise. Moreover, as E. Kutsch, in H. Gese et al. (Eds), FS K. Elliger, 126, points out,

confronted with as he tried to rework the prophetic material
into his own composition. The root was used twice in Jer.
34:18-20 so that any deviation from it by using another word
would most probably have created a feeling of uneasiness.
This uneasiness, however, faded off as the author reached
v. 17 where he felt free to have recourse to another - a
more common - word: *gzr*.

Supporting the dependence of Gen. 15 on Jer. 34 in favour
of an reverse relationship is the fact that Jeremiah did not
seem to show a particularly keen interest in the patriarchal
traditions - leave alone draw on them. The only text in the
book that makes an explicit reference to the patriarchs is
Jer. 33:26. But, even then, the prophet's concern was not
with the patriarchs "per se". It was rather with their descendants: "the seed of Abraham, Isaac and Jacob" of whose
fortunes YHWH, out of His mercy, would work out a restoration[43].

If it is true that Gen. 15 depended on Jer. 34, how then
is their difference in the number of animals used for the
rite to be explained? Gen. 15 lists three animals while Jer.
34:18 records the use of only one. It may well be that the
author of Gen. 15, like Ezk. 39:18, intended to make a loose
reference to Israel's entire sacrificial system[44]. All the
three animals, we note, were among the four victims prescribed for the various types of offerings in Lev. 9:3-4[45].
O. Procksch observes that all these were domestic animals
which Israel, once settled in the land, could use in her
various sacrifices[46]. The author's intention seems to become
clearer through the inclusion of the two birds, *tôr* and

---

gzr does appear in a covenant context. So also Z. Falk, JSS, 14
(1969), 39-44.

43 Cf. R.P. Carroll, Jeremiah, 639.

44 J. Van Seters, Abraham in History and Tradition, 258, says, "The specific designation of the kinds of animals and the treatment of the
birds resembles cultic regulations for sacrifice." On Ezk. 39:18, cf.
the comments of G.A. Cooke, Ezekiel, 421.

45 For a sin offering *śeᶜîr ᶜizzîm* is used; for a burnt offering either
ᶜēgel or *kebeś* (both a year old and without blemish); and for a peace
offering *śôr* or *'ayil*.

46 Cf. O. Procksch, Genesis, 103.

gôzal, prescribed as substitutes for the above-listed animals in case of poverty.

Besides being a loose reference to Israel's sacrificial system, the list of three animals and two birds could also well reflect the author's intention of allowing one victim for each of the five promises without, however, being specific about the attribution[47]. This was probably why he dropped off one animal from the sacrificial list prescribed by the Mosaic law.

If the above dual intention of the author has been correctly detected, then it seems reasonable to suspect that his list of animals and birds, meant to fit in with his intention, is an expansion of the original requirement which the report in Jer. 34 reflects.

In view of this relationship, it seems likely that the introduction of *hā'ayiṭ* in Gen. 15 as an attempt by foreign elements to foil the ritual prepared for by Abraham - especially if their swooping down was to consume the carcasses of the cut animals - was inspired by the announcement of God's punishment for the people's transgression in terms of turning them *lᵉma'ăkāl lᵉ'ôp haššāmayim* in Jer. 34:20[48]. However, by not qualifying the action of the birds of prey on the carcasses, the author of Gen. 15 left it to his audience to interpret it.

Another point that finds its clarification in the light of the relationship we have traced concerns Abraham's peaceful death in Gen. 15:15, strangely announced in the midst of a prophecy about his descendants. For in the context of Jer. 34:18-20 there is also an announcement of Zedekiah's peaceful death despite the catastrophe to befall his city: *bᵉšālôm tāmût* (v. 5). Furthermore, both announcements add a note of honour surrounding the deaths talked about - in Zedekiah's case: *ûkᵉmiśrᵉpôt 'ăbôteykā hammᵉlākîm hāri'šonîm*

---

47 The five promises are: great reward, blood-heir, great posterity, land for Abraham and land for his descendants.
48 The full phrase is *lᵉma'ăkāl lᵉ'ôp haššāmayim ûlᵉbĕhemat hā'āreṣ* and is one of the Deuteronomist's metaphors for a curse: cf. Dt. 28: 26. It is found elsewhere in Jer. e.g. 15:3; 16:4; 19:7.

'ăšer-hāyû l^{e}pāneykā kēn yiśr^{e}pû-lāk (Jer. 34:5) and for
Abraham: tiqqābēr b^{e}śêbāh ṭôbāh (Gen. 15:15b).

2. Is. 7:1-17

The most specific evidence of Isaiah's influence on Gen.
15 seems to have come from Is. 7:1-17. The protagonists of
both stories were faced with a situation of threat: Abraham
his childlessness and thus the eventuality of losing his position as well as possession to a foreign heir; Ahaz the imminent end of his reign and dynasty through the usurpation
of his throne by a non-Davidic king (Is. 7:6). Confronted
with such a situation, both protagonists were eager to work
out a stable future for themselves. Abraham's eagerness is
reflected in his question and remark to YHWH in Gen. 15:2-3.
Ahaz's visit to the "upper pool" (Is. 7:3) was part of his
precautionary measure to arm himself against the Syro-
Ephraimite conspiracy to depose him[49].

It was in the context of such a situation of threat that
YHWH came to the rescue of His chosen ones. Except for its
prophetic medium in the Isaian passage, YHWH's intervention
is depicted in much the same way in both chapters. Dispelling their fear with the same formula - 'al-tîrā' (Gen.15:
1b; Is. 7:4) - He gave them much the same kind of assurance
expressed negatively: lō' yirāš^{e}kā zeh (Gen. 15:4a) and lō'
tāqûm w^{e}lō' tihyeh (Is. 7:7b)[50]. It is striking that in both
cases the assurance was given with great solemnity, introduced in Gen. 15:4 by w^{e}hinnēh d^{e}bar-yhwh 'ēlaw lē'mōr and
in Is. 7:7 by kōh 'āmar 'adōnāy yhwh. The solemnity of the
assurance served to underline YHWH's serious and unquestion-
able commitment to His word.

---

49 Cf. H. Wildberger, Jesaja Kapitel 1-12.
50 With 'al-tirā' followed by an assurance from YHWH, we encounter the
    basic elements of the oracle of salvation traced by J. Begrich, ZAW,
    52 (1934), 81-92. Begrich's classification of Is. 7:4-9 as an expand-
    ed oracle of salvation applies well to Gen. 15:1-4.

After elaborating on YHWH's assurance to Ahaz in Is. 7:8a,
9a[51], Isaiah made the following declaration: *'im lō' ta'ămînû*
kî lō' tē'āmēnû (Is. 7:9b). Two significant points must be
noted here. Firstly, there is a switch to the use of plural
verbs. It indicates that Isaiah somewhat "took off" from his
personal encounter with Ahaz and addressed the "house of
David" or even his audience. Secondly, the declaration is
conditional. It reflects the prophet's and therefore YHWH's
respect for the audience's freedom in giving their response.
From this point of view it was a challenge thrown to the audience to take their stand in a situation of crisis. There
is thus a certain "theologizing" here. Gen. 15:6 too is
marked by the same literary phenomenon of the author's "taking off" from the story to turn to the audience[52] and "theo-
logize".

The point to consider now is: what exactly is being
"theologized" in both our texts and what relationship is
there between them? The double question centres around the
two key concepts in each text: *ta'ămnînû* and *tē'āmēnû* in
Is. 7:9b and *he'ĕmin byhwh* and *ḥšb ṣedāqāh* in Gen. 15:6.

A clear common denominator between the two verses is the
recurrence of *'mn-hiphil*[53]. However, Is. 7:9b uses it in an
absolute way while Gen. 15:6 with *be*. The absolute use of
'mn-hiphil seems constantly to mean "to be firm; to hold

---

51 The conjunction *kî* in v. 8a is to be read as expository. H. Simian-
   Yofre, Messianic Hope, 51, offers four reasons in favour of this
   reading: (a) It eliminates the implicit affirmation of the interpretation that Jerusalem is the head of Judah which would be the central
   point of an elliptical reading of vv. 8a,9a. For such an interpretation, cf. O. Procksch, Genesis, 116; E. Würthwein, in Id, FS K. Heim,
   61; also in Id, Wort und Existenz, 140. F.D. Hubmann, BN, 26 (1985),
   43-44. suggests that the Immanuel sign which he interprets as referring to Ahaz's son serves to complement vv. 7-9a, thereby supporting
   the elliptical reading of vv. 8a,9a. (b) *qwm* in v. 7 can be read as
   durative, referring to the stability of a kingdom. (c) Vv. 5-6 would
   be the protasis of vv. 7a,8a,9a and not the reason for v. 4. The conjunction *ya'an kî* introduces an accusation which awaits the pro-
   nouncement of condemnation, not sufficiently expressed by v. 7 without vv. 8a,9a. (d) If vv. 8-9 are the subject of v. 7, then the con-
   traposition with the ambitious pretensions of these nations in v. 6
   becomes much clearer.
52 Cf. pages 47-48 above.
53 Many studies have been made on *'mn-hiphil* in the OT. Cf. the two long

one's stand on something; not to be moved (physically or
emotionally)"[54]. Its sense in Is. 7:9b would therefore seem
to be that Ahaz and his house and even the audience should
not despair ("emotionally moved") and should therefore not
be physically moved into any action.

This sense ties in well with the opening exhortation the
prophet was asked to give Ahaz in Is. 7:4[55] where *hašqeṭ*
means refraining from any physical move[56] and *lᵉbābᵉkā 'al-
yērak* not allowing oneself to be emotionally weakened. However, if through Isaiah YHWH could advocate passivity for
Ahaz at this stage of the threat, it was because He Himself
was going to intervene in the latter's favour. His assurance
in v. 7 bore evidence to this plan of His. All that He asked
of Ahaz was to put his whole confidence in His fidelity and
power to intervene by not succumbing further to the tempta-
tion to have recourse to any human strategy as he had already started to do by inspecting the "upper pool". Thus, the
exhortation in Is. 7:4 and the first part of the conditional
declaration in Is. 7:9b seem to convey more than a merely
physical and psychological firmness. Ultimately, they root
this firmness in YHWH's promise of a favourable intervention
(v. 7)[57], thereby expressing one's reliance on YHWH alone.

Used with *bᵉ*, *'mn-hiphil* expresses "confidence in something or someone" and puts its emphasis on "the foundation
or grounds (a person or thing) of the confidence"[58]. Thus,
the sense of *'mn-hiphil* in Gen. 15:6 is that Abraham believed in all of YHWH's promises presented in the chapter

bibliographical lists in H. Wildberger, VT Suppl., 16 (1967), 327,
footnote 1, and A. Jepsen, TDOT, I, 292f.
54 H. Simian-Yofre, Messianic Hope, 57. The texts analysed are: Job 29:
24; 39:24; Hab. 1:5; Ps. 116:10; Is. 28:16.
55 H. Irsigler, BN, 29 (1985), 99-103, stresses the connection between
the sense of *'mn-hiphil* as "Festigkeit gewinnen" in v. 9b and v. 4.
H. Wildberger, Jesaja Kapitel 1-12, 285, also maintains a close link
between these two verses.
56 Here, the physical move was to appeal to Tiglath-Pileser, King of
Assyria, for help; so H. Wildberger, Id, 280.
57 So H-P. Müller, VT Suppl., 26 (1974), 37; cf. also H. Irsigler, BN,
29 (1985), 100.
58 H. Simian-Yofre, Messianic Hope, 56. Cf. also H. Wildberger,
VT Suppl, 16 (1967), 380f.

because they came from YHWH Himself. It expresses Abraham's
exclusive reliance on YHWH. There seems therefore to be a
certain amount of coincidence in sense between the 'mn-
hiphil in Is. 7:9b and that in Gen. 15:6.

What is the consequence of a total reliance on YHWH? Is.
7:9b answers the question in terms of non-reliance on Him:
kî lō' tēʾāmēnû, involving the use of 'mn-niphal and thereby engaging in a play on words.

In the OT, 'mn-niphal used of a human person seems to express two fundamental qualities[59] - "worthy of trust"[60] and
"enduring"[61]. Both meanings are possible in Is. 7:9b. Considering Isaiah's exhortation to Ahaz and his house to "stand
firm" by relying on YHWH, recourse to any "YHWH-excluded"
strategy in the handling of their crisis would be tantamount
to a betrayal of Him. Consequently, YHWH would in turn regard him as "not worthy of trust".

Taking into account YHWH's assurance lō' tāqûm wᵉlō'tihyeh

---

59 So H. Wildberger, Jesaja Kapitel 1-12, 59: "der Doppeldeutung dieser
    Wurzel" (nʾmn) is "fest gegründet" and "zuverlässig, treu". When used
    of YHWH's relationship to His people, 'mn-niphal expresses His fide-
    lity to them and in a particular way His fidelity to the house of
    David - thus, H. Simian-Yofre, Messianic Hope, 57.
60 Texts that bear this meaning may be categorized into religious and
    profane uses. Examples of the first category are found in 1 Sam. 2:35
    where the priest described as neʾĕmān is considered as one who acts
    according to YHWH's heart and mind; and Ps. 78:8 in which an entire
    generation of Israelites failed to exhibit a neʾĕmānāh spirit because
    of their rebelliousness. Profane uses of 'mn-niphal with the first
    meaning are those that have to do with human relationship. One clear
    example is found in Neh. 13:13 where those considered neʾĕmānîm were
    appointed treasurers over the storehouses whose "duty was to distri-
    bute to their brethren". Given the kind of job involved, the quality
    expressed by 'mn-niphal would quite clearly be trustworthiness. The
    same quality seems to be the underlying requirement for the witnesses
    Isaiah was looking for in Is. 8:2. Prov. 11:13 seems to confirm this
    understanding of 'mn-niphal when it defines a neʾĕmān as one who does
    not reveal secrets and keeps what is hidden. In 1 Sam. 22:13-14,
    David's unfailing loyalty to Saul for which he was renowned was ap-
    pealed to by Ahimelech in order to clear Saul's suspicion that David
    was involved in a conspiracy against Saul.
61 In YHWH's promise to David concerning his house (2 Sam. 7:16), 'mn-
    niphal has the sense of "being enduring" or "permanent"; cf. also
    (1 Sam. 25:28); 1 K. 11:38; Ps. 89:37; Is. 55:3. This sense of perma-
    nence seems also to apply to the house of YHWH's faithful priest in
    1 Sam. 2:35 and even to the great plagues and sicknesses in Dt. 28:59.

(Is. 7:7a), failure to rely on YHWH would result in the non-applicability of the assurance. In other words, Isaiah's addressees, particularly Ahaz and his house, would run the risk of being stripped of their royal status by their foes in coalition. As YHWH's traitors, they could no longer expect to enjoy His protection or favourable intervention. Thus, they would not "endure".

In Gen. 15:6b, we find a statement on the consequence of positive reliance on YHWH: $wayyaḥ\overset{e}{s}^{e}beh\bar{a}$ $l\hat{o}$ $\bar{s}^{e}d\bar{a}q\bar{a}h$. It was YHWH's act of reckoning ($ḥ\overset{s}{s}b$) Abraham's total reliance on Him as $\bar{s}^{e}d\bar{a}q\bar{a}h^{62}$. At first sight, v. 6b does not seem to have anything to do with the idea of $t\bar{e}'\bar{a}m\bar{e}n\hat{u}$ in Is. 7:9b. However, in the light of Is. 1:21,26, a close link between $\bar{s}^{e}d\bar{a}q\bar{a}h^{63}$ and $t\bar{e}'\bar{a}m\bar{e}n\hat{u}$ becomes apparent.

Is. 1:21[64] laments the fact that Jerusalem, the $qiry\bar{a}h$ $ne'\bar{e}m\bar{a}n\bar{a}h$ precisely because $\bar{s}edeq$ $y\bar{a}l\hat{i}n$ $b\bar{a}h$ has now become a $z\hat{o}n\bar{a}h$. On the ground of the well-known OT use of harlotry as a figure of speech to express infidelity (thus, e.g. Hos. 1:2; 2:7; 3:3; 4:12-15; 9:1)[65], $ne'\bar{e}m\bar{a}n\bar{a}h$ would therefore mean fidelity - expressing the city's relationship with YHWH. This relationship is closely associated with $\bar{s}edeq$. As if to emphasize the close association between the two words, v. 26b repeats them in predicting the name of the city as $^{c}\hat{i}r$ $ha\bar{s}\bar{s}edeq$ $qiry\bar{a}h$ $ne'\bar{e}m\bar{a}n\bar{a}h$.

Basically, $\bar{s}^{e}d\bar{a}q\bar{a}h$ ought not to be taken as "declarative

---

62 Cf. the argument for YHWH as subject of $ḥ\overset{s}{s}b$ in v. 6b on pages 23-25 above. See also Ges.-K., par. 122q and 135p.

63 Like $'mn$, the theme of $\bar{s}edeq$ / $\bar{s}^{e}d\bar{a}q\bar{a}h$ has been widely studied. Among the more prominent works we have: G. Quell, G. Schrenk, TDNT, II, 174-178, 185-187, 195-198, 212-224; E. Achtmeier, IDB, IV, 80-85; G.von Rad, The Problem of the Hexateuch, 125-130 and 243-266; H.H. Schmid, Gerechtigkeit; Id, in J. Friedrich et alii, FS E. Käsemann, 403-414; Id, EvT, 40 (1980), 396-420; W. Zimmerli, in FS E. Käsemann, 572-592; H.G. Reventlow, BEvT, 58 (1971), 10; U. Luck, WuD, 12 (1973), 71-89; and J. Reumann, Righteousness in the New Testament, 12-22. While taking into account some of the relevant major conclusions, our consideration focuses only on the relationship between $\bar{s}^{e}d\bar{a}q\bar{a}h$ and $'mn-niphal$.

64 For the relationship between Is. 7:9 and 1:21,(26), cf. R. Smend, VT Suppl., 16 (1967), 288.

65 Cf. H. Wildberger, Jesaja Kapitel 1-12, 60.

justice in the Lutheran sense or the first justification in
the Catholic sense, the passage from sin to grace"[66] but rather in the sense of fidelity to a relationship by fulfilling its obligations. At the level of one's relationship
with YHWH, fidelity is expressed by the observance of YHWH's
laws which include fundamental social demands expressing
one's fidelity to one's community (cf. Ezk. 18:5-9).

Fidelity to YHWH qualifies one as "worthy of trust" before
Him. In turn, YHWH will observe His part of the relationship
by protecting the *ṣaddîq* so that he will "endure"[67]. It is
with this understanding that Hab. 2:4b affirms, *w^eṣaddîq
b^e'ĕmûnātô yiḥyeh*, while Ezk. 18:9 declares, *ṣaddîq hû' ḥāyōh
yiḥyeh* on one who *b^eḥuqqôtay y^ehallek ûmišpāṭay šāmar
la'ăśôt 'ĕmet*[68].

The idea of righteousness as a reckoning of fidelity that
secures permanence is also found in Ps. 106:31 which, as we
have seen, bears the closest affinity with Gen. 15:6b. The
imputation of righteousness to Phinehas was made on the
ground of an action[69]. It is clear that the "plague being
stayed" was YHWH's response to Phinehas' fidelity and consisted in His withdrawal of the punishment unleashed on the
people for their sins. In its final analysis, *ṣ^edāqāh* meant
the survival of Phinehas and through him the people. The
whole of v. 30 is then subsumed in the use of *ḥšb*[70] in the
niphal 3rd fem. sing. in v. 31.

---

66 Cf. R. de Vaux, La Genèse, 83.
67 Cf. also Ps. 31:24.
68 Prov. 10:25,30 and 12:28 also affirm the longevity of the righteous
person.
69 Acting upon YHWH's prohibition of intermarriages with pagan women to
preserve Israel from idolatry (cf. Dt. 7:1-5), Phinehas killed a Mi-
dianite woman whom an Israelite had taken to his family (cf. Num.
25:1-13).
70 On the basis of the use of *ḥšb* in three texts belonging to P, viz.,
Lev. 7:18; 17:4 and Num. 18:27, G. von Rad maintains that there was
a liturgical use of the word. On the basis of the temple entrance
liturgy contained in Pss. 15 and 24, which spell out the criterion
that only those possessing integrity and righteousness may go up to
dwell on YHWH's holy mountain, he presumes that on every offerer
satisfying the criterion, a priest would pronounce a declaratory
statement of righteousness which might well have been, "It shall be

Pursuing the point further, we should not be surprised to
find the idea of death and survival in the remaining two
texts that use the verb ḥšb in a moral sense, viz. 2 Sam.
19:20 and Ps. 32:2. In the case of Shimei, David's clemency
towards him spared him from the death he deserved for having
cursed the Lord's anointed:: lō' tāmût (2 Sam. 19:24). In
Ps. 32:2-4, bodily corruption is indirectly tied to non-
imputation of guilt.

From the above consideration, both ne'ĕmānāh and ṣᵉdāqāh
appear to share a common meaning, namely, "being trustwor-
thy" and "enduring". In Gen. 15:6, there is room for the
understanding of ṣᵉdāqāh as "being enduring". The promise of
a son (v. 4) in response to Abraham's anxiety, "I am going
(to my death) childless" (v. 2bA), followed by that of innumerable descendants (v. 5) expresses the idea of longevity –
continued by Abraham's family line. Moreover, the patriarch
himself would have a long life (v. 15).

However, ṣᵉdāqāh, used with ḥšb, also has a moral connotation as Ps. 106:31; 2 Sam. 19:20 and Ps. 32:2 show. Abraham's attitude of faith in YHWH motivated him to remain
faithful and obedient to his God. Thus, the moral connotation of ṣᵉdāqāh is also applicable to the patriarch.

It may therefore be asserted that what Is. 7:9b says in a
negative way, Gen. 15:6b expresses in a positive way and
goes beyond. Isaiah's use of tē'āmēnû, while motivated by
his wish to play on words[71] is also determined by the content of his story. The promise of endurance of survival is
certainly relevant to one facing a threat of extinction.

---

counted to him for righteousness." Cf. von Rad, Old Testament Theo-
gy, I, 377-383. All the texts constituting the foundation of von
Rad's view have no bearing on Gen. 15:6b because they lack either
(i) ṣᵉdāqāh or ᶜāwōn (all the three priestly texts) or (ii) ḥšb
(Pss. 15 and 24), both of which are essential constituents of Gen.
15:6b. Ps. 106:31, cited for support, does not refer to the validity
or non-validity of a sacrificial offering and its respective effects
on the offerer. Neither does it declare the worthiness or unworthi-
ness of someone seeking entry into the Temple. The verb ḥšb therein
may therefore not be considered as having a liturgical meaning.
M. Oeming, ZAW, 95 (1983), 182-197 also disagrees with this view expressed by von Rad.
71 Cf. H. Wildberger, ZThK, 65 (1968),139.

Moreover for us who seems to lack faith in YHWH, there is
not much use appealing to such a "spiritual motivation" as
$ṣ^ed\bar{a}q\bar{a}h$ to get him to believe. An appeal to his current exi-
gency would stand a greater chance of securing Ahaz's positive response.

To describe the virtue of a man whose faith in YHWH is
outstanding and whose life is not so much threatened by extinction as blessed with YHWH's promises, $ṣ^ed\bar{a}q\bar{a}h$ is a more
appropriate term than $'mn-niphal$. This was probably at the
back of the mind of the author of Gen. 15 when he "theologized" about Abraham's faith.

Before affirming any sort of relationship between Gen. 15:
6 and Is. 7:3-9, we need to rule out the possibility of an
influence from Hab. 2:4b: $w^eṣaddîq\ be'ĕmûnātô\ yiḥyeh$. There
are disagreements about the sense of $b^e\ 'ĕmûnātô$. The RSV
translates it thus: "by his faith", taking "his" to refer to
the $ṣaddîq$. In a footnote it admits the possibility of the
sense of "faithfulness" for $'emunāh$[72]. The LXX takes the expression in a different sense: $ek\ pisteōs\ mou$ (= "by my
faith"), quite obviously referring to YHWH since the statement is considered as YHWH's[73].

To my mind, the best solution so far is the one proposed
by J.G. Janzen[74], viz., "by its reliability". The pronominal
suffix refers to the $ḥāzôn$ ("vision") in v. 3aA. This solution takes into account the entire context of Hab. 2:4b as
well as other biblical traditions. The prophet accuses YHWH
of "failing to live up to a prior word announced through

---

72 W.E. Rast, CTM, 10 (1983), 169-175, basically agrees with the RSV but
   thinks that "faithfulness" alone does not adequately express the full
   meaning of $'ĕmûnāh$, as it "would stress that future possibilities
   would pivot around the $ṣaddîq$ himself" (173). For Rast $'emunāh$ would
   emphasize the $ṣaddîq$'s "faithful trust" that God would finally act as
   He has promised in His vision to the prophet.
73 While on this basis Kittel proposes a variant reading $be'ĕmûnātî$,
   D.H. van Daalen, in E.A. Livingstone (Ed), Studia Evangelica, VII
   524, does not think this proposal necessary. For, "throughout the OT
   changes from direct to indirect speech are exceedingly common. We can
   therefore not take it for granted that, as YHVH was introduced speaking in vs. 2, he must be referred to in the first person." Van Daalen
   fails to give textual support to his reason.
74 J.G. Janzen, HTR, 73 (1980), 53-78.

prophetic agency"[75]. On the ground of Jer. 15:18, this could
be interpreted as an experience of YHWH's deceitful ways[76].
Thus, in Hab. 2:2-4, YHWH vouches for "the vision as a reliable witness and testifier which does not lie"[77]. In support of this, Janzen cites six texts from Proverbs dealing
with the credibility of witnesses[78]. Against the possible
objection that the most natural antecedent to the pronominal
suffix is *ṣaddîq* rather than *ḥāzôn* on account of its greater
proximity, Janzen offers two arguments. Firstly, from a linguistic viewpoint, proximity in a literary text goes beyond
linear nearness to reach the "several images, themes, and
even complex structures and contents of meaning" presented
"simultaneously to the reader or hearer"[79]. Secondly, in the
context, the themes of vision and the nature of the response
to it are prevalent[80], This vision, though apparently
"slow", will "surely come" (v. 3b). It merely "awaits its
time" and "will not lie" (v. 3a). It is therefore a reliable
vision.

   The reliability of the vision is of course founded on YHWH
who grants it. In this sense, it expresses YHWH's own reliability and thus coincides with the sense of *ek pisteōs mou*
rendered by the LXX. As pointed out by van Daalen, the LXX
translates *'ĕmûnāh* by *pistis* and *alētheia* in an equal number of texts[81]. This itself shows that the two Greek words
are not clearly distinguished in the LXX in the reference to
'ĕmûnāh. Used of God, they emphasize His reliability.

   In the context of Hab. 2:2-4, the *ṣaddîq* is one who gives
a positive response to YHWH's vision. He is confident that
it will come to be fulfilled "in its appointed time" and

---

75 J.G. Janzen, HTR, 73 (1980),60.
76 Jeremiah's accusation in metaphorical terms *'akzāb* and *māyim lō'*
   ne'ĕmānû in Jer. 15:18 gives the reason for his pain. In effect,
   Jeremiah is accusing God of being deceitful as His ways are un-
   reliable. Cf. Janzen, id, 59.
77 Id, 59.
78 The six texts are: Prov. 6:19; 2:17; 14:5,25; 19:5,9.
79 Janzen, id, 61.
80 Id, 68.
81 D.H. van Daalen, in E.A. Livingstone (Ed), Studia Evangelica, VII,
   525. He thinks that the different Greek words used for *'ĕmûnāh* seem
   to indicate different translators rather than shades of meaning.

therefore patiently "waits for it" (v. 3). Since YHWH will
intervene to resolve his crisis[82], he "will live".

To be sure, Gen. 15:6 and Hab. 2:4b do coincide in sense:
the righteous one is one who trusts in God's promises and
will "live" or "endure". But there is still a gross difference between them. The fact that 'mn is used of two different objects in both texts is already indicative of their
difference. No doubt, both texts do bring out YHWH's trust-
worthiness. Nevertheless, in Hab. 2:4b the real emphasis
is on the reliability of the vision and YHWH's trustworthi-
ness on which it is grounded is drawn only as an implicit
conclusion. In Gen. 15:6, byhwh explicitly affirms this qua-
lity of YHWH's. Moreover, in Gen. 15:6 Abraham's faith is
highlighted while in Hab. 2:4b it is very faintly implied
and, even then, it is not so much faith in YHWH as confidence in His vision.

To sum up, the force of 'mn in Hab. 2:4b is too weak for
Gen. 15:6 to draw on. Therefore, we are still left with
Is. 7:3-9.

Basically, therefore, a close literary and theological affinity exists between Gen. 15:1-6 and Is. 7:3-9, especially
v. 9b[83]. The only significant difference lies with their human protagonists: Abraham, a man of great faith, and Ahaz,
his opposite. But then, in view of the above-traced affinity, it is reasonable to postulate that the two protagonists
are intended to form an antithetic parallelism, that is, as
type and anti-type.

The two figures, Eliezer and the son of Tabeel, present
another parallelism between the two texts under considera-

---

82 The crisis is clear from the prophet's lament in Hab. 1:2-4. Whatever
   be the historical situation faced by the prophet and his people, this
   crisis "was deeper than a simply external one... how trust and obedience toward God could be maintained at all in the present", says
   W.E. Rast, CTM, 10 (1983), 169.
83 R. Smend, VT Suppl., 16 (1967), finds such a close similarity between
   Gen. 15:6 and Is. 7:9 which he postulates as "die Entstehung des
   wichtigsten alttestamentlichen Begriff für das religiöse Glauben von
   uns haben" (288), that he thinks it would be difficult not "den Autor
   von Gen. xv 6 'mogelijk een Jesajaleerling' zu nennen" (290) - an ex-
   expression he borrows from Th.C. Vriezen, Geloven en vertrouwen, 17.

tion. Seen as potential "usurpers", both of them were feared by the two protagonists of our narratives. In addition, both were of Aramaean origin[84]. In view of this the qualification of Eliezer as a "Damascene" (Gen. 15:2bB) seems to be redundant. Yet, it is given. It would be difficult not to accept this inclusion as due to the recurrence of *dammeśeq* in Is. 7:8a.

The second part of the Ahaz narrative does not lack traces of a parallelism with Gen. 15. In Is. 7:11, although explicitly advised, Ahaz refused to ask for a sign[85]. Abraham, on the contrary, made his request in Gen. 15:8. Thus, the antithetic parallelism we have traced between the two protagonists is stretched further.

Regardless of Ahaz's refusal, a sign was given him: the Immanuel, a son prophesied to be born of *hā'almāh* (Is. 7: 14)[86]. This semeiotic character of a son is very likely behind the presentation of the promise of a blood-heir as a sign in Gen. 15. The formulation of the latter, *'ăšer yēṣē' mimmē'eykā*, is exactly the same as that found in YHWH's promise of an offspring to David given within the overall promise of an eternal dynasty in the "locus classicus" of the promise (2 Sam. 7:12). It is possible that the author of Gen. 15 was reminded of this "locus classicus" by the word *'mn-niphal* in Is. 7:9b, which is also found in 2 Sam. 7:16

---

84 For Eliezer as an Aramaean name, cf. H. Cazelles, RB, 69 (1962), 230; and A. Caquot, Sem., 12 (1962), 58. On Tabeel, O. Kaiser says, "The account of the plan to overthrow the dynasty and appoint a prominent Aramaean as puppet king for the alliance in v. 6, whether it is historical or projects back into the past problems in post-exilic Jerusalem, indicates the theme which stands in the foreground"; cf. Isaiah 1-12, 139. H. Wildberger, Jesaja Kapitel 1-12, 266, states, "Die Namenform ist gewiss nicht zufällig aramäisch."

85 H. Simian-Yofre, Messianic Hope, 65, points out that in Is. 7:11, while Isaiah advised Ahaz to ask for a confirmative sign, the king interpreted the *'ôt* as anticipatory. On the ground that he would not tempt God, he refused to ask for it. But in actual reality, he did not need it (= the anticipatory sign) because he had already decided to rely on his own plans rather than accept Isaiah's suggestion.

86 Since Ahaz twisted Isaiah's advice to mean an anticipatory sign, the prophet now offered him one. The sign of the Immanuel is "ambiguous and polyvalent... which the king will have to interpret with all the same difficulties (or worse) as today's exegete faces" (H. Simian-Yofre, id, 65).

and by the similarity of content (i.e. promise of a son) Is.
7:14 bears with 2 Sam. 7:12. Or, it may even be possible that
he gave the Immanuel promise a dynastic interpretation[87].
This led him to borrow his formulation of the promise of a
son to Abraham from 2 Sam. 7:12.

The rather close literary and theological contact Gen. 15
bears with the prophetic literature and more specifically
with Jer. 34:18-20 and Is. 7:1-17, favours its dependence on
the latter. If dependence had gone in the reverse direction,
there would quite naturally have been no prophetic traits in
Gen. 15. On the contrary, the two specific prophetic texts
would have suffered certain marks left by the author of Gen.
15 whose central concern was very different from that of the
two prophets. No such mark, however, could be traced. In
fact, the two prophets paid no attention to the patriarchal
traditions about the promises made to Abraham highlighted in
Gen. 15.

It seems quite clear that the author of Gen. 15 used his
prophetic source only as a vehicle of his own theology built
on the traditions about the promises made to Abraham and
about Israel's early history. It is to these traditions that
we must now turn.

---

87 This should not be surprising especially since the expression bêt
dāwid is found twice in the chapter, viz., vv. 2 and 13. H. Wildberger, Jesaja Kapitel 1-12, 281, writes, "Irgendwie, wenn auch nicht
deutlich fassbar, steht zweifellos die Zionstheologie hinter Jesajas
Mahnungen... Das ist der Grund, warum das 'Haus Davids' angesprochen
wird." Cf. also H. Irsigler, BN, 26 (1985), 88. For this latter and
for F.D. Hubmann, BN, 26 (1985), 43-44, the Immanuel referred to
Ahaz's own son.

PART TWO

GENESIS 15: THEOLOGICAL COMPENDIUM
OF PENTATEUCHAL HISTORY

CHAPTER 1

GENESIS 15 KNEW THE PENTATEUCH
ALMOST IN ITS FINAL FORM

Before attempting to define the relationship Gen. 15 bears
to the Pentateuch, it is obligatory to show that the author
of the chapter knew the Pentateuchal corpus, if not in its
final canonical form, at least very close to it.

I. Expressions Claimed As Traces Of
The Deuteronomic / Deuteronomistic And
Priestly Schools In The Chapter

From the viewpoint of documentary hypothesis, there is a growing consensus among scholars that Gen. 15 reflects a Deuteronomic / Deuteronomistic influence[1]. It suffices to recall that the two most important promises of descendants (v. 5) and land (vv. 18-21) are couched in Deuteronomic / Deuteronomistic language: metaphor of stars (cf. Dt. 1:10; 10:22; 28:62)[2] and delineation of land (cf. e.g. Dt. 1:7; 7:1; Jos. 9:1; 12:8).

The traces of P claimed by some scholars[3] in the following expressions in Gen. 15 are less sure than those of the Deuteronomist: "four hundred years" (v. 13bC); $bir^e ku\check{s}$ $g\bar{a}d\hat{o}l$ (v. 14bB); and Abraham's burial $b^e\acute{s}\hat{e}b\bar{a}h$ $\d{t}\hat{o}b\bar{a}h$ (v. 15b). For P's chronology for the duration of the Israelites' slavery in Egypt in Ex. 12:40f has "four hundred and thirty years"; $r^e ku\check{s}$ seems to be a common expression for wealth[4]; and apart from Gen. 25:8 (=P), $\acute{s}\hat{e}b\bar{a}h$ $\d{t}\hat{o}b\bar{a}h$ is also found elsewhere[5].

---

1 M. Anbar, JBL, 101 (1982), 39-55, has attempted to demonstrate that Gen. 15 is totally Deuteronomic. Though, as he admits, the data sifted for his consideration "are not unequivocal" (39) - and I would add, not equally convincing - to my mind, his work not only sums up but reinforces the position favouring Deuteronomic/Deuteronomistic influence.

2 M. Anbar, id, in footnote 30, makes the following observation: the use of the metaphor in Gen. 22:17; 26:4; and Ex. 32:13 may well have been due to a Deuteronomistic influence (thus, J. Skinner, Genesis, 279-280) for these verses are thought to be secondary (thus, H. Gunkel, Genesis, 236, 239-240; J. Skinner, id, 328, 331, 363f; B.S. Childs, Exodus, 558-559).

3 So H. Gunkel, op. cit., Cf. also J. Skinner, op. cit., 282; A. Caquot, Sem., 12 (1962), 63.

4 Cf. Gen. 13:6; 14:11,12,16,21; 31:18; 36:7; 46:6; Num. 16:32; 35:3; Dan. 11:13,24,28; 1 Chr. 27:31; 28:1; 2 Chr. 20:25; 21:14,17; 31:3; 32:29; 35:7; Ezra 1:4,6; 8:21; 10:8.

5 Thus, Jdg. 8:32; Ruth 4:15; 1 Chr. 29:28; Ps. 92:14.

Two reasons, more important when compared to the above-
considered traces of a Deuteronomic / Deuteronomistic hand
and more certain than the aforementioned expressions in respect of P, may be advanced for the influence of the two
sources on the chapter. They are found in YHWH's self-
predication in v. 1bB and the exodus and the promise of land
donation formula in v. 7 vis-à-vis vv. 18-21.

II YHWH As "Shield"

The metaphorical description of YHWH as "Shield" is found
a good number of times in the OT[6] but only twice in the Pentateuch, viz., Gen. 15:1 and Dt. 33:29. The latter is the
concluding half of the framework[7] into which Moses' hymn
comprising a list of traditional blessings on the individual
tribes is inserted. Presented very much in the style of
Jacob's blessings on the twelve eponymous ancestors of the
twelve tribes of Israel[8], this hymn places Moses in continuity with the patriarchal line and therefore qualifies his
task of leading the Israelites as the working out of YHWH's
oath to the patriarchs. That Israel should be made up of
twelve tribes means that the promise of innumerable descendants has been fulfilled[9]. The promise of land is now approaching its total fulfilment since the Israelites have
reached the brink of the promised land.

The use of the metaphor "sword" in Dt. 33:29, coupled
with another metaphor "sword" and followed by "enemies",
clearly takes on a military overtone. The salvation of the
people achieved by YHWH refers thus to the military victories over Israel's enemies in her journey towards the promised land: the battles that YHWH "fought for them"[10]. But

---

6 Cf. footnote 1 on page 17 above.
7 The opening half is constituted by vv. 2-5. The rest of the concluding half is vv. 26-28. Cf. D.N. Freedman, in G. Rendsburg et alii,
   Essays in Honor of Cyrus H. Gordon, 25-46; also D.L. Christensen,
   Bib., 65 (1985), 382-389.
8 It must also be noted that the tribe of Simeon is omitted. "The traditional total of twelve is maintained through dividing Joseph into
   Ephraim and Manasseh, while keeping Levi, the tribe normally omitted
   from the tribal lists when Joseph is considered as two tribes," explains A.D.H. Mayes, Deuteronomy, 396.
9 The same meaning is intended in the eponymic lists of Jacob's twelve
   sons in Gen. 35:23-25; Ex. 1:2-4; and the blessing in Gen. 49.
10 Cf. Ex. 14:14,25; Dt. 1:30; 3:22; 20:4.

all these saving acts were oriented towards the fulfilment
of YHWH's promises to the patriarchs. This is probably why
Moses' final words to his people are couched in the style of
a patriarchal blessing. Understood thus, Dt. 33:29 expresses
the fulfilment of the divine promises to the patriarchs as
well. YHWH is "Shield" not only because He has been protec-
ing the Israelites from their enemies but also because He
has been steadily fulfilling His promises.

It is important to note that Dt. 33:29b focuses not so
much on YHWH's saving acts for His people but on YHWH Himself[11]. In like manner, the first part of the verse depicts
Israel as ʿam nôšaʿ byhwh. Focusing on the person rather
than on the acts underscores the relationship between YHWH
and Israel and the dynamism of the relationship. For acts of
favour, however great, belong to past history once they have
been achieved. But the person of YHWH remains. He is stead-
fastly faithful. This means that He will continue to bring
His promises toward their total fulfilment and guide the Israelites into the promised land. Thus, the Israelites whose
part in the relationship is passive - a people saved by
YHWH - can continue to have confidence in their God.

It is probably to drive home this point that the hymn
comes just before Moses is recorded to be given a panoramic
view of the promised land on the eve of his death during
which YHWH reasserted to him His oath to Abraham, Isaac and
Jacob (Dt. 34:1-4). In this context, the mataphor "Shield"
is linked to the divine oath which in v. 4 is specifically
spelled out as the gift of <u>land</u> to Abraham's <u>descendants.</u>

In Gen. 15:1bB, the metaphor is used in YHWH's self-

---

11 In fact, the entire framework of the hymn, as pointed out by Christensen, Bib., 65 (1985), 388f, is built on the following chiastic
   structure that spotlights on the person of YHWH as King and God in
   Jeshurun:
   V. 2:   A - YHWH's March of Conquest from the Southland
       3-4   B - YHWH's Protection and Provision for His People
       5:          C - YHWH is King in Jeshurun!
       26:         C1 - There is none like God, O Jeshurun!
       27-28: B1 - Israel's Security and Blessing
       29:     A1 - Israel, a People delivered by YHWH

predication. Put structurally in parallelism with v. 7, the
self-predication takes on the connotation of YHWH's guidance
of Abraham. In our presentation of the literary unity of the
chapter[12], we saw how v. 7 is oriented towards v. 18 and v.1
is entirely left elastic enough to encompass the whole chapter. Thus, the guidance theme in v. 7 is oriented towards
the promise of land (v. 18b) and the divine self-predication
is oriented towards both the central promises of innumerable
posterity (v. 5) and land (v. 18b).

But that is not all. The exhortation 'al-tîrā' in v. 1bA
that accompanies YHWH's self-predication signals a situation
of fear faced by Abraham. Vv. 2-3 clarify what this fear was
all about. In this context, YHWH's self-predication takes on
the natural concept of "Shield" as an implement of protection: YHWH promised to protect Abraham from his potential
usurper and successor. Again, on account of its elastic character, this self-predication extends itself into the second
section to encompass YHWH's protection of Abraham's descendants by liberating them from oppression (vv. 13-16). YHWH's
protection of Abraham and his descendants, as the chapter
presents it, is also oriented towards the central promises
of innumerable descendants and land donation.

YHWH's self-predication in v. 1bB not only expresses His
guidance and protection of Abraham and his descendants to
guarantee His promises but more so underscores His very being as the foundation of this guarantee. The assertion of
Abraham's faith in v. 6a with YHWH rather than His promises
as its object lends support to this understanding. Because
YHWH was YHWH, Abraham could and did have confidence in Him.

It seems quite clear that the two texts, Gen. 15:1bB and
Dt. 33:29, make a similar use of the metaphor "Shield" to
found the certainty of the fulfilment of the promises in
YHWH's own being. There seems in all probability to be a case
for maintaining that both the texts employ the term "Shield"
to sum up YHWH's relationship to Israel as her protector

12 Cf. Part 1: Chapter 2, II, pages 43-58 above.

manifested through the gradual working out of His oath to
her fathers. While in Gen. 15 it is given an elasticity that
allows it to be stretched to include the very last promise,
in Dt. 33:29 its end is left open so that even after Moses'
death in Dt. 34, the Israelites will continue to see the
fulfilment of the promises under Joshua's leadership. Abraham's faith in Gen. 15:6a serves as a good paradigm for the
descendants to have full confidence in YHWH.

It must be noted here that while a good number of OT
texts, especially the Psalms[13], use the metaphor "Shield"
for YHWH to designate Him as protector and saviour, only two
texts, namely, 2 Sam. 22:31 and Ps. 18:31, connect it with
YHWH's promise: YHWH's promise proves true." These two
verses occur in two slightly variant versions of David's
song of deliverance from Saul's hands (2 Sam. 22:2-51; Ps.
18:3-51). But the statement about YHWH's fidelity to His
promise is of a general kind and certainly without any specific reference to YHWH's fulfilment of the patriarchal
oath[14].

The relationship between Gen. 15:1bB and Dt. 33:29b is too
close and too strong for their use of the metaphor "Shield"
to be coincidental. The fact that the former is not far from
the beginning of Pentateuchal history would favour an intention somewhat to form an inclusion with the latter.

---

13 Cf. footnote 1 on page 17 above.
14 BHK even suggests that the stich, "YHWH's promise proves true" is an
   addition.

III. Verse 7 Vis-à-vis Verses 18-21

Gen. 15:7 reflects a basic tenet of Israel's faith. Though it is recalled in many texts throughout the Bible, the formulation of this tenet of faith together with YHWH's self-predication is found, apart from Gen. 15:7, only in Ex. 6:6; 7:5; 20:2; 29:46; Lev. 19:36; 25:38,42, (55 where the self-predication is given after the exodus formula); 26:13; Num. 15:41[15] and Dt. 5:6. Except the Ex. 20:2 and its parallel in Dt. 5:6[16], all the other texts belong to P.

From the texts listed above, it is obvious that the exodus tradition has acquired a somewhat stereotyped formulation: *'anî ('ānōkî) yhwh 'ĕlōhêkem 'ăšer hôṣē'tî 'etkem mē'ereṣ miṣrayim* and that generally any qualification centres around the Israelites' slavery in Egypt. It is significant that though none of these texts except Lev. 25:38 links the formula with YHWH's gift of the land[17], Gen. 15:7 should do so. That is not all. Its formulation of Abraham's exodus, right till the last but one word, bears a very close affinity with Lev. 25:38 not only in the choice but also in the order of words[18], as the following schema shows:

Gen. 15:7	Lev. 25:38
'ănî yhwh	*'anî yhwh 'ĕlōhekem*
'ăšer hôṣē'tîkā	*'ăšer-hôṣē'tî 'etkem*
mē'ûr kaśdîm	*mē'ereṣ miṣrāyim*
lātet lekā 'et-hā'āreṣ hazzō't	*lātēt lākem 'et-'ereṣ kena'an*
lerištāh	
	lihyôt lākem lē'lōhîm

---

15 Num. 15:41 comes quite close to Lev. 25:38 but lacks *lātēt lākem 'et-'ereṣ kena'an*.

16 Both Ex. 20:2 and Dt. 5:6 being introductions to the decalogue leave out *lihyôt lākem lē'lōhîm* probably in view of the first commandment. They also omit the naming of the land of Canaan in favour of qualifying Egypt as the land of slavery.

17 Ex. 29:42 links the exodus formula with YHWH's dwelling in the midst

However, there are also differences between the two texts.
The first has to do with the places involved and is required
by the particular situations of the addressees concerned:
'ûr kaśdîm and *hā'āreṣ hazzō't* for Abraham who was presumably living in Canaan (Gen. 13:18), and *'ereṣ miṣrāyim* and
'ereṣ kᵉnaᶜan for the Israelites. The land of Abraham's origin is, significantly enough, not referred to in the same
way as Gen. 12:1 but specifically named *'ûr kaśdîm* which also figures in just one other text in the Pentateuch, viz.,
Gen. 11:31, a text universally accepted as P's[19]. Thus, a
further relationship with P may be posited here.

The endings of the two texts of our concern offer another
important difference. Gen. 15:7 not only omits *lihyôt lākem
lē'lōhîm* but also introduces *lᵉriśtāh*. There are two possible sources for this expression. One is Gen. 28:4, another
P text, in which the infinitive construct of *yrś* is used
with *ntn* to express land possession[20] : *lᵉriśtᵉkā 'et-'ereṣ
mᵉgureykā 'ăśer-nātan 'ĕlōhîm lᵉ'abrāhām*, to which Lev. 20:24
in the Holiness Code refers back[21]. If Gen. 28:4 is the
source of *lᵉriśtāh* for Gen. 15:7, the latter's dependence on
P gains further ground.

However, this does not seem to be so, because the more
likely source appears to be offered by the Deuteronomistic
literature of which the combination of the land donation
formula with *lᵉriśtāh* is a marked characteristic[22]. The use
of *yrś*, whether in its *qal* or *hiphil* conjugation, to mean
"driving out" or "dispossessing" nations is an exclusive
trait of the Deuteronomistic writings[23]. A vital part of

---

of the people while Num. 15:41 adds, *lihyôt lākem lē'lōhîm* - a qualification Lev. 25:38 also includes.

18 Cf. N. Lohfink, Die Landverheissung als Eid, 61; C. Westermann,
Genesis, 265; M. Anbar, JBL, 101 (1982), 45.

19 Cf. e.g. H. Gunkel, Genesis, 158; G. von Rad, Genesis, 153; J. Van
Seters, Abraham in History and Tradition, 258.

20 One other text belonging to P where there is a combination of
and *yrś* is Ex. 6:8. But there *yrś* occurs as a derivative of *môrāśāh*.

21 Cf. N. Lohfink, ThWAT, III, col. 981.

22 Thus, M. Weinfeld, Deuteronomy and the Deuteronomic School, 341f.
Cf. Dt. 2:31; 3:18; 5:28; 9:1,6; 12:1; 15:4; 19:2,14; 21:1; 25:19.

23 Cf. Dt. 2:12,21,22; 9:1; 11:23; 12:2,29; 18:14; 19:1; 31:3. See
N. Lohfink, ThWAT, III, cols. 958 and 961f.

YHWH's grant of land to the Israelites was His driving out
(*yrš-hiphil*) of the nations. It was only after this that His
people could succeed them in the occupation (*yrš-qal*) of the
land[24]: Dt. 9:3,4,5; 11:23; 18:12.

The list of peoples in Gen. 15:19-21, each of which is
governed by *'et* as the direct object of *nātattî* (v. 18b),
qualifies the land. This means that the land donation by
YHWH must involve a certain "driving out" or "dispossessing"
of these nations as Jos. 3:10 ascertains. This understanding
is in itself a trace of the Deuteronomistic influence. Because of the orientation of v. 7 towards v. 18, it also
shows that *l*^e*ristāh* in v. 7 is most probably a borrowing
from the Deuteronomistic usage.

The omission of *lihyôt lākem lē'lōhîm* might have been necessitated by the author's desire to present the unilateral
character of YHWH's oath. The expression is customarily
linked with the bilateral Sinai covenant[25]. Its use in Gen.
15 would therefore run the risk of clouding the unilateral
nature of YHWH's oath. In its place, he might have been inspired by the Deuteronomic / Deuteronomistic land donation
formula to use *l*^e*ristāh*.

That the exodus tradition contained in Lev. 25:38 was a
well-known one is borne out by the extensive reference to it
in the OT. That it was originally connected with the people
of Israel and with Egypt is clear from the somewhat stereotyped formulation it has assumed in all the Pentateuchal
texts except the text of our concern. On the ground that of
all these texts, Lev. 25:38 (=P) should come closest to ours
not only in the exodus formula but also in the land donation
(minus possession) formula, that the same P text contains
the original tradition and that *'ûr kaśdîm* is found in our
text as well as in Gen. 11:31, also belonging to P, it may
be postulated that Gen. 15:7 is dependent on P.

The simultaneous influence of P and the Deuteronomic /

---

24 Cf. N. Lohfink, ThWAT, III, col. 962.
25 Cf. thus Ex. 6:7; Lev. 26:12; Dt. 7:6; 27:9; (29:12); Jer. 11:4;
   24:7; 30:22; 32:38...

Deuteronomistic literature on Gen. 15 means that its author
must have had at his disposal the entire Pentateuchal corpus.

CHAPTER 2

RECAPITULATION OF PATRIARCHAL HISTORY

Patriarchal history is so shaped by the theologoumenon of
the divine oath to the patriarchs that it seems best to
start off our examination of its recapitulation in Gen. 15
by first considering the importance it gives to the divine
oath. Since this latter is a matter of faith, a study of the
faith response of the patriarchs to it - which is another
theologoumenon by itself - is in order.

I. Divine Oath To The Patriarchs

The importance of the theologoumenon of the divine oath to the patriarchs is underscored by its literary positions in the presentation of the patriarchal history in Genesis[1]. To appreciate the significance of these positions, it would be useful to have before us a clear picture of (i) the literary framework that holds the patriarchal history together and (ii) the distribution of the divine oath texts within this history.

On the basis of the long-detected literary indicator, w^e'*elleh tôl*^{e}*dôt*[2], the patriarchal history may be delineated between Gen. 11:27 and 37:2. It is composed of two cycles marked off at Gen. 25:19 by another occurrence of the same literary indicator. Since Gen. 11:27-32 serves as the transition from the "Urgeschichte" to the patriarchal history[3] and another w^e'*elleh tôl*^{e}*dôt* at Gen. 25:12 introduces Ishmael's genealogy, the Abraham cycle may be traced from Gen. 12:1-25:11[4] and the Jacob cycle from Gen. 25:19-37:1. The two cycles are fused together by an artificial story com-

---

1 R. Rendtorff, Das überlief. Problem, 40-65, believes that the promises belong to the redactional level of the patriarchal narratives in Genesis and have been inserted where they are now to serve the redactor's theological intention. Cf. also Id, JSOT, 3 (1977), 2-10; and Id, Hen., 6 (1984), 1-14. Z. Weisman, JSOT, 31 (1985), 56, sees the importance of the divine oath in terms of providing "the patriarchal narratives with a literary spine that joins them together into a genealogical and conceptual unity."

2 This is a heading which might have been borrowed from the title of a Priestly "Book of Genealogies" (cf. Gen. 5:1) - cf. H. Gunkel, Genesis, 134; G. von Rad, Genesis, 68 and 151f. It "is a characteristic formula which introduces the major sections throughout Genesis", writes D. Sutherland, ZAW, 95 (1983), 337. These major sections are 5:1; 6:9; 10:1; 11:10,27; 25:12,19; 36:1,9; 37:2. According to R. Smend, Die Erzählung des Hexateuch, 15, *tôl*^{e}*dôt* may designate "Nachkommenschaft" or "Stammbaum" or "Geschichte". For a detailed discussion of the stylized formula, cf. F.M. Cross, Jr., Canaanite Myth, 301-305.

3 C. Westermann, Genesis 12-36, 166.

4 D. Sutherland, ZAW, 95 (1983), 337-343, has attempted to trace a con-

posed around the figure of Isaac apparently reduplicating
some episodes from both cycles.

The divine command that opens the patriarchal history in
Gen. 12:1 involves a journey into the land of YHWH's choice
and sets the direction for its entire history. Settlement in
this land or possession of it is obviously a vital goal of
this journey. Thus, journey and settlement are the two pola-
rities between which the patriarchal history unravels
itself[5]. Consequently, one way of tracing the literary organization of the patriarchal history is to treat these pola-

---

centric pattern in the organization of the Abraham narratives on the
basis of the redactor's central concern with a tension between promise and obstacles to promise. Applying to the Abraham cycle the observation made by J.P. Fokkelmann, Narrative Art in Genesis, 239, viz.
that "in the Jacob cycle the genealogies form an 'outer frame' to the
cycle", Sutherland suggests that the Abraham cycle "should not be concluded with the death of Abraham" but "come to an end immediately before the genealogy of Nahor" in 22:15 (cf. pages 337, 338). Sutherland's analysis, however, is not quite successful as (i) it leaves
out a great deal of narratives; and (ii) it does not seem to be able
to handle the odd element, "Abraham and Abimelech in conflict over
territory"; and (iii) it leads to a fundamentally unacceptable conclusion: "Abraham's role in the unit is not primarily one of faithfulness. Rather, it is one of disbelief and confrontation" (343). How
does this conclusion square up with Gen. 12:4; 17:22-27; 22:1-19, all
of which are about Abraham's total obedience in faith? How does it
face up to explicit affirmations about the patriarch's faith and obedience in Gen. 15:6; 22:12 and 26:5,24? More attractive attempts have
been made by M. Fishbane, JJS, 26 (1975), 15-38, and J.G. Gammie, in
M. Buss, Encounter with the Text, 117-132. Both of them also see a
concentric pattern in the organization of the Jacob narratives. For
the former, the concentric pattern is the result of a "literary ima-
gination" whereby "various traditions and motivations have been
deftly combined to balance and comment on each other - through key-
words, but especially the variations on the theme of deceit; frater-
nal strife; wrestling; strife for a blessing; fertility; meals; pacts
and interludes" (page 32). Gammie launches off his composition from
the predominance of the strife motif and other sub-motifs (e.g. deceit; decline in the status of the first-born, etc.). The concentric
arrangement is marked by "ironic reversals" (e.g. "Jacob who is told
when blessed by Isaac that his mother's sons will bow down to him (D
27:29) ends up by bowing down to his brother (D1 33:3,11)" (page 124).
A great pity about these two attempts is that they have ignored the
Abraham cycle. If the "synchronic whole" (Fishbane, 18) is the authors' concern, then they should have taken the Abraham cycle into
account.

5 In connection with the itinerary found in 12:8, C. Westermann, Genesis
  12-36, 181, notes that the departure and rest (or tent-pitching) constitute the typical rhythm of nomadic life.

rities as indicators . On the basis of these indicators, the
following pattern emerges as the framework wherein the patriarchal history in Genesis is presented.

TRANSITION

11:27 : w^{e}*ēlleh tôl^{e}dōt teraḥ*

 31 : *wayyiqqaḥ teraḥ* ... $\boxed{wayyēṣ^{e}{}'\hat{u}}$ ... *'ad-ḥārān*
   $\boxed{wayyēš^{e}b\hat{u}}$ *šām*

ABRAHAM CYCLE

A
  12:1 : $\boxed{lek-l^{e}k\bar{a}}$ *mē'arṣ^{e}kā* ... *'el-hā'āreṣ 'ăšer 'ar'ekā*

   4a : $\boxed{wayyēlek}$ *'abrām ka'ăšer dibber 'ēlâw yhwh*

  13:12 : *'abrām* $\boxed{y\bar{a}šab}$ b^{e}*ereṣ-k^{e}nā'an*

   18 : $\boxed{wayyēšeb}$ b^{e}*'ēlōnê mamrē'*

B
  20:1 : $\boxed{wayyissa'}$ *miššām 'abrāhām 'arṣāh hannegeb*

  22:19 : $\boxed{wayyēšeb}$ *'abrāhām bib'ēr šaba'* ...

C
  24:1-4: w^{e}*'abrāhām zāqēn* ... *'el-'arṣî* ... $\boxed{tēlēk}$ ...
          'iššāh ... l^{e}*yiṣḥāq*

  25:1-10: Death of Abraham and Burial at Machpelah

   11 : $\boxed{wayyēšeb}$ *yiṣḥāq 'im-b^{e}'ēr laḥay-rō'î*

  25:12 : w^{e}*'ēlleh tōl^{e}dōt yišmā'ē'l*

JACOB CYCLE

  25:19 : w^{e}*'ēlleh tôl^{e}dōt yiṣḥāq*

A
  26:1 : *wayhî rā'āb bā'āreṣ* ... $\boxed{wayyēlek}$ *yiṣḥāq* ... g^{e}*rārāh*

   6 : $\boxed{wayyēšeb}$ *yiṣḥāq bigrār*

B
  26:17 : $\boxed{wayyēlek}$ *miššām yiṣḥāq*

    $\boxed{wayyiḥan}$ b^{e}*naḥal-g^{e}rār* $\boxed{wayyēšeb}$ *šām*

C
  26:23 : $\boxed{wayya'al}$ *miššām b^{e}'ēr šaba'*

   25 : $\boxed{wayyeṭ}$ *-šām 'ohŏlô*

Bridged by the Isaac Episode

---

6 The verbs used to describe the journeys of the patriarchs are very
 varied. The most common ones are: *hlk* (12:4; 13:3; 22:2,3,19; 26:1,17;
 28:5) and *ns'* (20:1; 29:1; 35:5,16). For the idea of settlement, the
 most frequently used verb is *yšb* (13:12,18; 16:3; 20:1; 22:19; 24:62;
 25:11; 26:6,17; 35:1; 37:1). Other verbs include *gwr* (20:1; 21:34;
 26:3); *škn* (26:2); *ḥnh* (26:17; 33:18) and *lwn* (28:11).

D ⎡ 28:1-2: *wayyiqrā' yiṣḥāq 'el-ya'ăqōb ... wayyō'mer ... qûm* $\boxed{lēk}$
  │   5b : $\boxed{wayyēlek}$ *paddenāh 'ărām*
  └ 29:14 : $\boxed{wayyēšeb}$ *'immô ḥōdeš yāmîm*

E ⎡ 31:17f: *wayyāqom ya'ăqōb ...* $\boxed{lābô'}$ *... 'arṣāh kᵉnā'an*
  └ 33:18 : $\boxed{wayyiḥan}$ *'et-pᵉnê hā'îr*

F ⎡ 1 ⎰ 35:1 : *qûm* $\boxed{'ālēh}$ *bêt-'ēl*
  │   ⎱ $\boxed{wᵉšeb}$ *-šām*
  │
  │ 2 ⎰ 3 : *wᵉnāqûmāh* $\boxed{wᵉna'ăleh}$ *bêt-'ēl*
  └   ⎱ 37:1 : $\boxed{wayyēšeb}$ *ya'ăqōb ... bᵉ'ereṣ kᵉnā'an*

Now that the literary organization of the patriarchal history has been obtained, a table showing the distribution of the component promises of the divine oath will serve to bring out the importance of their role in this history.

TEXTS	BLESSING FOR SELF & OTHERS		LAND	DESCENDANTS	GUIDANCE[7]	SON
12:2-3	x	x		x	x	
12:7			x			
13:14-17			x	x		
15:1[8]	x				x	
4-5				x		x
7			x		x	
18			x	x		
17			x	x	x	x
18:9-14						x
18		x		x		
22:15-18	x	x	x	x		
24:7			x			
26:3-4	x	x	x	x	x	
26:23-24	x			x	x	
28:3-4	x		x	x		
28:13-15	x	x	x	x	x	
32:13				x		
35:11-12			x	x		

---

7 The promise of "guidance" here follows R. Rendtorff's understanding
of "Führung" (cf. Das überlief. Problem, 49-51) as comprising YHWH's
assurance of presence, aid or protection which is at times expressed
in His self-identification and, in 17:7f, through His promise to be

From the literary framework and table given above, a few
facts regarding the divine oath emerge and a few conclusions
regarding its significance may be drawn therefrom. Firstly,
YHWH made or renewed His oath to each of the patriarchs at
major turning points of his life, at the first of which the
oath was given its full content, namely, promises of blessing, land, descendants and guidance. The first turning
point was important as it marked each patriarch functioning
as patriarch "sui iuris". For Abraham, it was YHWH's calling
of him to leave his country and people for the promised land
(12:1) that marked YHWH's choice of him as patriarch. His
first contact with the land (12:7) may be included with this
stage of his life since it was at this point that the land
was identified[9]. In the case of Isaac, the patriarchal status was operative only after Abraham's death (25:1-11) and
thus the oath in 26:3-5 (after the introduction of his family in 25:19-34)[10] whilst for Jacob it was after he had taken
leave of his father (28:5). As settlement in the land was
the goal of the life of each patriarch - marked by the fact
that both the Abraham and Jacob cycles as well as the Isaac
episode conclude with their settlement in the land - the
return to the land was also an important milestone. The
association of the divine oath with it points to the importance of the oath as well.

God. Jacob's vow in 28:20-21 provides the best example of the equation of "being God" with guidance. Jacob expected YHWH to "be with
him and keep him in this way that he was going" and provide him his
needs of food and clothing. In this way YHWH would prove Himself to
be Jacob's God.

8 As we shall see shortly, "great reward" has the same meaning as
   "blessing".

9 I.M. Kikawada, in Proceedings of the Sixth World Congress of Jewish
   Studies, I, 229-235, argues for the unity of these nine verses. Concluding his article, he writes, "Only this kind of beautifully constructed literary unity can provide a fitting introduction to the
   equally well composed Patriarchal History of the Book of Genesis"
   (235).

10 The oath in Gen. 26:3-4 repeats that in 22:16-18 almost "verbatim".
   A. Weisman, JSOT, 31 (1985), 62, interprets this as "an attempt to
   introduce Isaac as the legitimate heir of all the national promises
   made to his father and to present the stories about Isaac as condi-
   tioned by those about Abraham."

Secondly, the fact that discounting Gen. 15 and taking
Gen. 12:7 together with 12:2-3, all the promise texts are
almost equally divided between the two cycles - seven in the
Abraham and six in the Jacob cycle - is indicative of the
equal importance of the promise theme in each of them.

Thirdly, even for each of the patriarchs themselves, the
divine oath was thought to be vital. Thus when Abraham sent
his servant to look for a wife for Isaac (24:7), the oath of
land donation was his reason for insisting on the potential
wife to be brought into Canaan. When Isaac commissioned Jacob to find himself a wife (28:1-4), he too recalled the divine promises. He prayed for their fulfilment. In view of
the probable understanding that a son's marriage was part of
the preparation to take over from his father[11], the two com-
missionings would have been considered as important events
in the patriarchal history. Jacob's recalling of the divine
oath was done in his prayer for deliverance from the hands
of Esau as he was preparing to meet him (32:10-13). The
meeting was critical in that Jacob ran the risk of having
himself and his entire family exterminated by Esau. If this
had happened, it would have been the end of the divine oath.

Fourthly, YHWH Himself is presented as recalling His oath
on the basis of which He decided to reveal to Abraham His
plan to destroy Sodom and Gomorrah (18:18f). As the plan did
not seem to be definitive since He still needed to check out
what He had heard about the sinfulness of the two cities
(vv. 20-21), His disclosure to Abraham appeared to be aimed
at involving Abraham in His deliberations: thus, Abraham's
intercession (vv. 22-23). Here, the recalling of the promise
of blessing for others and that of descendants is significant. The former served as the basis for Abraham's interces-
sory role, notwithstanding the fact that it ended up in
failure. The latter promise was connected with the patriarch's role as a teacher of righteousness for his descen-

---

11 Taking a wife would simply mean enabling the working out of the promise of numerous descendants and guarantee the continuation of patriarchal history.

dants (v. 19). The destruction of Sodom would furnish a good
example of the terrible punishment for not "keeping YHWH's
way by doing righteousness and justice" (vv. 19bA)[12]. Thus,
in a passage which apparently has nothing to do with Abraham[13], the promise theme is introduced to give the patriarch
a vital role to play. As a consequence, the passage takes on
a profoundly theological character[14].

Fifthly, the promise of a son is given an extensive cove-
rage in the Abraham cycle after his settlement in the land
(17:15-21; 18:9-15). It finds its fulfilment in 21:1-7.
Though important, this promise would not be an end in itself but rather serve as the first stepping stone to the
fulfilment of the promise of a great progeny. Perhaps it
might have been for this reason that it is presented immediately after Abraham's settlement in the land - the first
stepping stone to the fulfilment of the promise of land donation. Given this understanding, the account of Abraham's
sacrifice of Isaac (22:1-19) can also be considered a major
turning point in Abraham's journey of faith: thus, the renewal of the divine oath in Gen. 22:15-18.

Finally, a word must be said about the divine oath to Jacob in Gen. 35:11-12 since by looking back to 28:13-14
through the two names of Abraham and Isaac[15] it strengthens
the continuity from Abraham to Jacob and may be taken as the
concluding oath to the patriarchal history. In fact it also
bears several elements of close correspondence to the divine
oath to Abraham in chapter 17: (i) a change of name from Jacob to Israel (35:10; cf. 17:5); (ii) ʾanî ʾel šadday
(35:11aB; cf. 17:1); (ii) the almost similar formulations of
the promises of descendants and land donation (35:11-12;

---

12 Cf. G. von Rad, Genesis, 204f; also J. Van Seters, Abraham in History
   and Tradition, 213.
13 J. Van Seters, id, 213f, asks, "Why tell Abraham about Sodom, since
   he didn't live there?"
14 So G. von Rad, Genesis, 204f; C. Westermann, The Promises to the
   Fathers, 72-73.
15 G. von Rad, Genesis, 334, states, "Apparently a primary concern of
   our text is to show that the promise to Abraham was renewed completely to Jacob."

17:6,8)[16]; and (iv) p^erēh ûr^{e}bēh (35:11aB; cf. 17:2b,6a)[17].
In view of the continuity between the two patriarchs, the
command p^erēh ûr^{e}bēh given to Jacob may be interpreted as
entrusting to him the responsibility of fulfilling the promise of descendants made to Abraham in Gen. 17:2b,6a. Jacob's fulfilment of this responsibility is presented in Gen.
35:22b-26 in which his twelve sons are listed out. Given
the eponymic character of the names of these sons, it seems
likely that the twelve tribes of Israel are here presented
in embryo[18]. In terms of the promise of descendants, the
Jacob cycle fulfils the Abraham cycle. In addition, there
is the fact that this final promise was given on Jacob's
arrival at Bethel, marking the climax of his journey back to
the "land of his birth" (cf. 31:13), thereby signalling the
initial fulfilment of the promise of land donation: "To your
descendants I will give this land" (12:7; 24:7).

The final recurrence of the divine oath in the patriarchal
history may thus be said not only to hark back to the initial one at the opening of this history in Gen. 12:2-3,7 but
also to serve as its first flowering. In between these two
end points, the divine oath is implanted at major crossroads
in the two cycles thereby setting the direction of the patriarchal history. The theme of the divine oath thus stands
out strikingly as not only the red thread but also the
"mould" of the patriarchal history.

---

16 The use of gôy and m^{e}lākîm together serves to emphasize the grandeur
   and innumerability of Abraham's posterity to be effected through
   Jacob; cf. J. Hoftijzer, Die Verheissung, 11.
17 The close correspondence between 35:9-13 and 17 seems to be further
   corroborated by the same expressions whereby the vision is introduced
   and concluded: wayyērā' ... 'el (35:9; 17:1) and wayya'al me'al
   (35:13; 17:22).
18 Cf. G.W. Coats, Genesis, 244.

II. The Theme Of Faith

Although the word for "faith" is used only once in the entire patriarchal history - that is, in Gen. 15:6 - its reality deeply marks this history. The faith of the patriarchs
is expressed principally in two ways: their obedience to
YHWH's commands and their response to His promises.

1. Obedience to YHWH's Commands

Patriarchal history begins on a positive note about Abraham's unquestioning obedience to YHWH's call of him (Gen.
12:1-4). With an unspecified land as its destination, this
call amounted to a test of faith[19] which carried on even after Abraham's arrival in the land- marking the physical attainment of the goal of the journey - the donation of which
was then promised for the future (12:7). Gen. 22 narrates
another similar demand of faith on Abraham in the sacrifice
of this son. As for the first test, this one came at a time
when, in possessing a son, Abraham had attained the physical
ability to have the promises worked out. In both cases, the
patriarch passed the test[20]. In the latter case, Abraham's
obedience was affirmed (v. 12) and constituted the reason
for a renewal of the divine oath (vv. 15-18). Later on in
Gen. 26:5,24 he is presented as a model of obedience on
whose account the divine promises passed into Isaac's hands
(cf. also 28:4).

Jacob's decision to return to Canaan (Gen. 31:17) was a

---

19 H. Gunkel, Genesis, 164, calls this "eine Glaubensprobe".
20 H. Gross, in G. Braulik, FS W. Kornfeld, 31-32, points out that
   whilst God's command in Gen. 12:1-3 demands of Abraham to cut himself
   off totally from his past ties, that in Gen. 22 asks him to sacrifice
   his entire future.

response to YHWH's command (31:3). Just as he was on the
point of achieving the goal of his journey, he went through
practically the same test of faith as Abraham did. For his
inevitable encounter with Esau was clouded with ambiguities
as he ran the risk of losing everything he had. But like
Abraham, he passed the test as, with a prayer, he decided to
carry on with his journey (32:10ff).

2. Response To YHWH's Promises

The patriarch's response to YHWH's promises[21] took several
forms. The most obvious one was their faithful execution of
whatever requirement demanded of them by YHWH when He made
these promises. Thus, Abraham's obedience to YHWH's call
can also be taken as his acceptance of the divine promises
attached to the call (Gen. 12:2-3). It expressed his faith
in these promises. In like manner, his acceptance of circum-
cision for himself and his household was expressive of his
positive response to all the promises made in Gen. 17.

The other forms of response are less clear and would require a detailed analysis. They are: the building of an altar, the erection of a stone pillar, the planting of a tama-
risk tree and the calling on of YHWH's name. The following
table shows their distribution in the patriarchal narratives
as well as the places and/or promises, if any, with which
they are associated.

---

21 Here we would like to note that Gen. 18:18; 24:7; 28:3-4 and 32:13
   merely present a recalling of the divine oath by YHWH, Abraham, Isaac
   and Jacob respectively in view of providing a reason for a certain
   course of action: thus, the oath in 18:18 explains why YHWH decided
   to involve Abraham in His deliberations; 24:7 justifies Abraham's
   insistence on Isaac's prospective wife to be brought to the land of
   Canaan; in 28:3-4, the oath is the foundation of Isaac's blessing on
   Jacob at the point when Jacob assumed his position as patriarch; and
   32:13 presents the oath being used by Jacob as the basis of his
   intercession for deliverance from Esau's hands. Thus in these texts
   the divine oath is not recalled for its own sake. As such it does not
   require a response.

TEXTS	ALTAR	TREE	PIL-LAR	YHWH'S NAME	PLACE (=SANCTUARY)	CONNECTION WITH APPARITION OR PROMISE
12:7b	x				Shechem (Oak of Moreh)	- Apparition⎫ - Promise of⎬v. 7a land⎭
12:8	x			x	Between Bethel and Ai	- No apparition - No promise
13:4	Re-called			x	Between Bethel and Ai	- No apparition - No promise
13:18	x				Oaks of Mamre (= Hebron)	- No apparition - Promise of land & descendants (vv. 15-16) with symbolic possession (v. 17)
21:33		x		x	Beersheba	- No apparition - No promise
26:25	x			x	Beersheba	- Apparition (v. 23) - Promise of guidance, blessing & descendants (v. 24)
28:18			x		Bethel (Luz)	- Dream (v. 12).. YHWH's visible presence (13aA) - Promise of land, descendants, blessing and guidance (13aB-15)
33:20	x				City of Shechem	- No apparition - No promise
35:6-7	x				El-Bethel (Luz)	- No apparition - No promise - But: a looking back to Jacob's vow in 28:18 (cf. 35:1)
35:14			x		Bethel	- Apparition (v. 9) - Promise of descendants and land (vv. 11-12)

The table unveils one fact, that is, all the texts are
connected with one sanctuary or another in the land of Canaan. Gen. 12:8 and 13:4 do not identify the exact locus but
their emphasis on Bethel through their double mention of it
seems intended to associate the response with this sanctuary. On the ground of the natural association of cult with
sanctuary, it is very likely that the patriarchs' actions
recorded in the texts tabled above were cultic acts.

Were these acts carried out in response to something divine? From one half of the tabled texts (12:8; 13:4; 21:33;
33:20 and 35:6-7) they would appear not to be, as these
texts do not record any divine phenomenon at all. The other
half of the texts (12:7; 13:18; 26:25; 28:18; 35:14), however, do present divine apparitions and/or promises. Of them
12:7 and 35:14 depict these acts as the patriarchs' response
apparently to a divine apparition. But the response recorded
in 13:18 could only be to the promises in vv. 14-17 as there
is no mention of an apparition. There is thus a need to examine these texts in detail.

Two facts not tabulated above must be brought into consideration. Firstly, in Genesis, there are texts which contain
divine apparitions to which a patriarch did not make any
cultic response such as those tabled above: thus, 18:1; 31:3
(vis-à-vis vv. 11-13); 32:2f; 32:25-31. This yields a negative consequence: a divine apparition did not seem to require a patriarchal response. Secondly, from the promise
texts we have considered in the previous subsection and in
the early part of the present subsection, it appears that
every making or renewal of a divine oath to a patriarch
called for one form of response or another. It is therefore
likely that the cultic acts in the tabulated texts containing divine promises were in response to these promises[22]
rather than to the apparitions. This is probably why 13:18
can dispense with any notice of an apparition. In 12:7 and
35:14 (vis-à-vis v. 1), although the building of an altar is
to YHWH who appeared to the patriarchs in the sanctuary con-

---

22 So C. Westermann, Genesis 12-36, 181, and G.W. Coats, Genesis, 108.

cerned, it must be borne in mind that the apparition was for
the purpose of making the promises. 12:7a has YHWH appear to
Abraham to promise him the land. The apparition referred to
in 35:14 (vis-à-vis v.1) harks back to 28:10-15 where in a
vision granted him in a dream YHWH promised Jacob land, descendants and guidance (vv. 13-15). It is hardly possible to
separate the vision from promises as its purpose. Consequently, the vision in 12:7 and 35:14 would seem to be a
summary way of resuming the promises made in the vision and
the cultic act a response to these promises.

We have now to examine the remaining five texts which do
not record any apparition of promises. What sense do we make
of the cultic acts therein? It is noteworthy that three of
these texts (12:8; 13:4; 21:33) record Abraham's invocation
of YHWH's name. In the OT, such an invocation often expresses one's trust in YHWH - either in an act of supplication
(1 K. 18:24; 2 K. 5:11; Ps. 116:4; Lam. 3:55) or in that of
thanksgiving (1 Chr. 16:8 // Ps. 105:1; Is. 12:4) for the
manifestation of His power. In a few of these texts, it is
even associated with the divine oath to the patriarchs or
with the patriarchs themselves (1 K. 18:36; 1 Chr. 16:13-18
// Ps. 105:6-11). In the context of the Abraham cycle, the
invocation of YHWH's name could only have to do with the
divine oath to him. It would thus express Abraham's recalling of YHWH making these promises to him and his faith in
Him. For the patriarch, YHWH's power would be manifested in
His fulfilment of His promises to him. It may therefore be
concluded that Abraham's invocation of YHWH's name serves as
a substitute for the explicit record of the divine promises.
The patriarch's activity would be considered as a response
to the promises recalled. The fact of this response in deed
preceding the statement about the patriarch's invocation of
YHWH's name is not a problem. For the statement could well
be intended as an explicit declaration about both his mental
recalling of the promises and his response in deed expressing his faith in these promises.

In this connection it is noteworthy that 26:25 presents
Isaac invoking YHWH's name in a context where the Lord re-

newed His promises in an apparition to the patriarch. It
will be recalled that the Isaac story serves as a bridge
between the Abraham and the Jacob cycles. Part of the literary device to do so is, as we have noted earlier, to repeat
some episodes from each cycle. It is not surprising that in
retelling an episode from either cycle, one related element
or another from elsewhere in the same cycle may be inserted
into the episode. One clear example of this seems to be our
present text. Isaac's problem with the Philistines over
wells and his covenant with Abimelech at Beersheba (26:17-31)
echo those of his father's (21:22-34). Since this is Isaac's
only contact with the sanctuary reported, the promises YHWH
made with him at Gerar in the land of the Philistines
(26:3-4) which echo those found in 22:15-18 are here presented in a shorter manner. The notice about his invocation of
YHWH's name would be an explicit declaration about his faith
in YHWH's promises as manifested in his response to them
through his building of an altar.

The Jacob cycle has two texts recording Jacob's building
of an altar without an explicit mention of an apparition,
making of promises or invocation of YHWH's name: 33:20 and
35:6-7. There are, however, possible indications of an implicit reference to the invocation of YHWH's name. For the
place names in both texts involve the use of YHWH's title:
El-Elohe-Israel (33:20) and El-Bethel (35:7). In Gen. 21:33,
the title El Olam is appended to Abraham's invocation of
YHWH's name, thereby qualifying the name itself. Extra-
Pentateuchal books also furnish data that may clarify the
use of divine titles in relation to the invocation of YHWH's
name. One such datum is the thanksgiving song in 1 Chr. 16.
It begins with an exhortation to "give thanks to YHWh and
call on His name" (v. 1) and ends with "Blessed be YHWH,
Elohe-Israel" (v. 36). YHWH's name is here given as Elohe
Israel, which is the same title found in Gen. 33:20. In Gen.
17:7,8, YHWH promised to be God to Abraham and his descendants. Not only is it possible but it also seems quite probable that the naming of the sanctuary as El-Elohe-Israel is
an indirect calling on of YHWH's name, thereby calling to

mind His promises. By the same token, the naming of El Bethel
which through a double use of El in Gen. 35:7 emphasizes the
divine title could be taken as serving the same function as
El-Elohe-Israel in 33:20. If our interpretation is correct,
Jacob's building of the altar was not out of place as it
would be a response to the promises.

To sum up, the cultic acts tabled above seem in all likelihood to be the patriarchs' positive responses to the divine promises, i.e., their acceptance of these promises.
Together with the responses that take the form of an execution of a divine command, they provide evidence that every
making or renewal of the divine promises met with the acceptance in faith by the patriarchs. Since, as we have seen,
the theme of the divine oath has exerted such an important
influence on the patriarchal history as presented in Genesis,
the patriarchs' response to it must necessarily become important as well.

III. Recapitulation Of Patriarchal History

Of the two cycles making up the patriarchal history, only
the Abraham cycle enjoys an explicit reference in Gen. 15.
V. 7 with its statement about the patriarch's exodus from Ur
of the Chaldaeans harks back to Gen. 11:31. The fact that
this exodus was guided with a view to giving the land of
Canaan to the patriarch and his descendants is a reflection
of His promise of guidance in Gen. 12:1 when He called the
patriarch to "go to the land I will show you." V. 15 projects the account of his death in Gen. 25:7-11. The promise
of a son in v. 4 is made twice in Abraham's life:
Gen. 17:15-21 and 18:9-15, and its fulfilment is recorded
in Gen. 21:1-7. Apart from these explicit points of contact with the Abraham cycle, all the others are veiled by
the subtle style and metaphorical language of Gen. 15.

The first subtle element is the word "reward" (śākār) in
YHWH's opening promise in Gen. 15:1. The use of this word
here is not in its usual sense of a recompense for an act of
favour or service[23] rendered but, as we have seen in an earlier chapter[24], in a rather elastic manner so as to encompass all the other promises to follow in the chapter. Since
son and descendants are the contents of two of these promises, appeal may be made to Ps. 127:3 where śākār is also

---

23 There are at least sixty texts in the OT which use the root śkr in
   this sense. The favour or service rendered ranges from a marital
   right like sleeping with one's legitimate husband as in the case of
   Leah, for which right Leah had to give Rachel the mandrakes found by
   Reuben (Leah's son) (cf. Gen. 30:16), to the hard military war fought
   for God by Nebuchadnezzar and his army (cf. Ezk. 29:18-20). Payment
   for the favour or service is also very varied in form: in kind (e.g.
   Leah's mandrakes); in movable property (e.g. the spotted and striped
   flock in Gen. 31:8); in cash (e.g. the thirty shekels of silver in
   Zech. 11:13); and in immovable property (e.g. the land of Egypt in
   Ezk. 29:20).
24 Cf. Part 1, Chapter 2, page 43 above.

used in connection with sons to obtain a clearer understanding of the word in Gen. 15:1bC. Ps. 127:3 reads,
hinnēh naḥălat yhwh bānîm śākār pᵉrî habbāṭen.

The next psalm, Ps. 128, presents as happy (*'ašrê,* v. 1)
and blessed (*yᵉbōrak,* v. 4) the one who fears YHWH. The
blessing partly takes the form of the wife's fertility in
the bearing of children (v. 3)[25] and continuity through posterity (v. 6). In the light of Ps. 128, *śākar* presented in
terms of "sons" and "fruit of the womb" in Ps. 127:3 may be
understood as blessing[26]. This concept of *śākar* as blessing
may well apply to Gen. 15:1bC.

Gen. 28:4 also identifies the blessing of Abraham with the
possession of the land given to him. On the ground of the
understanding of *śākar* as blessing in Gen. 15:1bC, a parallel obtains between Gen. 28:4 and Gen. 15:1bC vis-à-vis vv.
7 and 18. In fact, the theological description of the promised land smacks of blessing from YHWH.

On the basis of the concept of *śākar* as blessing, Gen.
15:1bC with its elasticity for inclusion of the various promises contained in the chapter may well be intended to hark
back to the promise of blessing in Gen. 12:2aB, intentionally left unspecified so as to allow for a wide range of possibilities in the course of the patriarchal history. Furthermore, it is clear that Gen. 15:7 goes back to Abraham's
exodus from Ur of the Chaldaeans at the beginning of the
Abraham cycle (Gen. 11:31; 12:1). Thus, Gen. 15:1bC and 15:7
together with the notice in v. 15 about his death that marks
the end of the cycle may be said to recapitulate the entire
Abraham cycle.

The word *śākar* in Gen. 15:1bC seems also to furnish a literary point of contact with the Jacob cycle. In this latter, it is used several times for the wages Laban owed Jacob
for the patriarch's services to him: Gen. 29:15; 30:28,32,
33; 31:7,8,41. Obviously in these texts *śākar* refers to a

---

25 Cf. also Dt. 7:13.
26 In Genesis there are texts that consider blessing in terms of fertility and numerous descendants: thus, 17:16,20; 22:17; 26:24 and 28:3.

material recompense.

However, despite all the cheating[27] that went on between them, the two protagonists of the story became rich as a consequence of God's blessing on them. Laban acknowledged that YHWH had blessed him because of Jacob (Gen. 30:27). In his final encounter with his uncle, the patriarch asserted that Laban, if not for YHWH's presence with Jacob, would have sent him away empty-handed (Gen. 31:42).

Jacob was truly a man blessed by God. He managed to obtain his father's blessing before the latter's death (Gen. 27:4, 7,10,19,23,25,27). At this stage the blessing consisted essentially in his superiority over others and the return of a curse or a blessing on those who curse or bless him (Gen. 27:29). Before his departure to look for a wife[28], Isaac's blessing on Jacob was given in terms of posterity (Gen. 28:3) and possession of land (Gen. 28:4). It is significant that the blessing here was explicitly identified with "the blessing of Abraham" (28:4). By this it is clear that Jacob inherited God's blessing on Abraham - the blessing expressed in terms of *śākar* in Gen. 15:1bC.

In the Jacob cycle, the blessing saw its realization through the children born to Jacob in Gen. 29:31-30:24. Once Jacob had all these children, he asked to be sent back to his homeland (Gen. 30:25) thus initiating the fulfilment of the promise of land. In Gen. 31:3, YHWH supported Jacob's request. The Jacob cycle ends with Jacob "dwelling in the land of his father's sojournings, in the land of Canaan" (37:1).

In the minds of Laban and Jacob, the *śākar* for the latter's service to the former was thought of very much in terms of a material recompense[29]. This seemed also to be the initial understanding crossing Abraham's mind when he asked

---

27 Laban and Jacob accused each other of cheating: Gen. 31:26; 31:7,41. M. Noth, Pentateuchal Traditions, 99, maintains that the Jacob-Laban story is constructed on the motif of the "deceived deceiver".

28 Departure from Isaac meant a certain independence for Jacob. Taking a wife meant having the possibility to have descendants. Both were necessary for Jacob to function as heir to the promises.

29 Cf. Gen. 29:15; 30:28,32,33; 31:7,8,41.

YHWH, "What will you give me?" (Gen. 15:2aB). But the real
meaning of *śākar* was the blessing that could only come from
YHWH - posterity and land. It went very much beyond the material recompense that Jacob deserved for his services to
Laban. On this score it was "very great" (Gen. 15:1bC).

YHWH's promise of a very great reward to Abraham in Gen.
15:1bC seems clearly to take up the motif of *śākar* understood as Jacob's wages in the Jacob-Laban story though giving it a new twist to embrace the double promise of posterity and land.

The author of Gen. 15 shows his literary skill in his recapitulation of the double struggle in the Jacob cycle. That
against Esau is more reflected in the struggle for succession to Abraham whilst that against Laban in the Aramaean
origin of the potential rival. In unifying the double struggle by presenting only one single rival and one struggle, he
succeeds in preserving the Jacob cycle as a coherent whole.
In finally pushing aside the rival in favour of the promised
blood-heir, he exhibits his fidelity to the orientation of
the cycle whose coherence and unity lie in the predominance
of the theme of the divine oath.

CHAPTER 3

FROM CANAAN TO EGYPT [1]
(GEN. 37:2 - EX. 1:14)

I. Recapitulation Of Gen. 37:2 - Ex. 1:14

Gen. 15:13, with its verbs *ʿbd* and *ʿnh*, sets a literary
contact with Ex. 1:1-14 where the two verbs (cf. vv. 11,12,
13,14) characterize the plight of Abraham's descendants in
Egypt. The insistence in Gen. 15:13aB-C on their foreign
status through the progressive doublet - *gēr* from the viewpoint of the descendants and *lōʾ lāhem* from the viewpoint of
the land - begs the question: how did they land up in Egypt
in the first place? The answer is furnished by the Joseph
novella[2] in Gen. 37:2-50:26 which appears precisely to explain how Jacob left the promised land and settled in Egypt
"to become the people of Israel"[3] which is the "terminus a
quo" of the exodus traditions. If suffices here to note that
Gen. 37:2-50:26 and Ex. 1:1-14 together serve the literary
purpose of providing a transition from the patriarchal history to the exodus tradition[4].

---

1 The expression is borrowed from G.W. Coats, From Canaan to Egypt.
2 This is the genre some scholars classify the Joseph narrative under:
   thus, H. Gunkel, Genesis, 397; G. von Rad, Genesis, 428. G.W. Coats,
   Genesis, 265, while maintaining it as a novella because "like a tale,
   it narrates a plot from a point of crisis to its conclusion", also
   allows for the classification of a subsection (39:1-41:57) as a legend "whose narration focuses not on events, but on the central figure as an ideal who exemplifies particular characteristics."
3 T.L. Thompson, in J.H. Mayes and J.M. Miller, Israelite and Judean
   History, 210.
4 There are several literary elements that serve to blend Gen. 37:2-
   50:26 and Ex. 1:1-14 together as a transition from the patriarchal
   narrative to the exodus tradition. Ex. 1:1 opens with the same for-

The contact of Gen. 15:13aBC with the Joseph novella needs
at least a brief elaboration as it is not immediately clear.
The former's insistence on foreign status is also traceable
in the latter. In the Joseph novella, the foreign status of
the Hebrews in Egypt is highlighted in a number of ways.
Firstly, Joseph's own position as an alien is given relief
in the contrast between his race - he was called "the Hebrew
servant" (39:17; cf. also 41:12) - and his master's: an
Egyptian (39:1). To reduce or eliminate this gap in order to
qualify him for the appointment as Egypt's administrator,
Pharaoh gave him an Egyptian name (41:45) whereby "Joseph
was drawn completely into the Egyptian court circle and...
being placed within the protective sphere of an Egyptian
deity"[5]. The names Joseph gave his two sons seem to indicate his own awareness of his status as a foreigner (cf.
Gen. 41:51f).

In later episodes, Joseph's brothers too were not only
treated as aliens but also conscious of this status of
theirs. Thus in their meal with Joseph who had by now been
identified with the Egyptians, the "Hebrew brothers" had to
eat apart from him (43:32). In their dialogues with him, a
certain insistence was placed on their being from the "land
of Canaan" (42:7,13;; cf. also 44:8). Jacob's fear to go

---

mula as Gen. 46:8: $we^{\flat}$elleh $\check{s}^{e}m\hat{o}t$ $b^{e}n\hat{e}$ $yi\acute{s}r\bar{a}^{\flat}\bar{e}l$ $habb\bar{a}^{\flat}\hat{i}m$ $mi\d{s}r\bar{a}y^{e}m\bar{a}h$
and Ex. 1:6 picks up from Gen. 46:27 the fact about the same number
of Jacob's family members in Egypt. Ex. 1:7a notes the numerical increase of the sons of Israel in partially similar terms as Gen. 47:27.
While setting the stage for an entirely new scene, v. 8 provides a
clear connection with the Joseph story through the specific mention
of the name of Joseph. Where the division of Ex. 1:1-14 into two
parts is effected is "nicht ganz klar", according to Th. C. Vriezen,
VT, 17 (1967), 134. However, according to G.W. Coats, VT, 22 (1972),
131ff, it is between v. 6 and v. 7 since "the death notice in vs. 6
effectively concludes the patriarchal traditions by announcing the
end of a generation" and "vs. 7 introduces the protagonists for the
exodus tradition." To my mind, however, v. 7 with its resumption of
Gen. 47:27 seems to fit in much better with the literary character of
vv. 1-6: both seem to pick up from the Joseph story in Genesis. It
seems better, therefore, to take the break between v. 7 and v. 8.
5 Cf. G. von Rad, Genesis, 373. H. Gunkel, Genesis, 439, thinks that
"in Wirklichkeit war es selbstverständlich dass ein hoher Beamter
fremdländischer Herkunft wenigstens öffentlich die ägyptischen Götter
ehrte."

down to Egypt (46:3-4) could well be due to his deep awareness that he was going to a foreign land. In their request
for the land of Goshen, the twelve brothers acknowledged
their coming to dwell in Egypt as foreigners: lāgûr bā'āreṣ
bā'nû (47:4). Indicative of this constant awareness of
theirs were the hope and desire, despite the great prospe-
rity enjoyed in the land, to return to Canaan on the ground
of the divine promise of land donation (47:27,30; 48:3-4,21;
50:24).

However closely identified with the Egyptians, Joseph and
his own two sons would have their true home in Canaan. Thus,
Jacob adopted Joseph's two sons in order to give them an inheritance right in the land of Canaan equal to that of their
uncles' (48:5). Joseph himself was sure of Canaan as his final burial ground (50:25).

A point that merits consideration at this juncture is the
record in Gen. 15:13 of the four hundred years' duration of
the Israelites' sojourn in Egypt. This is thirty years short
of what Ex. 12:40-42, a P account, informs us. The character
of this latter as a summary appears from the fact that "it
calculates Israel's total stay in Egypt, marks the very day
of departure and concludes by returning to the theme of the
earlier speeches by stressing the continual observance of
this night 'for all generations'"[6]. Whether Gen. 15:13 de-
viated from the P information because it took its datum from
another source or because it attempted to round off the figure given by P, it is clear that it does give a chronological summary of the Israelites' slavery in Egypt.

While Gen. 15:13aB-C recalls Gen. 37:2-50:26 by highlight-
ing the foreign status of Jacob and his sons in Egypt, Gen.
15:13b characterizes the servitude nature of that sojourn as
depicted in Ex. 1:1-14 and gives information of its duration.

---

6 Cf. B.S. Childs, Exodus, 201.

II. The Divine Oath

Both the Joseph novella (Gen. 37:2-50:26) and Ex. 1:1-14
are heavily marked by the theme of the divine oath. At the
outset it may be noted that if Jacob had to take his family
down to Egypt, it was because by divine design the promise
of numerical increase would find its fulfilment there (Gen.
46:3b). In this connection it is striking that the circumstantial reason for the journey - the search for food in the
face of an outbreak of a severe famine - was not even given
a passing mention in YHWH's address to Jacob.

The fulfilment of the promise of numerous descendants was
in fact already within sight when Jacob and his family left
Canaan. The name list in Gen. 46:8-27 organizes the families
of Jacob's children "into their tribal groups in order to
depict the entire body"[7]. The final count of all the members
of all the families worked out to seventy - a number which
in tradition is intended as a "round figure, as an approxi-
mate, large number of men"[8]. Even though it is presented as
an exact figure in our text, it seems quite likely that it
envisages a multitude to come from it. An evidence to support this is Dt. 10:22. Moreover, Gen. 47:27, with the eponymic name "Israel" and its datum about Israel's numerical
growth, confirms this forward-looking intention[9].

Jacob's seventeen years in Egypt are passed over very
quickly in favour of his deathbed scene (Gen. 47:29-49:33) -
a critical moment in the patriarch's life. It is precisely
at this point that the patriarchal promises are brought in
(Gen. 48:4)[10]. Jacob's adoption and blessing of Joseph's two

---

7 G.W. Coats, Genesis, 298.
8 G. von Rad, Genesis, 398. Cf. Ex. 24:9; Num. 11:16; Jdg. 8:30.
9 In Gen. 47:27, "Israel" simultaneously refers to the individual,
   Jacob - thus, *wayyēšeb* (sing.) - and his descendants as the people of
   Israel - thus, *wayyēʾāḥāzû, wayyiprû* and *wayyirbû* (all pl.).
10 The two texts, Gen. 35:11-12 and 48:4, use several similar expres-

sons (Gen. 48:5-6,15-16) qualified them to inherit these divine promises[11]. The blessing points back to the patriarchal
traditions through Jacob's invocation of the God of Abraham
and the God of Isaac as well as through his praying for the
perpetuation of the patriarch's names and the fulfilment of
the promise of numerical increase in the two sons. Jacob's
farewell address to his sons (Gen. 49:1-28) depicts the qua-
lity of each tribe and is therefore a presentation of <u>all</u>
Israel[12], thereby looking ahead to the definitive fulfilment
of the divine oath promising a great posterity.

While focusing on the promise of descendants, the Joseph
novella does not sacrifice that of land donation. Thus in
Gen. 46:4, in addition to descendants, there is also the
promise of guidance both into and out of the land of Egypt
which, in view of the people's settlement in the land as the
purpose of the exodus, may be taken to imply the promise of
land as well. This implication finds its confirmation in Jacob's reassurance to Joseph of God's guidance back to the
"land of your fathers" (Gen. 48:21) and its repetition by
Joseph to his brothers (Gen. 50:24) which marks the end of
the Joseph novella.

The importance of the theme of the divine oath to the Joseph novella is effected by the literarily strategic position in which it is found[13]. Presented as the very reason
for the migration of Jacob and his family to Egypt which is
precisely what the novella is all about and as the patriarch's reassurance to Joseph and the latter's farewell

---

sions: *'ēl šadday; brk; prh* and *rbh; qᵉhal gôyim* (35:11) and *qᵉhal*
'ammîm (48:4) and the land donation formula.
11 The expression *wᵉ'attāh* is a consequential conjunction and thus expresses the idea of a legitimate inheritance of the promises in v.4.
Cf. C. Westermann, Genesis 37-50, 207.
12 M. Noth, Pentateuchal Traditions, 184, footnote 518.
13 Analysing the Joseph story from a narrative viewpoint, H.C. White,
Semeia, 31 (1985), 49-69, also reaches the conclusion that the focal
point of the story is the transmission of the patriarchal promise,
though he restricts the promise to that of land. His concluding affirmation is significant: "Every system utilized by the narrator to
explain the actions of his characters, including the drive toward
the restoration of broken communication between Joseph and his
brothers, is thus finally subordinated to the uttered promise and
its open future" (68).

address to his brothers, it becomes the focal point of the
novella. As a consequence, the original wisdom theme of the
novella - the ideal young man whose rise to power through
his wisdom and discretion has a didactic purpose[14] and
effects the reconciliation of his family with him as well as
salvation from a severe famine - is reoriented to serve the
denouement of the divine oath theme. Ultimately, it was the
divine promises of land and descendants that set the course
not only of the history of the patriarchs but also of that
of their descendants' - a point that finds confirmation in
Ex. 1:1-14.

Even though Ex. 1:1-14 contains no explicit reference to
the divine oath, the passage may be said to be infiltrated
by it. The list of the twelve eponymic names of Jacob's sons
in vv. 2-4 and the number seventy (v. 5) as in Gen. 46:8-27
envisage the multitudinous descendants that v. 7 talks
about. What signalled a fulfilment of God's promise posed a
threat to the new Pharoah who was bent on smashing it (vv.
8b-10). A fierce tension thus arose between God's promise
and Pharaoh's oppression of the sons of Israel. The promise
of innumerable descendants may thus be said to be the cause
of Pharaoh's harsh measure against the sons of Israel.

Equally important to the pericope, though not as directly
present as the above promise, is that of land donation. The
whole struggle that is recorded in the pericope and continued in subsequent chapters till chapter 14 in the Book of
Exodus is aimed at securing the liberation of the Israelites
in the exodus event. In turn the exodus event is geared towards the people's entry into and possession of the promised
land. The promise of land donation may thus be taken as the
motivating factor underlying the struggle in Ex. 1:1-14.

On the ground of the above two promises, the theme of the
divine oath may be said to serve as the starting point and

_____

14 G.W. Coats, CBQ, 35 (1973), 290, affirms this didactic function of
   the kernel of the Joseph story (Gen. 39-41).

the goal for difficult times facing the sons of Israel in
Egypt. In this sense, the theme has deeply penetrated Ex.
1:1-14.

III. The Theme Of Faith

G.W. Coats concludes his article, "The Joseph Story and
Ancient Wisdom", thus: "Indeed, in the middle of the picture
stands the entire scope of Israel's faith"[15]. This faith is
portrayed in various ways. The tragic experiences of the
protagonist - the bad treatment he received from his brothers, his forced departure from his family, his imprison-
ment in Egypt - were, humanly speaking, sheer ill-fate. For
both Reuben and Jacob, Joseph's disappearance was hope-
shattering (cf. 37:29,35-36). But the author of the novella
strikes an optimistic note in his remark about Joseph's success in Egypt: "The Lord was with Joseph" (39:2-5). Even
though Joseph should be cast into prison for his innocence,
"the Lord was with him; and whatever he did, the Lord made
him prosper" (39:23; cf. v. 21). Such a remark does not seem
to make much sense in Joseph's situation. If the Lord was
truly with Joseph, why did He not in the first place prevent
him from being thrown into prison, especially since he was
completely innocent? It would certainly call for an almost
blind faith to see God's hand controlling the entire situation.

Joseph himself, far from losing his faith in God despite
these bitter experiences of his, was still able to count on
His guidance in his interpretation of dreams (40:8; 41:16)
and express his belief in God's revelation to the Pharoah
regarding the step to be taken in the face of the famine to
follow on the forthcoming years of plenty (41:25,28,32). In
his appointment of Joseph to govern his house and people,
the Pharaoh also confessed his own faith in God (41:38f).

It is only now that God's purpose behind Joseph's bitter
experiences became clear. The name Joseph gave to his second

---

15 G.W. Coats, CBQ, 35 (1973), 297.

son expressed his faith in this (41:52). In the moving scene
of his self-revelation to his brothers (45:1-15), Joseph's
faith in God's providence found its clearest and most explicit expression (45:5-8). This faith was repeated in Joseph's
reassurance to his brothers (50:20) when they became appre-
hensive about a possible change of his attitude towards them
after their father's death (50:15-17).

In those sections in which the patriarch Jacob figures,
the faith element is anchored in the promise theme. Thus,
Jacob's journey from Beersheba (46:5) is presented as his
response to the vision in which God promised him numerical
increase and guidance. His adoption of Joseph's two sons was
also tied to the promise theme (48:3-5) thereby signalling
his faith that God would fulfill His promises in them, as
evidenced by the content of His blessing (48:15f,19). Finally, the assurance Jacob gave Joseph (48:21) and Joseph repeated to his brothers (50:24) could only have emerged from
their faith in God's fidelity to His promises! It is only in
this final scene that Joseph's faith in God was presented in
relation to the final oath to the patriarchs with which it
originally had nothing to do. By this Joseph's faith may be
said to reach its climax when it became a response to the
divine oath.

In Ex. 1:1-14, the redactor's faith reflecting Israel's
faith shows through in his insistence on the fulfilment of
God's promise of numerous descendants (v. 7) especially even
in the face of the Pharaoh's determination to shatter it
through oppression (v. 12).

CHAPTER 4

THE EXODUS TRADITION

I. Delineation And Unity Of The Tradition

The unit that concerns us now arches from Ex. 1:15, where
the previous unit left off, to Ex. 14:31[1], since this section of the Book of Exodus revolves around the theme of
"YHWH versus the Egyptian gods".

YHWH was initially represented by Moses whom He had made
"as God" to Aaron (4:16) and to Pharaoh (7:1). Pharaoh is
presented as personifying the Egyptian gods as YHWH's judgement on him is in fact seen as a judgement on all these gods
(12:12). In addition, Pharaoh is accorded the same status as
YHWH: "thus says Pharaoh" (5:10) in opposition to "thus says
YHWH" (4:22; 7:17,26; 8:16; 9:1,13; 10:3; 11:4); the Israelites "served" him (14:5,12) when they should be serving YHWH
(3:12,18; 4:23; 7:16,26; 8:16; 9:1,13; 10:3,7,24); and he
had "servants" (7:10,20; 8:17,25,27; 9:14,34; 10:6,7; 14:5)
as YHWH had.

The story starts off with no clear indication as to who
would emerge victorious in the struggle: "the more the people were oppressed, the more they multiplied and spread
abroad" (1:12). It then moves on to Pharaoh's clear victory
that left the Israelite foremen and Moses utterly helpless
(5:19-23) and continues with a series of manifestations of
YHWH's power but resulting only in the "hardening of Pha-

---

1 R. Rendtorff, Das überlief. Problem, maintains Ex. 1-14 as a self-
  contained unit in which "es sich.. im wesentlich um einen liturgis-
  chen Text handle" (155).

raoh's heart" (7:8-10:29). Finally, YHWH's decisive victory
is clearly asserted: it was acknowledged by the Egyptians
(14:25) as much as by the Israelites (14:31).

From the viewpoint of its literary organization, the unit
is seen to contain two parts: Ex. 1-4 and 5-14[2]. But they
are tied together by the following parallel literary pattern: oppression of the Israelites (1:8-22//5:1-21); the
background of Moses, YHWH's human agent (2:1-22//6:14-27);
the people's cry coming to YHWH (2:23-25) or being brought
to Him by Moses (5:20-23); YHWH's commissioning of Moses (3:
1-4:17//6:1,2-8); Moses' encounter with Pharaoh (4:21-23//6:
10-13,28-30 and 7:8-10:29); and the people's faith response
elicited by signs (4:29-31//14:31).

A further bond between the two parts is furnished by the
progression from the first to the second. In the first part,
the focus is on YHWH acting through the agency of His servant Moses. In the second part, this focus is repeated till
12:28 after which it is shifted to YHWH acting directly
(12:29-14:31).

---

2 R. Rendtorff, Das überlief. Problem, 71, points out that "ein deut-
  licher Zusammenhang zwischen der Komposition von Ex. 1-4 und der
  Gesamtkomposition von Ex. 1-14 erkennbar (ist)", since with the decisive turning point in Ex. 2:23-25 YHWH manifested His concern for His
  people through various signs whereby Moses' worry "ob die Israeliten
  Mose 'glauben' werden" (Ex. 4:1,5,8,9) found a positive answer; "das
  Volk glaubte" (Ex. 4:31). Cf. M. Fishbane, in Text and Texture, 63-76,
  (although Fishbane takes the "Exodus Cycle" from Ex. 1 to Ex. 19);
  H.-C. Schmitt, VT, 32 (1982), 175f.

II. Faith Supported By Signs

The theologoumenon of "faith supported by signs" is very
much in play in Ex. 1-14. First of all, signalled by *'mn-
hiphil* in 4:31 and 14:31, it marks the end of each of the
two parts (chapters 1-4 and 5-14). In each of these texts,
the people's response of faith is elicited by signs. 4:31 is
preceded by a record of signs worked by Aaron in the sight
of the people (4:30). 14:31 notes the Israelites' faith at
the end of a dramatic event in the sea. The use of the verb
r'h in 14:30,31 to recapitulate the event as the working of
YHWH's mighty hand attributes a sign character to the event.

At the level of the parts too, the theologoumenon has its
role to play. The main thrust of Ex. 1-4 is the first step
taken by YHWH to liberate the Israelites from their situation of bondage. 2:23-25 presents a turning point[3] to introduce YHWH's commissioning of Moses[4] as this first step of
His intervention. For the commissioning to be effective, it
must meet the faith of both Moses and the people. In other
words, both Moses and the people must believe in his being
sent by YHWH to execute His plan of liberation for them.

As he was called, the first problem faced by Moses was one
of faith as is clear from his first objection (3:11). Behind
his question about his dignity lay his doubt about the divine origin of his mission. This was why YHWH gave him a

---

3 R. Rendtorff, Das überlief. Problem, 71. B.S. Childs, Exodus, 32f,
  maintains, "The verses relate primarily to what has already been re-
  counted and conclude the section by returning to the earlier theme of
  Israel's misery. However, the verses do mark a decided break, both in
  time and perspective, with what is past. First, the narrative takes
  the reader back to Israel in Egypt and records the passing of time.
  Nothing has improved since Moses' departure. Israel continues to
  groan under its burden. Secondly, their suffering has not gone un-
  noticed. God remembers his covenant with the patriarchs. But in both
  instances there is a glimpse toward the future as well."
4 So G.W. Coats, JBL, 92 (1973), 8.

sign that He had sent him (v. 12). From a comparative analysis of the text vis-à-vis two groups of texts dealing with
confirmative sign, B.S. Childs has demonstrated that the
sign in our text refers to the divine theophany in the burning bush (3:1-6)[5] which also served as a guarantee for Moses
that after rescuing the Israelites he would worship God "on
this mountain". This sign, for Moses himself, was thus aimed
at confirming his faith about his God-given mission.

Moses raised the problem of the people's faith in his
third objection (4:1). From YHWH's answer in v. 5, it seems
clear that this problem had to do with the divine authenti-
cation of Moses' mission, for the divine apparition of which
the sign was offered as a testimony would serve to legitimatize this mission. There is no doubt that v. 5 harks back to
3:1-6. Three signs were offered to confirm the people's
faith. They are described in 4:1-9, in which the verb *'mn-
hiphil* is used five times (vv. 1,5,8a,b,9) starting with a
negative usage and alternating with a positive one. The
three signs were: Moses' rod turned into a serpent (vv.3-4),
his hand turned leprous (vv.6-7) and the Nile water turned
into blood (v. 9). The failure of one sign to produce its
desired effect of enkindling faith led to the working of the
next one. Quite clearly, then, faith and sign in this pericope are inseparably tied to each other.

Faith in Moses as the divinely commissioned liberator for
the Israelites ultimately amounted to faith in YHWH Himself.
This is the implication of Ex. 4:31 whose absolute use of
'mn-niphil is most probably intended as faith in both YHWH
and Moses his servant.

In the second part (Ex. 5-14), we are told that in bringing the people's cry to YHWH (5:20-23), Moses was commissioned a second time by YHWH (6:1,2-8) . Here YHWH revealed
to Moses the main events of Israel's history and identified

---

5 B.S. Childs, Exodus, 56-60.
6 Ex. 6:2-7:7 is generally regarded as P's parallel to the account of
  Moses' call in Ex. 3:1-4:17. Thus, M. Greenberg, in Fourth World Congress of Jewish Studies, I, 151-154, points out that P's narrative of

Himself thrice: *'ănî yhwh*[7]. The force of this self-identification at the beginning and at the end of His speech was
to underscore His redemptive power and authority in His interventions in Israel's history[8] and provide a "guarantee
that the reality of God stands behind the promise and will
execute its fulfilment"[9]. The self-identification in v. 7bA
is given in connection with an assurance of the Israelites'
"knowing" of YHWH through their history, thereby transforming this history into a sign. The same affirmation is given
again in 10:2 in connection with the plagues.

In the "programmatic discourse"[10] in 7:1-5, YHWH also predicted that the Egyptians would come to know Him through His
actions against them (v. 5). This knowledge was certainly
the aim of the unleashing of the plagues in Egypt[11] as is
clear from its repeated proclamation in the accounts of the
plagues. The repetition is made "in a manner giving it increasing emphasis and meaning... This is a gradual revelation of the divine nature which will eventually be acknowledged even in Egypt"[12]. The divine nature finally revealed
is: YHWH the God of the Israelites is the supreme God in
full control of world history because the world is His and
He is present therein.

The failure of the plagues to secure the acknowledgement

Moses' call is "a reinforcement of Moses' message and mission, intended in the first place for Moses' ears, in the second, for the people
... and, finally, for Pharaoh." In this way they serve to introduce
the plagues narrative to come as this narrative revolves around the
theme of revelation by God of His name to Pharaoh, the Egyptians and
the onlooking Israelites. Cf. also M. Greenberg, in H. Goedicke,
Near Eastern Studies in Honor of W.F. Albright, 243-252. Moreover,
the parallel literary pattern we have traced between Ex. 1:8-4:31 and
Ex. 5:1-14:31 has an integral place for 6:2-7:7.

7 W. Zimmerli, in G. Ebeling, FS A. Alt, 179-209, has demonstrated the
   ancient liturgical background to this formula.
8 Cf. B.S. Childs, Exodus, 114-116.
9 B.S. Childs, Exodus, 115.
10 So J.L. Ska, Bib, 60 (1979), 24-27. He affirms that Ex. 7:1-4aA projects Ex. 7-11 and 7:4bB points to Ex. 12-14.
11 So M. Greenberg, Fourth World Congress of Jewish Studies, I, 153. For
   a survey of the main opinions about the nature of the Egyptian
   plagues and the sources of their accounts in Exodus, cf. J. Sievi,
   ThBer, 5 (1976), 13-35.
12 D.J. McCarthy, CBQ, 37 (1965), 346.

of YHWH by the Egyptians was due to the invariable hardening
of Pharaoh's heart. As announced in 4:21 and 7:3, Pharaoh's
stubbornness was YHWH's doing[13]. It prevented him and the
Egyptians from knowing YHWH through the plagues[14] and necessitated the working of further signs[15]. Thus, even at the
unleashing of the tenth plague, viz., the death of every
Egyptian first-born male[16], there was still no acknowledgement of YHWH by Pharaoh, though it forced him to set the Israelites free. With this, the stage was set for the manifestation of YHWH's glory over the Egyptians at which they
would know YHWH, as announced in 14:4,18 and realized in
14:25.

The fulfilment of YHWH's prediction about the hardening of
Pharaoh's heart and the hearts of the Egyptians and their
final acknowledgement of YHWH at their discomfiture in the
sea[17] in itself constituted a sign for the Israelites. It

---

13 The "hardening" vocabulary in Ex. 4-14 consists of: (i) *kbd*, usually
   in its *hiphil* conjugation (8:11,28; 9:34; 10:1), once in the *qal* (7:
   14) and once as verbal adjective (7:14); (ii) *ḥzq*, usually in the
   piel conjugation (4:21; 7:3; 9:12; 10:20,27; 11:10; 14:4,8,17), and
   four times in the *qal* (7:13,22; 8:15; 9:35); (iii) *ʿaqšeh* (7:3);
   (iv) *hiqšāh* (13:15). Whether YHWH is expressly presented as hardening
   the hearts of Pharaoh and the Egyptians (4:21; 7:3; 9:12; 10:1,20,27;
   11:10; 14:17) or Pharaoh himself (8:11,28; 9:34; 13:15) or the Pharaoh's heart itself hardened (7:13,14,22; 8:15; 9:35), Pharaoh's
   every resistance was YHWH's doing as YHWH had announced it before
   (4:21; 7:3). This is why even when YHWH is not presented directly as
   hardening Pharaoh's heart, the clause "as the Lord had said" is used
   to conclude the notice (7:13,22; 8:11,15; 9:35).
14 This seems to be characteristic of J's account. The execution of the
   plagues as well as their removal were aimed at revealing YHWH to Pharaoh (7:17; 8:6,18; 9:29; 11:7) but systematically Pharaoh's failure
   to know YHWH is expressed through the hardening of this heart (8:11a,
   28; 9:34) as signalled right at the beginning of Moses' encounter
   with Pharaoh (5:2).
15 This is P's trend of thought whereby the plagues are distinguished
   from the destruction of the Egyptians in the sea - a distinction already made in 7:4-5. P concludes each of his plague accounts with the
   hardening formula (7:13,22; 8:11b,15; 9:12) thereby presenting it as
   the ground for the next plague.
16 G. Hort, ZAW, 70 (1958), 54f, takes this plague as originally a destruction of the first fruits caused by the other plagues but later
   misunderstood to mean the first-born.
17 Opening his study, G.W. Coats, StTh, 29 (1975), 53-62, poses the
   question, "What really happened at the Sea of Reeds?" and observes,
   "Scholars interested in history and theology in traditions about Is-

was the "great work which the Lord did against the Egyptians" (14:31a). This served to confirm their faith in YHWH and His servant Moses.

From Ex. 1-14, it is clear that the historical events had served to manifest YHWH's power and lordship[18] and forced the Egyptians to acknowledge it. For the Israelites they led not only to their knowledge but also their faith in YHWH.

---

rael's early past face unusual problems in evaluating the sea tradition" (53). Historical solutions given vary. F.M. Cross, JTC, (1968), 16-19, thinks that the stormy sea had drowned the Egyptians from their barks or barges. J. Bright, A History of Israel, 120, proposes, "It appears that Hebrews, attempting to escape, were penned between the sea and the Egyptian army and were saved when a wind drove the waters back, allowing them to pass (Ex. 14:21,27); the pursuing Egyptians, caught by the returning flood, were drowned." L.S. Hay, JBL, 83 (1964) 297-403, argues for the victory of the Israelites over the chariot troops of the Pharaoh in a war. The Israelites' victory was made possible by the almost dry condition of the sea but damp enough to clog the Egyptian chariots which became an easy target for the Israelite archers, M. Noth, The History of Israel, 116f, explains the destruction of the Egyptians as due to "some unexpected disaster... veiled from our sight." R. de Vaux, The Early History of Israel, 384, affirms, "Bearing the epic character even of the prose account of Ex. 14 in mind, it would be foolish to try to discover what really happened. The fleeing Israelites are shown to be in a desperate situation and their rescue is attributed by them to a powerful and miraculous intervention by their God." It was this "miraculous intervention" by YHWH that constituted a sign element to corroborate faith - not only the faith of the exodus generation who witnessed it, but also the faith of the future generations of Israel, as G.W. Coats, StTh, 29 (1975), 58, rightly concludes after analysing the use of this tradition in various parts of the OT: "Indeed... history for the sea tradition cannot be confined to a box of time and space... Rather in the sea tradition the event demonstrates a distinct openness toward the future. It develops unique significance for each new generation."

18 R. de Vaux, The Early History of Israel, 357, affirms, "Yahweh was... a God who directed man's history and manifested himself... in historical events following one another in time and moving towards an end."

III. The Oath To The Patriarchs

The divine oath to the patriarchs has its importance in
Ex. 1-14. It is found explicitly in 2:24; 6:3-5,8 and 13:5,
11 and implicitly referred to in 1:7,12,20 through the mention of the people's numerical increase and in 3:6,15f
through the naming of the patriarchs.

1. Ex. 1:7,12,20

Its implicit but sure presence in 1:7,12,20 in the context
of the struggle between YHWH and the Egyptians defines it as
the root cause of the Israelites' plight in Egypt. For vv.
9-10 unveil the Pharaoh's plan of oppression as aimed at
preventing their numerical increase - at first through hard
labour (v. 11) and later through attempted male infanticide
(vv. 15f,22). The force of the oath explains the people's
survival and the continuation of the oppression (vv. 12-14,
20-22). Since the oppression constitutes the obvious beginning of the history of the people of Israel "per se", an obvious conclusion to draw is that the oath to the patriarchs
launches Israel's history off into its orbit. This finds
confirmation in the subsequent references to the patriarchal
oath in the current section of our consideration.

2. Ex. 2:24

we have already noted that Ex. 2:23-25 constitutes a transition from the situation of oppression to YHWH's intervention in Ex. 3-14. The whole tone of the brief passage builds
up to an expectation that YHWH was now going to do some-

thing[19]. That expectation comes, to be sure, from the reader's empathy for YHWH's sympathy for the people effected by
the series of four short clauses in vv. 23b,c,24a. But more
important than that is YHWH's remembering of His oath to the
patriarchs (v. 24b). In fact, the evoking of sympathy builds
up to YHWH's recalling of the oath as its climax. The oath
obliged YHWH to take a decisive course of action to break
His people's yoke, for which action v. 25 presents YHWH as
being ready. As such the oath set in motion all the subsequent interventions of His to free His people, starting with
His call of Moses in 3:1-4:17[20].

3. Ex. 3:6,15f

Of significance to our present consideration is the sequence constituted by Ex. 2:23-25 and 3:1-4:17, namely,
YHWH's awareness of the Israelites' sufferings followed by
His decision to deliver them. This sequence is reflected in
the following smaller units of the call narrative (3:1-4:17):
3:7-8; 3:9-10 and 3:16-17. In fact, 3:7 uses the same verbs
as 2:23-25 to express YHWH's noting of the situation: $\check{s}m^\epsilon$,
$r^\flat h$, and yd^ϵ, whilst 3:16 names the three patriarchs the divine oath to whom is recalled in 2:23-25. Through its lite-
rary contact with 3:7, 3:9[21] is also linked with 2:23-25.
Thus, it seems clear that God's decision to deliver the Israelites in 3:7,9 and 16 is, as in 2:23-25, rooted in His
oath to their patriarchal ancestors.

Moses' mission in 3:10 is given a sign to authenticate it

_____

19 Thus, C. Isbell, in D.J.A. Clines et alii, Art and Meaning, 52, affirms, "It is only with 2:23-25 that God is fully introduced into the
   narrative: we are told that God saw, remembered, heard, and knew. Only with 2:23-25 will the rest of the story begin to make sense. Why,
   for example, would "God" suddenly appear in Midian to enlist Moses?
   Verses 24-25 answer that question in advance."
20 So also D.M. Gunn, in D.J.A. Clines et alii, Art and Meaning, 82.
21 V. 9 bears two points of contact with v. 7: (i) $hinn\bar{e}h$ $\c{s}a^\epsilon\bar{a}qat...$
   $b\bar{a}^\flat\bar{a}h$ $^\flat\bar{e}l\bar{a}y$ (9a) // $w^e et$-$\c{s}a^\epsilon\bar{a}q\bar{a}t\bar{a}m$ $\check{s}\bar{a}ma^\epsilon t\hat{\imath}$ (7bA); and (ii) $w^e gam$-
   $r\bar{a}^\flat\hat{\imath}t\hat{\imath}$ $^\flat et$-$hallahas$ (9bA) // $r\bar{a}^\flat\bar{o}h$ $r\bar{a}^\flat\hat{\imath}t\hat{\imath}$ $^\flat et$ $^\epsilon\bar{o}ni$ $^\epsilon amm\hat{\imath}$ (7a).

as of divine origin (3:12). The sign is the theophany in the
burning bush (3:1-6) in which YHWH identified Himself as the
God of the three patriarchs (3:6). This identification would
be the name by which YHWH is "to be remembered throughout
all generations" (3:15b). In the context of the call narrative (3:1-4:17) as the sequence of 2:23-25, there is an al-
lusion to the patriarchal oath in 3:6 and 3:15f.

The indirect reference to the divine oath to the patriarchs in 3:6,15f presents this oath as the ultimate reason for YHWH's commissioning of Moses to liberate the Israelites. The import of YHWH's perpetual title as the God of
the patriarchs is far-reaching. It expresses the assurance
that out of His fidelity to His oath to the patriarchs, YHWH
would always intervene in favour of any generation that des-
cended from the patriarchs as He was doing for the Israelites of Moses' generation. In other words, YHWH's oath to
the patriarchs is presented as setting in motion an open-
ended history for their descendants.

4. Ex. 6:3-5,8

In a different way the people's suffering were here
brought to YHWH's attention (5:20-23) to introduce the second step of YHWH's intervention (6:1,2-8). In this second
commissioning of Moses, YHWH made a disclosure at two levels: to Moses personally (vv. 2-5) and to the people (vv.
6-8). At both levels, He used the formula *'anî yhwh* to give
weight to the declarations to follow.

The two levels are linked by the same sequence that, as
pointed out above, ties 2:23-25 and 3:1-4:17, namely YHWH's
awareness and His decision, together. In fact, 6:5 picks up
the vocabulary of 2:24. YHWH is thus presented as being ready for action. His oath to the patriarchs is the reason for
it - thus, the use of *lākēn* to introduce the second level.

YHWH's announcement of His plan to the people (6:6-8)
spells out His interventions at the various stages of the

people's history from His liberation of them till His guidance of them into the promised land. Their entry into the
land (v. 8), presented as the "terminus ad quem" of these
interventions, would seem to be the goal of Israel's history. With this entry as its object, the divine oath may thus
be taken as serving to provide the goal for Israel's history.

From Ex. 6:1,2-8, it seems clear that YHWH's oath to the
patriarchs serves the double purpose of being the source and
goal of Israel's history. Each of the various stages of this
history spelt out in the divine speech would therefore be
genuinely rooted in the oath as well. On this score, the
oath is the operating force for the entire history of Israel
worked out stage by stage.

5. Ex. 13:5,11

Immediately after their exodus resulting from the striking
of the tenth plague[22], Moses instructed the people to commemorate the two events through two cultic practices: the an-
nual eating of the unleavened bread (13:3-10) and the offering of the first-born (13:11-16). These two instructions are
presented in parallel fashion[23].

---

22 D.J. McCarthy, JBL, 85 (1966), 137-158, advances the hypothesis that
the plagues narrative with Ex. 14 as its climax was originally independent of the passover legenda in ch. 12. Ex. 14:5a,b (in which šlḥ
means "allowed to go free" rather than "sent away") is a residue of
an account of a stealthy escape that had been dropped off "in order
to make room for the different account of Israel's departure connected
with the Passover" (155). In an earlier article, McCarthy, CBQ, 27
(1965), 336-347, claimed that a concentric scheme binding 7:8-9:7
together excludes the tenth plague from the plagues narrative. Pursuing further G.W. Coats' study, VT, 17 (1967), 253-265, in which the
author maintains that the Reed Sea event really belongs to the wilderness theme, B.S. Childs, VT, 20 (1970), 406-418, notes that Coats'
conclusion is true for the JE level. However, there was a shift from
this wilderness theme to the exodus theme so that by P's time, the
Sea event had already occupied a central place within the Exodus itself. By introducing the major themes of the plagues narrative, viz.
Pharaoh's obduracy, the stretching out of hand, the Egyptians' recognition of YHWH, P painted the exodus as a two-phased event: the slay-
ing of the first-born and the victory at the sea.
23 The series of parallels are: $w^e h\bar{a}y\bar{a}h\ ki\text{-}y^e b\hat{\imath}\text{'}\check{a}k\bar{a}\ yhwh\ \text{'}el\text{-}\text{'}ere\c{s}$
$hakk^e na\text{'}\check{a}n\hat{\imath}$ + oath of land donation (v. 5 // v. 11); a cultic obser-

It is important to note that both cultic commemorations
were to be carried out only after the Israelites' entry into
the land (13:5,11) since it was in connection with this entry that the divine oath of land donation was explicitly recalled. In both cases, the oath functioned to give the people the certitude that they would enter the land. It was towards this entry that the exodus, resulting from the death
of every Egyptian first-born male, was oriented. In other
words, the exodus was a necessary first step in a process
whose "terminus ad quem" would be entry into the land. That
is to say, the divine oath to the patriarchs, apart from
providing certitude, was also the operative force behind the
two inter-related events that had just taken place. This
takes us back once again to the importance of the divine
oath to the patriarchs to the history of their descendants.

A second noteworthy element concerns the implicit or indirect association of the oath with Israel's cultic practices
depicted in the instructions. At this level of indirect association, the catechetical instruction attached to each
rite[24] explained its significance in terms of the two related events (vv. 8,14-15). That means to say the foundation
role of the divine oath for the two events spilled over to
the cult that was to commemorate them. It may thus be said
that the divine oath lay at the root of the two cultic
practices talked about in Ex. 13. Yet in commemorating the
events of Israel's history, the cult at the same time perpe-
tuated memory of the oath as well. The oath deserved this
perpetual memory because the Israelites owed their survival
and liberation to it. Such was its importance for the people
that it was given a place in their cult - that important moment in which they entered into a conscious contact with
their God.

---

vance (vv. 6-7; vv. 12-13); the son's (sons') question regarding the
meaning of the cultic observance (vv. 8a, 14a) and the answer in
terms of the exodus (vv. 8b, 14b-15); an external reminder ^{c}al-$y\bar{a}d^{e}k\bar{a}$
and $b\hat{e}n$ $^{c}\hat{e}ney\bar{a}k\bar{a}$ (vv. 9 and 16).

24 For catechesis in the form of cultic-aetiological legends, cf. J.A.
Soggin, VT, 10 (1960), 341-347.

To sum up, the importance of the divine oath is underscored in Ex. 1-14. Explicitly referred to in 2:23-25, it
marked every subsequent intervention by YHWH in Israel's favour as motivated by His fidelity to it. This is particularly evident in the important first step in the intervention (3:1-4:17) as well as its reinforcement (6:2-8)[25]. When
the actual liberation had attained its first phase, attention was once again called to this oath to remind the
liberated ones that their liberation was YHWH's doing in
fidelity to His oath. This reminder would be served by their
cult in the land which again the oath assured they would
possess.

---

25 See M. Greenberg, Fourth World Congress of Jewish Studies, I, 153.

IV. Recapitulation In Gen. 15:14

Gen. 15:14 presents the exodus as a consequence of YHWH's judgement: $dān$ $'ānōkî$ $w^e'aḥărê-kēn$ $yēṣ^e'û$. While $yēṣ^e'û$ clearly refers to the exodus event (cf. Ex. 12:42; 14:11), the connection between v. 14aB and the events that led up to the exodus is not so obvious. The key word of v. 14aB is $dān$ - a word not found in the narration of any of the events.

However, in Ex. 6:2-8[26], which narrates God's call of Moses and thus spells out His mission for him, and in Ex. 7: 1-5, which is a "programmatic discourse"[27], the events leading up to the exodus are announced as the $š^ep\bar{a}ṭîm$ $g^ed\bar{o}lîm$ (Ex. 6:6; 7:4) by which YHWH would deliver the Israelites. The point to consider is whether there is any relationship, and if so, what sort of relationship it is, between dyn and $špṭ$ in the OT.

The root $špṭ$ has a very broad range of usages in the OT[28]. Its occurrence in the context of Ex. 6:2-8 and 7:1-5 sets the criterion for the kind of usage to be selected for consideration here. In the given context, we are basically concerned with the use of $špṭ$ in connection with the deliverance of the Israelites from the Egyptian bondage (Ex. 6:5-6; 7:4) and the revelation of God therein (Ex. 6:7; 7:5). From this, it is clear that the texts of relevance here are those where $špṭ$ denotes a certain action of God on an oppressor in favour of the oppressed whereby something of Him is revealed.

The Book of Ezekiel contains a number of passages which

---

26 For the literary position of Ex. 6:2-8 in the exodus tradition, cf. J.L. Ska, ZAW, 94 (1982), 530-548.
27 J.L. Ska, Bib, 60 (1979), 23-35.
28 Cf. the extensive study by G. Liedke, Gestalt und Bezeichnung alttestamentlicher Rechtssätze, 62-100.

provide an analogous context for the use of *špṭ*: 5:10,15;
11:9; 14:21; 16:41; 25:11; 28:22,26; 30:14; 38:22[29]. Of
these, the text that comes closest to Ex. 6:5-6 and 7:4 is
Ezk. 30:10-19 in that if presents YHWH's *š^epāṭîm* being unleashed against the Egyptians and their gods and resulting
in their acknowledgement of YHWH (Ezk. 30:19). In Ezk.
30:10-19, YHWH's *š^epāṭîm* consisted of His complete destruction of His foes[30]. The same concept of *š^epāṭîm* emerges from
the oracles against Moab for her word against the house of
Judah in Ezk. 25:11 and against Sidon in Ezk. 28:22. In an
oracle against Jerusalem in Ezk. 14:21, the *š^epāṭîm* were
concretely spelt out as "sword, famine, evil beasts and pestilence".

In all the texts listed above, *š^epāṭîm* is governed by the
verb *'āśāh,* thereby referring to an action by YHWH. From the
context, it is clear that YHWH's *š^epāṭîm* were the concrete
acts that He carried out as a punishment for what in His
judgement were offences against Him (here, Judah and Israel
were not exempted) or against His people. In legal termino-
logy, they were the sentences YHWH passed in His judgement
of His offenders the execution of which led to the acknowledgement that He was YHWH.

In some texts, the word *mišpāṭîm* is also used to express
such sentences passed in judgement (2 K. 25:6; Ps. 105:5;
Jer. 1:16) or executed and leading to a certain knowledge of
YHWH - thus, Ps. 9:17: YHWH has made Himself known (*nôda'*)
in His execution of a sentence passed (*mišpāṭ 'āśāh*)[31] on
the wicked.

The root *dyn* - much less frequently used in the OT than
špṭ[32] - also betrays a number of usages[33]. Used with YHWH as

---

29 For some texts outside Ezekiel, cf. Num. 33:4; 2 Chr. 24:24; Prov.
   19:29. Joel 4:2,12 use *špṭ* in its verbal form as in Ezk. 38:22.
30 Thus, V. Hamp and G.J. Botterweck, in TDOT, III, 188.
31 For the expression *'āśāh mišpāṭ,* cf. also Gen. 18:19; 2 Sam. 8:15 //
   1 Chr. 18:14; 1 K. 10:9 // 2 Chr. 9:8; Jer. 9:23; 22:3,15; 23:5;
   33:15; Ezk. 18:5,19,27; 33:14,16,19; 45:9; Ps. 99:4.
32 For statistics, cf. G. Liedke, in THAT, I, col. 446; V. Hamp and
   G.J. Botterweck, in TDOT, III, 187.
33 This is treated in both the articles referred to in the above footnote.

subject it could refer to a divine act of mercy towards a
needy individual - e.g. Rachel (Gen. 30:6) and the psalmist
(Ps. 54:3). Or, it could mean YHWH's vindication of His people (Dt. 32:36; Ps. 135:14) or even punishment of them (Is.
3:13f; Ps. 50:4). There are texts which employ *dyn* to express YHWH's judgement on the nations or the whole earth
(Pss. 7:9; 9:9; 76:9; 96:10; 110:6).

The last series of texts above are of special significance
for our present purpose because they use *dyn* in parallelism
to *špṭ*. On the basis of this parallelism, one may suspect
some sort of relationship between the two roots. In Pss. 9:9f
and 76:9f, *dyn* and *špṭ* appear in the context of YHWH's stand
for the oppressed. Other passages bearing such a usage of
špṭ[34] indicate YHWH passing or executing a sentence so that
it seems clear that Pss. 9:9f and 76:9f also allude to
YHWH's action against the oppressors in His defence of the
oppressed. The occurrence of *dîn* as the object of *šmˤ-hi-
phil* in Ps. 76:9 suggests that there is also a sentence uttered or passed. Thus, it would seem that in such parallel
uses, *dyn* and *špṭ* bear the same meaning. This finds confirmation in Ps. 140:13 where *dyn* and *špṭ* are also found in
parallelism:

I know that YHWH *yaˤăśeh dîn ˤonî*

mišpāṭ ʾebyōnîm.

The psalmist's association of YHWH's protection of the poor
and needy with his own knowledge of Him is noteworthy as it
is this knowledge that gives the former the condifence that
YHWH will deliver him from evil men (v. 1). Viewed from this
angle, YHWH's *dîn* and *mišpāṭ* do certainly involve an act of
judgement against the psalmist's oppressors.

There is an analogous situation between Gen. 15:14 and Ex.
6:2-8 and 7:1-5. In all three texts, the Israelites were oppressed and YHWH was bent on delivering them. Abraham's
faith in Gen. 15:6, which arches both forward and backward
to cover both sections of chapter 15, is his acknowledgement
of YHWH corresponding to that in Ex. 6:7 and 7:5. On the

---

34 Ezk. 25:11; 28:22; 30:14; 38:22; Joel 4:2,12.

ground of the analogous situation in the three passages
as well as their reference to the same exodus event in the
history of Israel, it seems clear that YHWH's act depicted
by *dîn* in Gen. 15:14 refers to the whole series of plagues
leading up to the utter destruction of the Egyptians in the
sea[35] that Ex. 6:2-8 and 7:1-5 announce. The sea event recorded in Ex. 14[36] was a sign of YHWH's complete victory
over the Egyptians[37] thus revealing His glory. It was as a
consequence of this final catastrophe that the complete
"redemption" (Ex. 6:6) in the form of an exodus from Egypt
(Ex. 7:4) which had begun with the plagues was definitely
achieved[38]. This is the point of Gen. 15:14: *'aḥărê kēn*
yēṣ^eʾû. Thus, Gen. 15:14 reflects the author's intention to
recapitulate the entire exodus tradition.

---

35 Cf. J.L. Ska, Bib, 60 (1979), 191-215.
36 J.A. Soggin, in A. Caquot et alii, Mélanges bibliques et orientaux en
   l'honneur de M. Mathias Delcor, 379-385, points out that there are
   three reports of the Sea event in Ex. 14: viz., vv. 21aB.bA; 21aA.bB-
   22b; 24-25. The Song of Victory in Ch. 15 may contain a fourth account.
37 G.W. Coats, VT, 18 (1968), 457, argues for an escape of the Israelites by stealth in the motif of despoiling. This "secret escape with
   spoil constitutes an alternative climax for the Exodus theme." His
   interpretation of *šăʾal* as a "borrowing" with clear supposition that
   "objects so obtained would be returned" also posited the Israelites'
   intention to deceive their masters as in actual reality they wanted
   to despoil them. "The Israelites would have been forced to complete
   their deception by stealth, by escaping without the knowledge of the
   Egyptians." The question is, why should the Israelites have to deceive when YHWH was obviously intervening on their behalf by "giving
   them favour in the sight of the Egyptians"? J. Morgenstern's theory
   as advanced in JBL, 68 (1949), 1-28 - that the despoiling was originally the borrowing by the Israelite women of bridal outfit and orna-
   ments from the Egyptian women in their anticipated role of brides -
   has to answer solid objections raised by S. Goldman, From Slavery to
   Freedom, 203-206.
38 So B.S. Childs, VT, 20 (1970), 409; and D.J. McCarthy, JBL, 85 (1966),
   150-154.

CHAPTER 5

THE SINAI TRADITION

I. Delineation And Unity Of The Tradition

1. Delineation

The Sinai narrative begins with Ex. 19:1 which marks a literary break from the preceding episodes and seems to form a superscription to the following ones[1]. An explicit notice about the departure from Sinai is found only in Num. 10:11f indicating thereby that the Sinai narrative ends in Num. 10:10[2]. Prior to this in Num. 9:15-23, a detailed presentation is given of how the tabernacle together with the cloud and fire operated to provide divine guidance in the wilderness. There is thus a harking back to Ex. 40:16-38 - a link which is necessary at this stage since after a long stretch of the most varied minute laws in Leviticus and "unsystematized collections of divine ordinances on a wide range of subjects" in Num. 5:1-6:27 and 8:1-9:14 the reader will most probably have lost sight of the Sinai setting.

Since it is obvious that Gen. 15 is not concerned with laws, the legal material in Leviticus and Numbers may be

---

1 So B.S. Childs, Exodus, 366.
2 In providing the heading "Preparations for Departure" for Num. 9:1-10:10, F.L. Moriarty, in R.E. Brown et alii, The Jerome Biblical Commentary, I, 89, seems to imply that the Sinai Tradition ends in 8:26. However, insofar as the people had not departed from Sinai, the passage in question seems to belong to the Sinai Tradition rather than the tradition about the journey to the Promised Land.
3 M. Noth, Numbers, 3.

dropped from the present consideration. Num. 1-4 too is to
be dropped because the census in chapters 1-2 is geared towards the conquest of the land[4] - a stage which Gen. 15 does
not reach, whilst the "organization of the Levites in 3:1-
4:49"[5] focuses on the tabernacle and is thereby "absorbed"
by the other chapters on the tabernacle, viz. Ex. 25-31 and
35-40. Being the new mode of YHWH's presence after Sinai[6],
the instructions about and the erection of the tabernacle in
these two sections in Exodus have relevance for Gen. 15.
Concretely, we have to reckon with the entire block of Ex.
19-40 in our present discussion.

2. Unity

Despite the literary as well as traditio-historical com-
plexities underlying the narrative[7], it does reflect a certain overall thematic and literary unity. as this unity cla-
rifies certain points of our analysis, a brief exposition of
it is in place. Our exposition is to a great extent based on
B.S. Childs' observation[8].

Thematically, Ex. 19-40 presents the God-people relationship between YHWH and Israel (Ex. 19:5) sealed by means of
a covenant (Ex. 24). Israel's part in the covenant is governed by the *tôrāh* (Ex. 20:1-17; 20:22-23:33). YHWH's part
was His unfailing presence in glory with Israel, in the beginning on Mt. Sinai and later on, in the tabernacle, after
it had been made (40:34-38). The worship of the golden calf
in Ex. 32 was Israel's choice of an alternative representa-

---

4 Cf. D.J.A. Clines, The Theme of the Pentateuch, 53
5 Heading borrowed from M. Noth, Numbers, 26.
6 Cf. R.W.L. Moberly, At the Mountain of God, 47.
7 Thus, J.A. Soggin, A History of Israel, 130, affirms, "However, the
  section about Sinai... is far from being a unity; indeed it is one of
  the most complex sections in the whole of the Hebrew Bible." An important monograph attempting to grapple with this problem is W. Beyerlin,
  Origins and History of the Oldest Sinai Traditions. The two most recent studies are those of Th. Booij, Bib, 65 (1984), 1-26; and
  A. Phillips, VT, 34 (1984), 39-52; 282-294.
8 B.S. Childs, Exodus, 340-368.

tion of God's presence constituting thereby an anti-type to
the tabernacle of God's choice[9]. Chapters 33-34 present a
renewal of the divine presence as well as of the covenant
followed by the making of the tabernacle in chapters 35-40.

Childs observes that at the level of organization there is
a broad pattern, namely, theophany-law-covenant, that loosely sets the contents of the episode into two parallel parts.
To this pattern may be added an extra element contributed by
A. Phillips' remark that the anti-Canaanite epilogue in
23:20-33 is a fitting introduction to the episode about the
golden calf[10]. Thus we have the two parallel parts:

	(i)	(ii)
Theophany:	19:1-25 & 20:18-20[11]	24:12-18
YHWH's commands:	20:1-17 (Deca-logue) 20:22-23:19 (Book of the Covenant)	25:1-31:18 (Instruct-ions for building the tabernacle)
Anti-Canaanite Motif:	23:20-23	32
Covenant:	24:1-11	34:1-28

Even the renewal of the covenant in 34:1-28[12] is also composed on the same pattern; theophany (vv. 1-9); anti-Canaan-

---

9 R.W.L. Moberly, At the Mountain of God, 47, points out a number of
  parallelisms between 25:1-9 (the preliminary directions for building
  the ark and the tabernacle) and 32:1-6, the people's plan to make a
  golden calf.
10 A. Philips, VT, 34 (1984), 291f. His reason for saying this is the
  long-observed background of the golden calf episode: the two sanctuaries of the northern kingdom, Bethel and Dan, each of which housed a
  golden calf, are evidence of an influence from the Canaanite practice.
  This episode is clear instance of the people's lack of loyalty to
  YHWH and accounts for the prefacing of the Book of the Covenant with
  a new introduction: the provisions on molten images (Ex. 20:23) and
  the simple altar (Ex. 20:24:26). This anti-Canaanite motif is picked
  up again in 23:20-33.
11 B.S. Childs, Exodus, 345, cites Wellhausen's acceptance of "Kuenen's
  suggestion to transpose 20:18-21 before 19:15-19, which rearrangement
  has been generally followed by his successors"; also cf. 351. This
  rearrangement was made apparently to make room for the Book of the
  Covenant.
12 J. Wellhausen, Die Composition des Hexateuchs, 334, has pointed out
  that the core of this chapter was originally J's parallel account of
  the covenant. Cf. B.S. Childs, Exodus, 607; D.J. McCarthy, Treaty and
  Covenant, 259.

ite commands (vv. 11-16)[13]; ritual laws (vv. 17-26); and
covenant (vv. 27f).

More specific observations concern first of all the con-
certed response of the people: "All that YHWH has spoken we
will do" (Ex. 19:8a). As it stands, it seems to be a response to YHWH's words in v. 5 which merely states a very
general condition of obedience for a special relationship
with YHWH. This response is found almost "verbatim" in 24:3,
7. The double response here may be indicative of a double
covenant from the two sources[14] but, if so, they have been
so well harmonized that, in B.S. Childs' words, "the covenant meal is now seen as a culmination of the rite in 3-8,
and not as a rival ceremony"[15]. In any case, the response
was to the same *kol-dibrê yhwh w*[e]... *kol hammišpāṭîm* (24:3)
referred to as *sēper habb*[e]*rît* (24:7), recapitulating both
the decalogue in 20:1-17 and the detailed laws in the Book

---

13 A. Phillips, VT, 34 (1984), suggests that 34:11ff reflect Hezekiah's
reform.

14 The two sources are found in vv. 1,9-11 and vv. 3-8. Cf. R. de Vaux,
Early History of Israel, 444, Vv. 3-8 have been commonly assigned to
the E source. D.J. McCarthy, Treaty and Covenant, 264, rejects source
division here altogether: "Indeed, the common attribution of 24:3-8
to E must defy the classic reasoning of the source critic by accepting as E a short section which insists on using Yahwe six times!
Even from a simple literary point of view the pericope is but loosely
tied to what has gone before."

15 B.S. Childs, Exodus, 502. Even E.W. Nicholson who strongly maintains
the original independence of the ancient tradition of Ex. 24:9-11 from
vv. 3-8, admits their "close relationship" in 24:1-11 whereby "Israel's
election is completed"; cf. VT, 32 (1982), 85. In his series of three
articles on Ex. 24:9-11, VT, 24 (1974), 77-79; VT, 25 (1975), 69-79;
and VT, 26 (1976), 148-160, Nicholson attempts to show that behind
the brief passage was an ancient tradition about a theophany which
originally had nothing to do not only with 24:3-8 but also with the
theophany in Ex. 19. How strongly he sticks to this view of his is
shown by his revision of his opinion regarding the significance of
"they ate and drank" in 24:11. In his first article, VT, 24 (1974),
77-97, he maintains that the expression means that "those who exper-
ienced this remarkable manifestation of God 'rejoiced' or 'worshipped'
in the presence of God" (97). But since the texts studied (e.g. Ex.
8:12; Dt. 12:7 and 14:26) have to do with the offering of sacrifices -
which would create a parallel situation with 24:3-8 thereby linking
24:9-11 to it - he abandons these texts in favour of texts like
1 K. 4:20; Jer. 22:15; Eccl. 5:16 and Am. 7:12, from which he derived
the meaning of "living" for "eating and drinking"; cf. VT, 26 (1976),
148-160.

of the Covenant in 20:22-23:33. One important conclusion we
draw from Childs' observations is that Ex. 19:1-8 seems
clearly intended to serve as a prelude to Ex. 19-24[16]. This
is probably why 19:1 literarily breaks off from the preceding narratives and seems to form a superscription to the
following ones.

But this is not all. As we have seen, Ex. 24:12-18 reports
a theophany to provide a context for the instructions about
the tabernacle. In the theophany YHWH was to give Moses a
written record of His commandments on two tablets of stone
(24:12) and the actual giving of the stone tablets is recorded at the end of the tabernacle instructions (31:18; also
32:15f). This serves to link Ex. 19-24 with Ex. 25-31 and
consequently with Ex. 32-34, since Ex. 32 presents the anti-
type of YHWH's chosen mode of presence to His people, and
Moses' instruction in 24:14 with its reference to Aaron au-
gurs the latter's responsibility in the episode about the
golden calf. Moreover the preparation of the tablets by Moses (34:1a,4) and the writing on them by YHWH (34:1b,28b)[17]
hark back to the earlier one in 24:12.

All these points of contact strengthen the impression that
Ex. 19-40 is intended to form a unit. Thus, the scope of material to which 19:1-8 is a prelude extends right up to
chapter 40. Since the extended material contains accounts of
further theophanies (24:12-18; 33:7-11; 33:18-23 vis-à-vis
34:5-9; 40:34-38), YHWH's announcement in 19:9 seems applicable to them as well. In fact, despite its verbal contact
in the word "thick cloud" with Ex. 19:16, this announcement
lacks any specific orientation and seems to open itself to

---

16 B.S. Childs, Exodus, 366. So also E.W. Nicholson, VT, 32 (1982), 84 –
   at least on Ex. 19:3-8.
17 A. Phillips, VT, 34 (1984), 45, thinks that "the new set of laws from
   Yahweh (Ex. xxxiv 11ff)... are inscribed on the two tablets apparently by Moses rather than God." However, R.W.L. Moberly, At the Mountain
   of God, 103, correctly observes that v. 28b is independent of v. 27
   where YHWH commands Moses to "write these words". Among the reasons
   advanced, the two strongest ones are: (i) v. 27 makes no mention of
   the stone tablets, and (ii) v. 28a seems clearly to be a rounding
   off of Moses' sojourn on Sinai and as such it should have come after
   v. 28b if this latter were meant to serve as the fulfilment of the

all the theophanies to come, all of which are also marked by
the presence of cloud (24:15,18; 33:9f; 34:5; 40:34,38).
Given an entire unit that begins with a theophany (19:10-19)
and ends with another (40:34-38), 19:9 is indeed an appropriate opening announcement. It must therefore be included
with 19:1-8 to form the overall prelude to the Sinai episode in Ex. 19-40[18].

---

command in v. 27. Falling back on 34:1, it is very likely that it was
again YHWH who wrote on the stone tablets.
18 H.-C. Schmitt, VT, 32 (1982), 177, affirms, "Ex. xix 9a ist... der
eine Art Präludium der Sinaierzählung darstellt und dabei eine
Brückenfunktion zwischen dem Exodus- und dem Sinaithema wahrnimmt."

II. Faith Supported By Sign

Like the "exodus narrative" (Ex. 1-14), the Sinai tradition also furnishes evidence of the theologoumenon of history taking on the character of a sign to support faith.
YHWH's announcement to Moses of His first theophany on Sinai
characterizes the theophany as a sign to elicit faith in
Moses: $ba\check{c}\check{a}b\hat{u}r...$ $w^{e}gam-b^{e}k\bar{a}$ $ya\,{}^{,}\bar{a}m\hat{\imath}n\hat{u}$ $l^{e\,\zeta}\hat{o}l\bar{a}m$ (19:9). The
sign character of the theophany is marked by the audibility
and visibility: thick cloud, thunder, lightning, trumpet
blast (v. 16) and fire and smoke (v. 18).

Moses was only an agent of YHWH. The entire theophany was
in fact intended to legitimatize this office of his. Such
being the case, faith in Moses was not to be an end in itself. It ought ultimately to lead to faith in YHWH whom he
represented for the people. This is quite clear from the
people's pledge of obedience in v. 8a. It was not to Moses
but to YHWH: $k\bar{o}l$ $^{,}\check{a}\check{s}er-dibber$ $yhwh$ $na\,{}^{\zeta}\check{a}\acute{s}eh$. Although the
word $h\,{}^{,}myn$ was not used, this was evidently a response of
faith. It corroborates the idea that faith in Moses amounted to faith in YHWH.

Another sign element figures in the account of the first
theophany on Sinai. 19:4a recalls a former sign alluded to
in 14:30-31: YHWH's destruction of the Egyptians - a sign
that elicited the Israelites' faith "in YHWH and in Moses
His servant" (14:31). V. 4b metaphorically presents YHWH
bringing the Israelites to Himself on Sinai[19], thus linking
the exodus with Sinai[20]. The exodus and Sinai - indeed, Is-

---

19 B.S. Childs, Exodus, 367, writes, "Moreover, God has continuously
   cared for his people and like a great bird watched over his fledge-
   lings until he brought them safely to his dwelling. The picture is
   of God's bringing his people to Sinai rather than of his going forth
   from Sinai (Ps. 68:7ff)."
20 Cf. H.-C. Schmitt's affirmation cited in footnote 18 above. It is not
   just v. 9a but the entire vv. 1-9 that serve this "Brückenfunktion".

rael's history reached thus far - constituted a sign to support her faith.

Presented in the prelude, this theologoumenon is intended
to cover the entire Sinai episode as well. In effect, therefore, it is the whole Sinai tradition that offers itself as
a complementary sign to the exodus event to elicit Israel's
faith in YHWH. Concretely there are evidences to this effect
in the episode.

The very first evidence is found in 20:22 which bears linguistic similarity to 19:3-4. YHWH's "talking from heaven"
quite clearly refers to His theophany (cf. 19:9)[21]. The use
of $r'h$ in favour of $šm^c$ seems to be intended to take after
19:4a, thereby underscoring the sign element of the theophany.

The next evidence is the people's response in 24:3,7 -
which clearly was a response of faith in YHWH. The theophany
in 19:10-24 and 20:18-20 led them to their acceptance to
listen to Moses as YHWH's spokeman for them (20:19). 24:3,7
verify the people's pledge.

A further evidence is furnished by the instructions concerning the building of the tabernacle. Ex. 29:46 suggests

---

A difficulty arises here because authors generally maintain that vv.
3b-8 form a unit by themselves. W. Beyerlin, Origins and History of
the Oldest Sinaitic Traditions, argues for the E origin of these verses. H. Wildberger, Jahwes Eigentumsvolk, 9-16, thinks that the unit
is an independent tradition. M. Noth, Penteteuchal Traditions, 31,
footnote 112, maintains, "Ex. 19:3b-9a(9b) is again a supplement in
Deuteronomic style"; G. Fohrer, TZ, 19 (1963), 359-362, considers it
as post-deuteronomic. R. de Vaux, Early History of Israel, 339, 341,
holds it as a late composition, certainly not before the exile. But
the point that its insertion into its present position puts it in
link with other verses in the larger context must always be reckoned
with.

21 While the interpretation of "from heaven" as expressing YHWH's trans-
cendence is acceptable, it seems to me to be reading too much into
the text to draw a neat distinction between it and YHWH's "descending
on Sinai" (19:18,20) or His presence on the mountain itself "in the
thick cloud" (19:17; 20:21b). Cf. e.g. M. Noth, Exodus, 175f; J.P.
Hyatt, Exodus, 224f; and E.W. Nicholson, VT, 27 (1977), 428-430.
Th. Booij, Bib, 65 (1984), 9, asserts, "The heart of the matter is...
God's 'descending' (Ex. 19:11,18; 34:5) and imperative 'speaking' and
the covenant between him and Israel (Ex. 24:8; 34:27). The 'descending' and 'speaking' are part and parcel of one great theophany in
which the covenant was either made or renewed."

that YHWH was involved in the liberation of the Israelites
"to dwell among them". The tabernacle was, so to speak, to
provide Him a dwelling place in their midst (v. 45). As
such, it would serve as the visible sign of His involvement
in their history and would thus lead to their knowledge of
Him in terms of this involvement of His: $w^ey\bar{a}d^e\hat{u}$ $k\hat{\imath}$ $^{\jmath}\breve{a}n\hat{\imath}$
$yhwh$ $^{\jmath}\breve{e}l\bar{o}h\hat{e}hem$ (v. 46aA).

   Israel's acceptance of this sign character of the tabernacle came about when, repenting of her worship of the golden calf, she got down to building the tabernacle (Ex. 35-
40). Possession of the golden calf became a sin when Israel
lost sight of its sign character and began to worship it.
Interestingly enough, when it was considered as a god, the
golden calf was attributed the title "who brought you out of
Egypt" (32:4b,8b). That goes to show that involvement in Israel's history had become an important sign to support her
faith, here in the golden calf as her god, but when she re-
verted back to the tabernacle, in YHWH.

   YHWH's continuing involvement in Israel's history was by
means of His $nipl\bar{a}^{\jmath}\hat{o}t$ (34:10aB) and $n\hat{o}r\bar{a}^{\jmath}$ (34:10bB). In the
concrete context of Israel's repentance of her worship of
the golden calf, YHWH's $nipl\bar{a}^{\jmath}\hat{o}t$ and $nor\bar{a}^{\jmath}$ consisted of His
restoration of sinful Israel through a renewal of His cove-
nant with her. That was without parallel in history (34:10a)
and constituted the "fearful thing I will do with you" (34:
10bB). "It will, therefore, constitute a powerful testimony
to the character of God"[22] both for Israel herself as well
as for other peoples.

   To sum up, history marked continuously by YHWH's $nipl\bar{a}^{\jmath}\hat{o}t$
and $n\hat{o}r\bar{a}^{\jmath}$ took on the character of a sign of YHWH's active
presence with His people. Of this presence the tabernacle
was a sign. This presence itself ought to confirm Israel's
faith in YHWH her God, just as YHWH's guidance of Abraham
supported the patriarch's faith in Him.

---

22 This statement is a quote from R.W.L. Moberly, At the Mountain of
   God, 93. His interpretation of Ex. 34:10 is convincing.

III. YHWH's Oath To The Patriarchs

Israel's worship of the golden calf (Ex. 32:8) constituted a total breach of the Sinai covenant as is apparent from
YHWH's disowning of her through the expression *ʿammᵉkā ʾăšer
heʿĕlêtā mēʾereṣ miṣrāyim* (32:7b). From His repetition of
Aaron's words (v. 8aB) it would seem that as far as YHWH was
concerned, the people had already disowned Him. They deserved to be completely destroyed (v. 10).

Moses' intercession saved Israel from YHWH's consuming
wrath. It grounded itself on two basic tenets of Israel's
tradition: YHWH's responsibility in the exodus (v. 11)[23] and
His oath to the patriarchs (v. 13)[24]. In fact, Moses' insistence on YHWH's responsibility and the status of the Israelites as His people, despite YHWH's disowning of them through
His reference to them as Moses' people (32:7), could only be
due to his certitude of the force of the divine oath to
which he was going to appeal shortly. The appeal to public
opinion (v. 12) merely served to bridge the first with the
second tenet. Ultimately, however, the one and only reason
that counted for YHWH was His oath to the patriarchs: numerical increase and possession of the promised land. This
seems to be clear from YHWH's own words in 33:1-3 where,
while still disowning Israel, He made it quite clear that it
was to honour His oath of land donation to the patriarchs
that He would ensure their entry into the land.

---

23 Moses is presented in the chapter as the only one to attribute the
exodus to YHWH and call Israel *ʿammekā* vis-à-vis YHWH, i.e. YHWH's
people. The people attributed the exodus to Moses (32:1,23); Aaron
to "these gods" (32:4); YHWH to Moses (32:7; 33:1) and to "these
gods" when he cited Aaron's claim (32:8).

24 In his article, in G.W. Coats et alius, Canon and Authority, 91-109,
Coats argues for the view "that appeal to the favor Moses holds before God replaces an appeal to God's prior promises" (107). The entire argument ignores the position of the divine promises to the
patriarchs at the basis of Moses' favour before God - a position

The events recorded in Ex. 32-34 are significant for the
understanding of the vital role played by the patriarchal
oath in Israel's history. They unveil the most basic difference between the patriarchal oath and the Sinai covenant.
This latter could be broken as it did happen and if it had
been the only foundation of Israel's history, this history
would have stopped with the worship of the golden calf. On
the contrary, the divine oath to the patriarch not only
stayed the complete destruction Israel deserved but also
provided the basis for a renewal of the Sinai covenant (Ex.
34:10-28) thereby reviving history. Certainly for the
author of Gen. 15 this difference was of such importance
that in his work he decided to spotlight exclusively on the
patriarchal oath as the force behind Israel's history.

----

which seems clear from Ex. 32:10. YHWH's initial intention to make
a great nation of Moses - echoing His promise to Abraham - was certainly an expression of His favour on Moses. A connection between
this favour and the "prior promises" is thus established. The whole
mission of Moses as Israel's leader would have been meaningless without the promises to the patriarchs.

IV. Episode Recapitulated In Gen. 15

Apart from the element of cloud, there were other elements
connected with the theophanies in Ex. 19-40, namely, "fire
and smoke" (19:18), "devouring fire" (24:16-17) and "fire by
night" (40:38). All the three elements - fire, smoke and
cloud - occur in pairs in the various theophanies and with
fire as the common denominator in all pairs, it seems quite
likely that smoke and cloud are intended to be mutually
identifiable. Both may have the same function of screening
off the unbearable radiance of divine glory[25]. The figuring
of smoke alone in the manifestation of YHWH's glory as a
substitute for cloud is found in Is. 6:3-4.

The sealing as well as the renewal of the covenant of
Sinai are expressed in terms of the technical krt $b^e r \hat{\imath} t$
(24:8; 34:10,27). By it, as announced in the prelude (19:5-
6), the Israelites became YHWH's $s^e gull \bar{a}h$ as well as "a
kingdom of priests and a holy nation".

Gen. 15 bears several major points of contact with the Sinai narrative. The first one has to do with the close association of the fire and smoke/cloud with the divine theophany on Sinai (Ex. 19:18; 20:18). In fact, Ex. 20:18 uses
the words $lapp \hat{\imath} d \hat{\imath} m$ and $\langle \bar{a} \check{s} \bar{e} n$ in the description of the theophany. This calls to mind the significance we have noted
about the flaming torch ($lapp \hat{\imath} d$ $^{\jmath} \bar{e} \check{s}$) and the smoking fire-
pot ($tann \hat{u} r$ $\langle \bar{a} \check{s} \bar{a} n$) in Gen. 15:17 as representing YHWH's
presence[26]. It may even be questioned whether one can deny
that the fire-pot has anything to do with the kiln in Ex.
19:18, since the basic association with both is the belching
out of smoke.

Secondly, the Sinai narrative presents the Mosaic covenant

---

25 So for cloud; cf. J.C. de Moor, in IDB, Suppl Vol., 168.
26 Cf. page 56 above.

being not only sealed but also renewed within the setting of
a theophany (24:1-11; 34). The technical expression *kārat
b^erît* is used in both passages to depict the act of "making"
the covenant (24:8; 34:10,27). Gen. 15:18a couches the divine promise of land donation in v. 18b in the same technical term *kārat b^erît*. V. 17 of course sets this covenant making within a theophany so that the parallelism with the Sinai narrative is reinforced.

Gen. 15:1 has already recorded Abraham having a prophetic
vision. That vision would have been a perfectly fitting setting for YHWH to make His oath of land donation to Abraham,
as it was for the other promises of a great reward, a blood-
heir and innumerable descendants. A theophany is set into
the chapter. Its position in v. 17 and not earlier, as for
example, before the promise of land donation in v. 7 is also
significant. It is certainly intended as a connection with
the prediction about the fate of Abraham's descendants as
well as with the *kārat b^erît* in v. 18a. In actual reality,
the entire history of Abraham's descendants as predicted is
oriented towards the land donation promised in v. 18. This
in itself reflects the orientation of the Sinai narrative as
spelt out in its prelude (Ex. 19:4), in Moses' intercession
(Ex. 32:13b) and in YHWH's command (Ex. 32:34; 33:1).

The use of *kārat b^erît* in Gen. 15:18a is significant. For,
here it clearly refers to the divine oath promising donation
of land to Abraham's descendants. Elsewhere in the Pentateuch it denotes a bilateral covenant - either as a mutual
pact between two human partners (Gen. 21:27,32; 26:28; 31:44;
Ex. 23:32; Dt. 7:2) or as the covenant YHWH made with the
Israelites binding both in a God-people relationship (cf.
Dt. 26:17-19[27]; 29:12) with obligations for both partners.
Israel's part consisted in the faithful observance of the
"statutes and ordinances" (Dt. 5:1) concretely stipulated in
the decalogue (Ex. 20:2-17 // Dt. 5:6-21) and the detailed
laws of the Code of the Covenant (Ex. 20:23-23:33) as well
as the Deuteronomic Code (Dt. 12-26). YHWH's part was to

---

27 Cf. N. Lohfink, ZkTH, 91 (1969), 517-553.

bestow blessings on Israel in the land (Lev. 26:3-13; Dt. 28:1-6) or unleash curses (Lev. 26:14-20; Dt. 28:15-19) depending on whether or not Israel was faithful to the covenant[28].

In Dt. 5:2-3, a categorical distinction is made between the divine oath to the patriarchs and the $b^e r \hat{i} t$ which YHWH $k \bar{a} r a t$ with the Israelites in Horeb (= Sinai). In the entire Pentateuch, except for Gen. 15:18a, the former is never expressed in terms of $k \bar{a} r a t$ $b^e r \hat{i} t$. The usual expressions for the patriarchal oath are $\check{s} b^c$ [29], $b^e r \hat{i} t$ with qwm-$hiphil$[30], $dibber$[31] and on three occasions with $ni\check{s}ba^c$ $b^e r \hat{i} t$ (Dt. 4:31; 7:12; 8:18). The use of $k \bar{a} r a t$ $b^e r \hat{i} t$ in Gen. 15:18a therefore shows a clear deviation from its normal sense in the Pentateuch as well as makes a fundamental break with the customary way YHWH's oath to the patriarchs is expressed in the same body of written traditions.

Living at a time when the Pentateuch had taken almost its final canonical form, the author of Gen. 15 must have had to grapple with the "complex character of $b^e r \hat{i} t$-making"[32] in

---

28 It has long been acknowledged that the Hittite treaty form of which stipulations and blessings/curses constituted a vital part is reflected in the Sinai covenant. It suffices here to refer to the following major works in this field: G.E. Mendenhall, BA, 17 (1954), 26-46,29-76; K. Baltzer, The Covenant Formulary; D.R. Hillers, Covenant: The History of A Biblical Idea; D.J. McCarthy, Treaty and Covenant. For a review of studies on the covenant, cf. D.J. McCarthy, Old Testament Covenant.

29 Cf. e.g. Gen. 22:16; 26:3; 50:24; Ex. 13:5,11; 32:13; 33:1; Num. 11:12; 14:16,23; Dt. 1:8,35; 2:14; 4:31; 6:10,13,18,23; 7:8,12,13;...

30 Cf. e.g. Gen. 6:18; 9:9,11; 17:7,19,21; Ex. 6:4. Gen. 17:2 uses a variant ntn $b^e r \hat{i} t$.

31 Cf. Ex. 12:25; Dt. 1:11; 6:3; 9:28; 10:9; 12:20; 15:6; 19:8; 27:3.

32 Thus, D.J. McCarthy, in P.A.H. de Boer, Studies in the Religion of Ancient Israel, (VT Suppl., 23 [1972]), 83. On the concept of $b^e r \hat{i} t$ in the OT, McCarthy strongly maintains that it is basically relational. E. Kutsch, ZAW, 79 (1967), 18-35, equally strongly denies it. Kutsch thinks that $b^e r \hat{i} t$ can mean: (i) a commitment one has solemnly undertaken by means of a ritual curse; or (ii) a self-imposed obligation or an obligation one imposes on another "with whom" one "cuts" the $b^e r \hat{i} t$; or (iii) a mutual obligation two parties agree to take on themselves; or (iv) an obligation one imposes on two others. Kutsch's distinctions are further sharpened in his monograph, Verheisssung und Gesetz. J. Scharbert, in M. Carrez et alii, De la Torah au Messie, 163-170, suggests that krt $b^e r \hat{i} t$ in its oldest concept meant "to guarantee by means of an oath rite" and after the 7th Cent. B.C. it took on the sense of a "covenant".

the Pentateuch that today's scholars are confronted with. However, whatever might have been the history of the concept of $b^e r\hat{\imath}t$ prior to his time[33], the author, if he was in touch with the latest theological trend of his time, would un- doubtedly have known "the use of $b^e r\hat{\imath}t$ to point up the law and obedience as conditions for being the people of YHWH... characteristic of the Deuteronomic school"[34].

From what he had read of the episode about the golden calf in Ex. 32, the author of Gen. 15 must have realized the vul- nerability of such a $b^e r\hat{\imath}t$ on account of the people's frail- ty. However, the same written tradition informed him of the underlying force that enabled the renewal of the broken covenant and assured the continuation of history. In other words, the people's part in the bilateral $b^e r\hat{\imath}t$ could be dispensed with by YHWH's unilateral oath to the patriarchs.

Thus, in Gen. 15 the author's concern is YHWH's part, not Abraham's. This is why apart from making the necessary pre- parations for the animal rite Abraham had no part to play in the chapter. All for him was YHWH's grace[35] manifested in His unilateral oath of land donation to him. For his descen- dants, too, all was grace - also manifested in the same oath. The divine oath was thus the only thing that mattered for Israel. Hence, Gen. 15 spotlights on it.

However, as one deeply rooted in Israel's traditions, the author of Gen. 15 could not disregard the sacredness of the Sinai covenant since it was a divine institution. It is reasonable, therefore, to think that in using the phrase

---

33 L. Perlitt, Bundestheologie, suggests that the $b^e r\hat{\imath}t$-theology came from the Deuteronomic school. He asserts that basically $b^e r\hat{\imath}t$ means "Verpflichtung" which one may take on oneself or impose on another. As a theological term, it expresses either YHWH's commitment to Is- rael or Israel's obligation to YHWH by the faithful observance of the law. D.J. McCarthy, Bib., 53 (1972), 110-121, reviews Perlitt's work and strongly criticizes Perlitt's failure to take into account the pre-Deuteronomic levels in the history of $b^e r\hat{\imath}t$ as a theological concept.
34 D.J. McCarthy, Bib., 53 (1972), 121.
35 E. Kutsch, ZAW, 79 (1967), 29, asserts, "Wo $b^e r\hat{\imath}t$... verstanden ist als göttliche Zusage, als Verheissung, Selbstverpflichtung... $b^e r\hat{\imath}t$ ist hier Ausdruck seiner (= Gottes) Gnade," Cf. Ps. 89:29f; Jer. 33:21; 2 Chr. 13:5; 21:7.

kārat b^erît, he intended to express his respect for the sacredness of the institution, and in reinterpreting it as a
unilateral oath, he attempted to bring to the fore the right
foundation and goal of both the Sinai covenant and Israel's
history.

   Interpreted in this way, Gen. 15:17-18 sum up Israel's entire history recapitulated in vv. 13-14,16. For the two verses explicitly refer to the exodus and Sinai traditions
through the use of the cultic implements to represent the
divine theophanies in both traditions and the *kārat b^erît*
that goes back to the covenant at Sinai. They also present
the giving of land and allude to the journey towards it. It
is probably in view of this overall summing-up character of
theirs that the two verses are accorded their literary position in the chapter.

CHAPTER 6

ON THE THRESHOLD OF CANAAN

As the Israelites were on the point of making their entry
into the promised land, they encountered various nations.
These encounters, recorded in Num. 13-36, constitute the
subject of the present chapter.

I. Recapitulation In Gen. 15

In the context of the exodus and return to the promised
land, the reference to the Amorites in Gen. 15:16b seems
intended to take the reader back to the Israelites' victory
over them as they were approaching the land of Canaan: cf.
Num. 21:21-23 // Dt. 2:26-35; 3:1-8[1]. However, a number of
"issues" need to be clarified before the intention can be
ascertained.

Firstly, the reason for the delay in returning to the land
is the fact that the Amorites' guilt was still incomplete.
This ties in neatly with the traditional understanding of
the guilt of a people as a vital reason for their being cast
out of their land[2]. With regard to Gen. 15:16b, therefore,
the natural tendency is to take the Amorites as referring to

---

[1] There are more episodes connected with this stage of Israel's journey
through the wilderness than Num. 21:21-35. The delimitation of the
text for consideration is determined by the reference in Gen. 15:16
to the Amorites. As a matter of fact, Num. 20-21 are presented as a
block, with 20:1-21 serving "the purpose of an introduction to the
account of the march itself which begins in 20:22" (G.B. Gray, Numbers, 256). Z. Kallai, JJS, 33 (1982), 182, suggests that Num. 20-21
serve to "emphasize the circuitous route through the eastern desert
to avoid conflict with the Edomites and Moabites, as well as with the
Amorite kings which ended with the conquest and inheritance of their
territories". Between the two parallels in Num. 20:22-21:35 and Dt.
2:1-3:11, there are more territories (the "extras" being Moab and
Ammon) and explanations being recorded in the latter than in the former. W.A. Sumner, VT, 18 (1968), 216-228, argues for an artificial
structuring of the itinerary in Dt. according to a pattern: two peaceful encounters balancing two warlike ones, both being bridged by one
(with Ammon) that indicates a change from peace to war. R. de Vaux,
in A. Caquot and M. Philonenko, Hommages à André Dupont-Sommer, 335-
338, sees the traditions presented in Dt. being marked by Dt.'s pre-
dominant theological interest, namely, the gift of land in fulfilment
of the divine promises (cf. 1:6-8). The land was divinely given to
the Edomites, the descendants of Esau, Israel's brother (2:4-5) and
to the Moabites and Ammonites, descendants of Lot, Abraham's nephew
(cf. 2:9, 18f). Thus, the Israelites were forbidden to invade their
land as they did that of Sihon's and Og's.
[2] Cf. e.g. Lev. 18:24-25; Dt. 9:4-5; 18:12; 1 K. 14:24; 21:26;....

the entire population of the land of Canaan[3]. For Israel to
possess the land, the entire population ought to be cast out
and the incomplete state of their guilt did not warrant
their evacuation. Does the term "Amorites" in Gen. 15:16b
represent the entire population of Canaan?

To be sure, there is evidence of a biblical understanding
of "Amorites" as a generic term embracing all the inhabitants of the promised land[4]. However, in the context of Gen.
15, a generic understanding of the "Amorites" in v. 16b
would create a major problem of inconsistency with v. 21.
Vv. 19-21 provide a gentilic description of the land of
Canaan. Obviously, this list intends to name the individual
peoples inhabiting the promised land in order to depict the
totality of the land.

If the term "Amorites" in v. 16b were intended to be a
generic disignation, then it should not figure in v. 21. For
the gentilic list in vv. 19-21 would be its specification.
From what we have seen, such a "progressive doublet" would
be perfectly in harmony with the literary style of Gen. 15.
Thus, the fact that "Amorites" figures in v. 21 - and that
in a special sense - does not allow its recurrence in v. 16b
to be taken as a generic term.

However, this understanding gives rise to a second problem: if only one sector of the population is presented as
guilty, how would the total possession of the land be possible? The answer is furnished by the fact that the Pentateuch
closes with the Israelites' arrival at the threshold of the
promised land and not beyond. Since the Israelites had to
conquer the Amorites before entering Canaan via the Trans-
jordan, it is quite in order to present the incomplete guilt
of the Amorites as the reason for the delay of the fulfilment of the promise of land donation.

---

3 T. Ishida, Bib., 60 (1979), 470, proposes, "The designation 'Amorites'
  .... took the place of 'Canaanites' as a generic name for the whole
  population of pre-Israelite Palestine, when the term Canaan had become obsolete as the name of the country." He also points out that
  the term "Canaanites" lost its significance after the establishment
  of the Israelite monarchy.
4 Cf. Jos. 24:18; Jdg. 6:10; 11:22f; 1 Sam, 7:14; 1 K. 21:26.

The defeat of the Amorites and conquest of their land implied in Gen. 15:16b would thus seem to recapitulate the Israelites' journey through the wilderness till this point.
The singling out of the Amorites' defeat is merely confor-
ming to tradition. For in the OT tradition, there is no
doubt that the Israelites' victory over Sihon King of the
Amorites and Og King of Bashan was very well known[5]. In
fact, later reminiscences of Israel's wilderness period often boiled down to a recapitulation of these two victories:
cf. Dt. 1:4; 29:6. To the foreigners, for example, Rahab the
prostitute (Jos. 2:10) and the inhabitants of Gibeon who
sought to enter into a covenant with them (Jos. 9:10), the
Israelites were known by the two events. The superscription
in Dt. 4:44-49 includes a relatively extensive reminiscence
of them (cf. vv. 46f). Of great significance is Dt. 31:3-4 in
which YHWH's destruction of Sihon and Og is presented as the
model for His destruction of the nations of Cisjordan. There
is no problem in having just one gentilic designation for
the two well-known episodes because not only Sihon but Og
too was an Amorite[6] (cf. Dt. 3:8; 4:47; Jos. 2:10; 9:10;
24:12).

Confirmation of the above hypothesis is furnished by the
use of the word *maḥăzeh* in Gen. 15:1. If the word is found
only four times in the entire OT, of which two are in Num.

---

5 G.W. Coats, JBL, 95 (1976), 177-190, demonstrates that the episodes
  about the Israelites' victory over Sihon and Og as presented in Numbers are connected with the wilderness theme. Besides the texts referred to below, cf. also Jdg. 11:19; Pss. 135:11; 136:19f. On the
  basis of these two psalms, J.R. Bartlett, VT, 20 (1970), 272-274,
  concludes to a possibility of the traditions about Sihon and Og being
  preserved and communicated by liturgical material, probably in the
  sanctuary of Gilgal. Basing himself on the "battle report" ("Kamf-
  bericht" or "Schlactbericht') delineated by W. Richter, Traditionsgeschichtliche Untersuchung zum Richterbuch, 262-266, J. Van Seters,
  JBL, 91 (1972), 182-197, argues for an instance of the "form" in the
  episode about Israel's victory over Sihon in Num. 21:21-31 and finds
  further support from ANE annals. For a contrary view, cf. D.M. Gunn,
  JBL, 93 (1974), 513-518.
6 J.R. Bartlett, VT, 20 (1970), 268, thinks that "by the time of the
  exile, Sihon and Og are presented in the Israelite tradition as fel-
  low Amorites, neighbours and contemporaries" and suggests that this
  was a result of the link between two originally separate traditions
  about two kings (276).

24:4,16[7], it is difficult not to suspect a connection between Gen. 15:1 and Num. 24, especially since the episode
about the prophet Balaam in Num. 22-24 comes immediately
after the Sihon and Og episodes, although as M. Noth has noted, "it has nothing whatsoever to do with the conquest tradition"[8]. Num. 22:2 ties the story loosely and artificially
to the preceding episodes.

It is not surprising that the Balaam story would have been
of interest to the author of Gen. 15 because its dominant
theme of blessing (cf. Num. 22:12; 23:8,20; 24:1,9) not only
echoes YHWH's blessing on Abraham (Gen. 12:3; cf. also Gen.
27:29) but more so encompasses the vital contents of YHWH's
oath to Abraham central to Gen. 15 itself, namely, posterity
(Num. 23:10; 24:7a[9]) and land (24:18f). It was most probably
on account of this thematic relevance to his chapter that
the author of Gen. 15 took over the idea of prophetic vision. However, in doing so, he did not fail to exhibit his
freedom in the use of his source. Instead of presenting
Abraham seeing YHWH as Num. 24:4,16 do Balaam, he had YHWH's
word coming to Abraham in a vision. Placed at the beginning
of the chapter, the vision marks all the promises in it as
divinely authenticated in the same way as Balaam's oracles
enjoyed divine authority in view of his visions[10].

Although separated from each other, the reference to the
guilt of the Amorites (v. 16b) and Abraham's *maḥăzeh* in v.
1a seem quite clearly to recall the episodes in Num. 21 and
22-24. Given the context of Gen. 15:17-21, it is likely that
a wider scope of the wilderness tradition is intended. Since
YHWH's destruction of their oppressors meant the liberation
of Abraham's descendants geared towards their "return" to

---

7 The fourth text is Ezk. 13:7.
8 M. Noth, Numbers, 172.
9 On Num. 24:7a, H. Simian-Yofre, Messianic Hope, 29, points out that
   mayim in the OT "can biologically signify human seed, and as a consequence, ancestry" (cf. Is. 48:1), *nzl* "does not mean only to overflow
   .... but also to flow smoothly" (cf. Dt. 32:2; Jer. 9:17; Song 4:16),
   and the dual form of *d^eli/doli*, derived from *dly* II (= *dll* II: "to make
   to descend, to let hang, to suspend, to balance oneself") refers to a
   man's reproductive organ. Thus, Num. 24:7a does allude to posterity.
10 Cf. pages 65-68 above.

the promised land (v. 16a), so the passing of the smoking
fire-pot and flaming torch between the parts of the cut animals would quite naturally have its effect endure till the
arrival of Abraham's descendants in the land. That means,
the smoking fire-pot and flaming torch should also symbolize
YHWH's guidance of the Israelites in their journey through
the wilderness. This corresponds to the detailed information
in Num. 9:15-23 of how the tabernacle - the mode of YHWH's
presence - together with the "cloud by day" and the "appea-
rance of fire by night" (v. 16) operated for the Israelites,
to signal to them when to pitch and when to break camp, presumably till their safe arrival in the land. That means to
say that between vv. 16 and 17 Israel's entire journey
through the wilderness is recapitulated[11]. The reference to
the episodes about Sihon and Og in Israel's history was due
to the fact that they were well known in tradition. But added to that, it also enjoys the advantage of presenting the
Israelites right at the threshold of the promised land - the
point at which the Pentateuch comes to its close!

---

11 If we are able to think of Israel's wilderness tradition in terms of
   a journey through the wilderness, it is due to a basically unified
   itinerary chain provided by Exodus and Numbers, For a schematic presentation of the chain, cf. G.W. Coats, CBQ, 34 (1972), 142. G.I. Davies, TynB, 25 (1974), 46-81, thinks that these itineraries, modelled
   on archival documents describing royal campaigns, were official military records. In another article, VT, 33 (1983),1-13, Davies argues
   for a redaction under Deuteronomic and Deuteronomistic influence of
   the meagre itinerary material of the old narrative source(s) and of P.
   He holds this redactor responsible for the journey through the wilderness. For a fuller discussion of the arguments, cf. Davies' monograph, The Way of the Wilderness. Other important studies on the wilderness itineraries included: V. Fritz, Israel in der Wüste; R. de
   Vaux, in A. Caquot and M. Philonenko, Homage à André Depont-Sommer,
   331-342; F.M. Cross, Canaanite Myth and Hebrew Epic, 308-321; K.A. Kitchen, Hokhma, 2 (1976), 45-76; J.T. Walsh, CBQ, 89 (1977), 20-33.

II. Faith Supported By Signs

Within Israel's wilderness tradition, two texts explicitly
figure the theme of faith in terms of *h'myn* - both of them
in negative fashion. Num. 14:11b records the unfaith of the
people and 20:12 that of Moses. Both these texts belong to a
context that explains why the generation of the exodus as
well as Moses and his brother Aaron were barred from entry
into the promised land.

As a number of studies have shown[12], the various strata
underlying Num. 13-14 have left traces of their central concerns in the pericope. Our present interest is in the central issue in Num. 14:11b: the theologoumenon of faith supported by signs - *lō'-ya'ămînû bî bᵉkōl hā'ōtōt 'ăšer 'āśîtî
bᵉqirbô*[13]. The people's lack of faith was betrayed when they

---

12 Cf. S.E. McEvenue, Narrative Style, 117-127, seeks to demonstrate
   that P altered the action-packed concern of JE from an interest to
   raid the area of Hebron to be followed by a subsequent general attack
   with a view to conquering the land to a theological concern marked by
   his technical understanding of *'ereṣ kᵉnā'an* as "a theological territory". G.W. Coats, Rebellion in the Wilderness, maintains that the
   original overriding concern of Num. 13-14 was the murmuring motif
   that involved "an overt move to reverse the Exodus" (146) marked by a
   "decidedly pro-Judean flavor" (157) in making Caleb (made leader of
   the Judahites in Num. 13:6) the only exception allowed to enter the
   promised land (14:24b). A later deuteronomistic addition to J, indicated by its characteristic tendency to summarize (thus: "these ten
   times" in v. 22b), attempts to depict the absolute character of the
   punishment YHWH decides to mete out. The punishment served to explain
   Israel's forty-year sojourn in the wilderness which might have been a
   motif from another Israelite tradition. P went beyond J's overriding
   concern by transforming the episode into a spy story defined by S.
   Wagner, ZAW, 76 (1964), 255-269. P's purpose was "to take into consideration the current situation of the people." Simon J. de Vries, JBL,
   87 (1968), 51-58, offers a critical review of Coat's thesis and postulates that the earliest stage of the spy story was probably about the
   settlement of the Calebites turned Yahwists as they were assimilated
   into the tribe of Judah in the richest area of the land. The next
   stage turned the spy story into an unsuccessful conquest of the land
   (Num. 14:40-45).
13 H.-C. Schmitt, VT, 32 (1982), 179, affirms, "Dass in ihm auf den Un-

heard the unfavourable report about the promised land (13:
27-29, 31-33) despite Caleb's exhortation (13:30). They "mur-
mured against Moses and Aaron" (14:2-3). Their immediate
desire was to choose a captain to lead them back to Egypt
(14:4). This desire is indicative of something more than
meets the eye. Basically, as Coats has pointed out[14], it was
a total reversal of the exodus. Concretely it meant a rejection of YHWH customarily identified as the one who brought
the Israelites out of Egypt (Ex. 3:17; 6:6; 7:4; 20:2; etc.).
This rejection is explicitly stated in terms of n'$\d{s}$[15] in 14:
11a, 23b. In the concrete context of the evaluation of
YHWH's land, signalled by '$ere\d{s}$ $k^e n\bar{a}$ 'an[16], rejection of YHWH
took the concrete form of rejection of the land (v. 31)[17]
and the desire to stone Joshua and Caleb for their exhortation (v. 10).

Israel's unfaith in YHWH in Num. 13-14 was not an isolated
instance. Rather, it was the climax of a gradual process:
"they had put YHWH to the proof these ten times" (14:22b).
The number "ten" here is more than just a round number to
summarize[18]. It has the symbolic meaning of "many" as in
Gen. 31:7,41; 2 Sam. 19:43 and Dan. 1:20. This is why YHWH
took it very seriously, as evidenced by the severe punishment He intended to mete out on them (14:12) - it was later
toned down, but only slightly (14:20-25, 33-37), on account
of the forgiveness YHWH showed at Moses' intercession (14:
13-20). In contrast, Caleb was exempted from the punishment

---

glauben der Israeliten 'trotz all der Zeichen, die Jahwe unter ihnen
  getan hat' abgehoben wird, zeigt wieder, dass hier der gleiche Glau-
  bensbegriff, bei dem die Bestätigung durch Zeichen eine zentrale
  Rolle spielt, vorliegt wie in Ex. iv 1ff."

14 G.W. Coats, Rebellion in the Wilderness, 146.
15 The contexts in which n'$\d{s}$ is used of God "suggest that the action is
   regarded as tantamount to rejection of the whole covenant relationship"; cf. K.D. Sakenfeld, CBQ, 37 (1975), 321. In footnote 11, he
   proposes, "Perhaps the thrust of the term can be better understood
   in terms of 'abandon completely' rather than the English 'despise'
   in its more casual current usage."
16 For the theological connotation of this designation in P, cf. S.E.
   McEvenue, Narrative Style, 118-120.
17 The verb m's used of the land has the same significance as n'$\d{s}$. In
   Num. 11:20, m's is used of YHWH in the same same as n'$\d{s}$ in 14:11a,23b.
18 So G.W. Coats, Rebellion in the Wilderness, 150.

on account of his faith: "he has a different spirit and has
followed Me faithfully" (v. 24)[19]. Faith, therefore, was
YHWH's expectation of His people.

YHWH could make this demand because He had given support
through "His glory and signs wrought in Egypt and in the
wilderness" (14:22). With this the reader is brought back to
the episode about the miracle in the sea in Ex. 14. In fact,
Num. 14 shares many common literary and theological characteristics with Ex. 14. The first such characteristic has to
do with the setting of the two episodes. In both, the Israelites were threatened by a power much greater than they: in
one, the Egyptian army with their chariots and horsemen (Ex.
14:9-10) and in the other, the gigantic inhabitants of the
land with their fortified cities (Num. 13:28,32-33). Theologically, it was a conflict between these great powers and
YHWH's.

The Israelites' reactions to both situations were very
much the same as the following parallels show[20]:

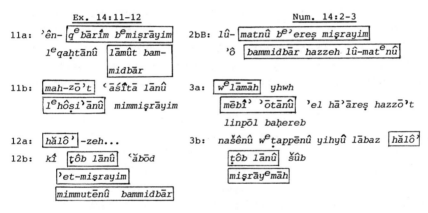

Ex. 14:11-12 / Num. 14:2-3

11a: 'ên- q^e bārîm b^e miṣrayim   2bB: lû- matnû b^e 'ereṣ miṣrayim
     l^e qaḥtānû lāmût bam-   'ô bammidbār hazzeh lû-mat^e nû
     midbār

11b: mah-zō't 'āśîtā lānû   3a: w^e lāmāh yhwh
     l^e hōṣi'ānû mimmiṣrāyim   mēbî' 'ōtānû 'el hā'āreṣ hazzō't
                                        linpōl baḥereb

12a: hălô'-zeh...   3b: naṣênû w^e tappēnû yihyû lābaz hălô'
12b: kî ṭôb lānû 'ăbōd   ṭôb lānû šûb
     'et-miṣrayim   miṣrāy^e māh
     mimmutēnû bammidbār

---

19 V. 30 includes Joshua in this exemption. No reason is given for this
   inclusion. From the historical datum provided by the Pentateuch (e.g.
   Dt. 31:1-34:9) as well as by Joshua (cf. 1:1-9), it was probably in
   view of his succession of Moses as Israel's leader.
20 The following two pairs bear not verbal but conceptual correspondence: (i) q^e bārîm (Ex. 14:11a) and matnû (Num. 14:2bB); (ii) hōṣi'ānû
   (Ex. 14:11b) and mēbî' 'ōtānû (Num. 14:3a). The final expression in
   Ex. 14:12b harks back to v. 11a and so corresponds to Num. 14:2bB.

It is clear from the above table that the parallelism borne by the two texts goes beyond verbal and conceptual correspondence. Their organization of ideas as well as their structure also support their parallelism. Coincidence would therefore hardly be likely.

Proceeding further, we find that Moses' intercession in Num. 14:14 uses two expressions that are found in Ex. 14 as well: $hōlēk$ $lipnêhem$ (cf. Ex. 14:19) and $ûb^e{}^{c}ammud$ ${}^{c}ānān$ ... $ub^e{}^{c}ammûd$ ${}^{>}ēš$ (cf. Ex. 14:24). YHWH's reply to Moses concerns all the men $hārō{}^{>}îm$ ${}^{>}et$-$k^eb\bar{o}dî$ $w^e{}^{>}et$-${}^{>}\bar{o}t\bar{o}tay$ ${}^{>}\check{a}šer$-${}^{c}\bar{a}śîtî$ $b^emiṣrayim$ $ûbammidbar$ (Num. 14:22). It certainly calls to mind the Israelites' vision of YHWH's destruction of the Egyptians in the sea as summarized in Ex. 14:31: $wayyar{}^{>}$ $yiśrā{}^{>}ēl$ ... ${}^{>}\check{a}šer$ ${}^{c}\bar{a}śāh$ $yhwh$ $b^emiṣrayim$. This was YHWH's glory ($k^eb\bar{o}dî$) over Pharaoh: $w^e{}^{>}ikkāb^edāh$ $b^epar{}^{c}\bar{o}h$ (Ex. 14:4; cf. also v. 18).

As we have already noted, in Ex. 14[21] YHWH's glory over the Egyptians in the sea was a sign (thus the verb $r{}^{>}h$ in v. 31) that brought to a climax all the signs He had worked in Egypt, namely, the plagues. The correspondence that Num. 14 bears with Ex. 14 would support the association of the signs (Num. 14:11b, 22) with the plagues of Egypt and the glory with the destruction of the Egyptians in the sea. However, whereas the Israelites came to believe in YHWH and His servant Moses (Ex. 14:31), here they not only failed to do so but also wanted to reverse the entire exodus tradition by requesting to return to Egypt (Num. 14:4). Obviously then an antithesis is set between Ex. 14 and Num. 14.

This antithesis has an important significance for Pentateuchal history. We have seen that Ex. 14:31 marks the end of one period of this history: Israel's oppression in Egypt and liberation from it[22]. But it also marks the beginning of the journey towards the promised land, possession of which is the goal of all YHWH's intervention in Israel's favour. Num. 13 narrates the evaluation of this land carried out in

---

21 Cf. Part 2, Chapter 4, pages 137, 139-141 above.
22 Cf. id, pages 135-136 above.

view of the achievement of this goal. That means, the final
goal of Israel's history as presented in the Pentateuch was
within sight! Like Ex. 14, Num. 13-14 should have signalled
the climax of this history by presenting the end of Israel's
wandering in the wilderness and the beginning of the conquest of the promised land. But instead, the episode in the
two chapters constitutes the peak of all Israel's murmuring
and marks the beginning of another gloomy period of her history: the protracted wandering in the wilderness[23] in order
to purge Israel of every single adult of the exodus generation, except Joshua and Caleb (14:30-34). Consequently, with
Israel's unfaith in Num. 13-14, Pentateuchal history took a
different course.

The antithesis between Ex. 14 and Num. 14 has left its
mark on Israel's history in the Pentateuch dividing it into
two major parts: the first characterized by faith which in
broad outline would correspond to the exodus tradition in
Ex. 1-14 and the Sinai tradition[24] in Ex. 19-40; Num. 1-10:
11; and the second marked by unfaith betrayed by Israel's
repeated murmuring which lies at the heart of the wilderness
tradition in Num. 10:12-36:13. On this ground, we may postulate that the theologoumenon of faith supported by signs has
penetrated Israel's entire history. Such is its importance.

Moving on to Num. 20:12 we read of unfaith being shown by
Moses and Aaron: *lō'-he'ĕmantem bî*. Whatever be the original
form of the story[25], Num. 20:2-13 has YHWH commanding Moses

---

23 G.W. Coats, CBQ, 34 (1972), 149, suggests that this may have replaced
   the original connection Num. 13-14 bear with the conquest tradition.
24 It will be recalled that Ex. 19:9 also presents the theologoumenon of
   faith supported by signs. The episode about the golden calf in Ex. 32
   ended with the people's repentance (33:4-6) and a renewal of the covenant (34:1-28). It was thus more of an isolated event than a continuous attitude of unfaith that we find in the wilderness tradition.
25 Another account quite likely of the same episode is found in Ex. 17:
   1-7. Both Ex. 17:1-7 and Num. 20:2-13 have basically to do with
   YHWH's response to the people's complaint about shortage of water by
   involving Moses and his rod in making a rock (although two different
   words are used; *ṣûr* in Ex. 17 and *selaʿ* in Num. 20) yield forth water.
   M. Noth, Numbers, 144, postulates that Num. 20:2-13 is composed of
   two versions of the episode as there are "two different results: on
   the one hand the announcement that Moses and Aaron are not to enter
   the promised land of Israel (v. 12) and on the other hand an expla-

and Aaron: *dibbartem ʾel-hasselaʿ* $l^{eʿ}ênêhem$ (v. 8) and the
latter doing something else: they addressed the people and
struck the rock twice with the rod (vv. 10-11). Their address to the people took the form of a rhetorical question
whose answer, in the given circumstances, was negative. For
the author of the episode, it constituted their failure to
"sanctify YHWH before the people" (v. 12aB)[26]. Taking the
lāmed in $l^{e}haqdîšēnî$ as explicative[27], it was this failure
that betrayed Moses' and Aaron's unfaith in YHWH. Their failure to build up the people's faith in YHWH[28] by not produ-
cing the sign commanded by YHWH was a manifestation of their
own unfaith in Him[29]. Their disqualification from leading
the people into the promised land (v. 12b) goes to show the
seriousness of their sin.

---

nation, partly explicit and partly clearly hinted at, of the names
'Meribah' and 'Kadesh' (v. 13). Even in the heart of the narrative
two parallel strands may be seen... (cf. especially v. 4 with v. 5
and v. 3a with vv. 2b and 3b)". He thinks that "the redactor has
elaborated upon the fundamental P narrative... by incorporating here
and there elements of that old narrative of corresponding content...
in Ex. 17:1bB-17". R. de Vaux, The Early History of Israel, 420,
attributes the pericope to J and P.

26 For the meaning of "to sanctify", cf. G.B. Gray, Numbers, 263. Gray
refers to the following texts for support: Is. 8:13; 29:23 Pss. 99:
3; 119:9.

27 Cf. P. Joüon, Grammaire, par. 124 o.

28 C.F. Keil and F. Delitzsch, The Pentateuch I-III, 130-131, consider
Moses' and Aaron's question as "inconsiderable words... which...
were certainly fitted to strengthen the people in their unbelief."

29 Beyond this, the exact nature of Moses' and Aaron's sin "must remain
doubtful" (G.B. Gray, Numbers, 258). J. de Vaulx, Les Nombres, 223,
225f, interprets the rock as symbolizing YHWH. "Et voici que Moïse
parle non pas 'au' rocher, mais 'du' rocher (jeu mot possible sur le
sense de *ʾel*, v. 8), il parle aux rebelles et non pas à Yahweh. Il
fait le geste rituel, quasi magique au lieu de s'addresser a Dieu
dans le priere." This interpretation has to reckon with three problems: (i) If the rock should actually represent YHWH it would be
difficult to understand why Moses is presented as striking it with
his rod; (ii) under the same condition it would not be necessary for
Moses to command the rock to bring forth water as it would have done
so on its own - just as the pillar of cloud by day and the pillar of
fire by night representing YHWH came and went of their own accord;
and (iii) v. 12 expresses the two brothers' unfaith in YHWH (*bî*) not
in the power of prayer. G.W. Coats, Rebellion in the Wilderness,
79-81, attempts to explain the vicarious nature of Moses' sin on the
basis of a close correspondence between v. 10 and Ps. 106:32. While
Coats is right in seeing the sin expressed in v. 10, his interpretation of the speech contained therein begs one or two questions. The

The sign element is alluded to by YHWH's command to Moses
and Aaron to "take the rod". In the entire command in v. 8,
the rod seems to be an odd element as nothing of its use is
stated. But its past connection with the working of signs
in Ex. 1-14 gives it the importance it has here. Its presence is intended to mark the rock's yielding of water as a
sign to support the people's faith as well as that of Moses
and Aaron.

Thus Num. 20:2-13 is marked, though negatively, by the
theologoumenon of faith supported by sign. Its importance
is complementary to that in Num. 13-14. There, it is predicated of the people and explains why they were barred from
entering the promised land. Here, it is predicated of Moses
and Aaron for the same reason[30].

---

verb *nôṣí'* does not imply striking the rock to bring out water, because only Moses alone "struck the rock" (v. 11). If at all a connection has to be made, it should rather be with "telling the rock"
which was YHWH's command to the two brothers in v. 8. In any case,
the address of the two brothers seems to be more of a rhetorical
question than posing a challenge on themselves, as would be implied
by Coats' interpretation. As regards the vicarious nature of the sin,
the people's rebellion was responsible for Moses' sin (Coats, Rebellion in the Wilderness, 81) only insofar as it occasioned it. But it
is clear that Moses was personally responsible for it. It seems more
likely that the other three texts (Dt. 1:37; 3:26 and Ps. 106:32-33)
reflect an attempt to cushion off the shock from the notion of Moses'
personal sin than that, as Coats maintains, they "exhibit the primary
form of the tradition" (Coats, id, 81). G.B. Gray, Numbers, 261f,
thinks that judging from subsequent allusions (e.g. Num. 27:14), there
was probably "an act of open rebellion" and the editor of Num. 20:12
has in fact "softened down the terms of the original story".
30 So M. Noth, Numbers, 146. G.W. Coats, Rebellion in the Wilderness,
79, affirms, "One of the strongest, if not the strongest, of all the
traditions about both Moses and Aaron is that they were not a part
of the generation that finally entered the promised land... This development would provide a traditio-historical foundation for the
disturbing fact that they died before reaching the land".

III. YHWH's Oath To The Patriarchs

Israel's wilderness tradition contains five references to
YHWH's oath to the patriarchs, namely, Num. 11:12; 14:16,23,
30[31]; 32:11.

Appealed to in a context in which Moses asked to be re-
lieved of his unbearable burden (11:10-15) due to the people's utter dissatisfaction (11:4-6), the patriarchal oath
in v. 12 serves as the climax of the three reasons Moses advanced for his request. The reasons take the form of rhetorical questions whose formulations are such that the responsibility of the people was thrown back to YHWH: He was the
one to "conceive them", "bring them forth" and lead them[32]
to the promised land, all because of His oath to the patriarchs. This oath of land donation therefore served as the
motivation for YHWH's past actions. In the current critical
situation it would motivate Him to further action - that of
providing for the people.

The three references to YHWH's oath of land donation to
the patriarchs in Num. 14 were made once by Moses (v. 16)
and twice by YHWH (vv. 23,30) - in both cases serving different purposes. In the case of Moses, the appeal to the
oath was clearly to advance an unfailing guarantee for
YHWH's forgiveness. Cited in his speculation about the
Egyptians' and the nations' cynical remark about YHWH's power to fulfill it, the oath served to support a very human
motivation: "face saving", so to speak, for YHWH. This would

---

31 Num. 14:40 as a promise text is uncertain. The sense of *'āmar* is not
clear. RSV renders it as "has promised" - a sense which *'āmar* does
not usually have. Moreover, if the divine oath were meant, *hā'āreṣ*
rather than *hammāqôm* would normally be used. G.W. Coats, Rebellion
in the Wilderness, 155, thinks that *'āmar* here means "command". If
so, v. 40 does not contain any oath.

32 Num. 11:12 is not of the very rare instance of the "mother image" the
OT uses for YHWH. Cf. also Is. 49:15; 66:13. The idea of leading is
expressed through the imagery of a nurse carrying a suckling child.

certainly be true as far as the unbelieving nations were
concerned. But for Moses, there was a deeper theological
motivation. His conjecture about the nations' reaction was
tied to his faith in YHWH's power (v. 17) and *ḥesed* as well
as mercy (18a). All these attributes had been manifested in
Israel's history "from Egypt even until now" (v. 19bB). This
history was but a working towards the total fulfilment of
the oath - as was clear even to the pagan nations (vv. 13-
16). For Moses YHWH had both total power and sense of fidelity to fulfill this oath. In the given situation, the
Israelites needed not just YHWH's forgiveness which YHWH
would have granted on the basis of His mercy but an assurance of a continuation of their history which at this point
had broken down. Moses' appeal to the divine oath secured
both needs.

However, the continuation of Israel's history required
some clarification which YHWH gave and in which He also referred to His oath but in direct association with His decision to bar the unbelieving generation from seeing the land
(vv. 23,30). His forgiveness of the people consisted in His
not "striking them with pestilence and disinheriting them"
(v. 12a). His fulfilment of His oath would be in the next
generation of His people: $w^e hebê^? t\hat{\imath}$ $^? \bar{o} t \bar{a} m$ $w^e y \bar{a} d^{e c} \hat{u}$ $^? et$-
$h \bar{a}^? \bar{a} re \d{s}$ (v. 31), thereby assuring the continuation of their
history.

In this context, YHWH's references to His oath served
primarily to clarify Moses' understanding of its fulfilment.
YHWH's vision of history went far beyond Moses'. His barring
of Moses' generation from entering the land did not mean
that He had not forgiven them nor that He would be failing
in fidelity.

In Num. 32:11 the reference to the divine oath occurs in
Moses' recalling the decision YHWH took in Num. 14:29-30.
The historical situation depicted in Num. 32[33] is one that
approaches the verge of an anti-climax to Israel's history.

---

33 Num. 32 is a late text. Cf. S.E. McEvenue, Bib., 50 (1969), 457.

The intention of the sons of Gad and Reuben to back out of
the conquest of the promised land and stay put in the land
of Jazer and the land of Gilead (vv. 1-5) would discourage
the rest of the tribes from pursuing the conquest. To Moses'
mind (vv. 8-13) the resultant situation would be as critical as that caused by the discouraging report made by the
evaluators of the land in Num. 13-14. Thus Moses strongly
vetoed the decision of the sons of Gad and Reuben.

In the context of Num. 32, Moses' recalling of the episode
in Num. 13-14 was to justify his opposition and the force
of the divine oath was to drive home the point that there
was no turning one's back on YHWH without sparking off further anger from Him (vv. 14-15). Concretely, that would mean
that out of fidelity to His oath YHWH was working out
Israel's history for her. The least Israel could do was to
co-operate by going along with it.

CHAPTER 7

THE TWO THEOLOGOUMENA
IN DEUTERONOMY

I. Faith Supported By Signs

In the entire Deuteronomy, the theologoumenon of faith
supported by signs is explicitly found in two places, viz.
1:32 and 9:23 - both times in negative fashion in contexts
recalling Israel's past. However, this scarcity of usage
does not mean that Deuteronomy plays down the importance of
this theologoumenon. For of its two recurrences one is connected with a very important stage of Israel's history
(1:32) and the other is expressive of her continuous attitude (9:23).

1. Dt. 1:32

Despite YHWH's past interventions in their favour in Egypt
(1:30) as well as in the wilderness (1:31), the Israelites'
attitude at Kadesh-barnea was unfaith: *ᵉênᵉkem maʾᵃmînîm
byhwh* (1:32). In using the expression *ûbaddābār hazzeh* to
refer to these interventions, Moses clearly intended not
only to oppose the Israelites' attitude to them but also to
present them as signs which should have elicited or supported an attitude of faith.
The occasion on which the lack of faith surfaced was an
important milestone in the Israelites' journey towards the
promised land. They were now nearing the final attainment of
the goal of their long march for which reason Moses could

command them to "go up and take possession" (v. 21). As in
Num. 13:1-14:45, a lack of faith on Israel's part at this
vital moment of her history, in all normal expectation,
would have brought to nought all that had taken place and
thus all of that history itself. Israel's faith was a necessary prerequisite for her history to forge ahead towards its
divinely set goal.

In recording Israel's unfaith at this point, Dt. 1:32
underscores this importance of the theologoumenon of faith
supported by signs to all of Israel's history which Moses
was recalling.

2. Dt. 9:23

Israel's lack of faith at Kadesh-barnea did not come as a
sudden eruption but rather as the climax of a long continuous attitude of rebelliousness. This is the point made by
9:23 which lists the unbelief at Kadesh-barnea as the final
episode in a series of episodes about the people's rebellions at various stations of their journey towards the promised land (9:8-10:11)[1]. The stations listed out are intended to serve as a representation of the entire journey
from Horeb to Kadesh-barnea. Their representative function
is signalled by Moses' remark in v. 7b: "from the day you
came out of the land of Egypt until you came to this place,
you have been rebellious against YHWH". It is further supported by the "Figur der Akzeleration"[2] in which the stations
are listed. Horeb and Kadesh-barnea are given an explicit
account because they mark the endpoints of the journey[3].

On the ground of their representative function, the state-
ment of unbelief, $w^e l\bar{o}$ ' he '$\check{e}mantem$ $l\hat{o}$, in 9:23 applies to
all the rebellions at these stations and thus Israel's con-

---

1 Dt. 9:1-10:11 has been considered a unit within chapters 5-11 with
  its own discernible structure. Cf. B. Peckham, in J. Plevnik, Word
  and Spirit, 3-59; A.D.H. Mayes, Deuteronomy, 194-195.
2 Cf. N. Lohfink, Das Hauptgebot, 211.
3 The episode at Kadesh-barnea is given a shorter account than that at

tinuous attitude of unfaith throughout her journey. The episode at Kadesh-barnea functions as the climax to all these
outbursts of rebelliousness. Thus, it is not just an isolated incident of unfaith and adds further weight to the
statement of unfaith in 1:32.

From these two texts about Israel's unbelief in YHWH, we
note that the wilderness period of her history has been
severely marked by her unbelieving attitude. This has also
shaped the course of her future history as 1:46-2:1 shows:

> "So you remained at Kadesh many days, the days that you
> remained there. Then we turned, and journeyed into the
> wilderness in the direction of the Red Sea, as the Lord
> told me, for many days we went about Mount Seir."

This amounted to a reversal of her history!

In the theological framework of Deuteronomy, Moses' recalling of Israel's unfaith was totally in order. Deuteronomy
is undoubtedly very much concerned about the observance of
covenantal law. In chapters 1-4, "Moses recapitulates Israel's past history in order to focus on the new and critical situation of the moment: a new generation, a new leadership, a new land. The concern of the Book of Deuteronomy is
how to actualize the covenant law in this new situation"[4].
1:32 presents a characteristic tendency of the old situation
and its unfavourable result in the hope of preventing the
new generation from the same pitfall. Chapters 5-11, rather
than presenting something different from chapters 1-4[5],
again review Israel's past with a view to calling on the new

Horeb probably because it has already been narrated in 1:19-46. The
Horeb episode bears a striking parallelism with the others: (i) w^e +
place(s) ... *hiqṣaptem 'et-yhwh* (vv. 8,22); (ii) Moses' prostration
before YHWH forty days and forty nights (vv. 18,25); (iii) YHWH's
readiness to destroy the people (vv. 19,25); (iv) YHWH hearkened to
Moses' intercession (vv. 19; 10:10). This parallelism may be intended
to corroborate the representative function as well.

4 B.S. Childs, Introduction to the Old Testament as Scripture, 214.
5 Strictly speaking, a literary delineation should be made between 1:6-
3:29 and 4:1-40 "wegen des besonderen Charakter von Dtn 4,1-40", to
use N. Lohfink's expression; cf. Bib, 41 (1960), 106. For a separate
study of Dt. 1:1-40, cf. Id, Höre, Israel, 87-120; and G. Braulik,
Die Mittel deuteronomischer Rhetorik, 1978. Braulik has successfully
argued for the unity of the chapter on the grounds of form, themes,
linguistic as well as stylistic features.

generation to a new commitment to the covenant. Once again,
Israel's sinful past marked by her unfaith in YHWH was an
obstacle to YHWH's covenant with her and ought therefore to
be avoided. Positively, that sinful past "is in effect cancelled out" and the new generation is called to a new response of faith in support of which YHWH's dealings with its
predecessors constitute the necessary signs. Concretely,
this faith response was to take the form of obedience to the
concrete laws in the promised land.

II. Divine Oath To The Patriarchs

Like the theologoumenon of faith supported by signs, that
of YHWH's oath to the patriarchs plays a very important role
in the theology of Deuteronomy. Much has been studied about
this theology and there is no need to repeat the generally
known facts "per se". It suffices here to present briefly
the relationship of the oath[6] to the main elements of Deuteronomy's theology with references to the texts where such a
relationship is expressed.

1. Election and Covenant[7]

As decendants of the patriarchs, the Israelites had been
chosen to be a people "holy"[8] to YHWH and to be His

---

6 For arguments for the identification of "your/our/their fathers" with
the patriarchs in the texts concerned, it suffices to refer to
D.E. Skweres, Die Rückverweise im Buch Deuteronomium, 101-110; 118-
121; 124-142; 157-171; 175-181.

7 The concept of election in Israel was originally applied to the Davidic king but became gradually democratized. The break-through came with
Deut. which applied it totally to the people. L. Perlitt sees Dt. 7
as "ein locus classicus der Erwählungstheologie..., als der Urheber
dieser Theologie den von der Daviddynastie her vertrauten Erwählungs-
gedanken zum erstenmal mit dem Begriff bḥr auf das Volk also ganzes
ubertrogen haben." Cf. Bundestheologie im AT, 57. On account of the
importance of this "Erwählungstheologie" as well as the "Aussonde-
rungstheologie", he sees v. 6 as taking "die ganze Paranese von Dtn 7
unter seine Flügel" (58). Much has indeed been written on Israel's
election. Among the more important studies are: H.H. Rowley, The Biblical Doctrine of Election; Th.C. Vriezen, Die Erwählung Israels nach
dem AT; K. Koch, ZAW, 67 (1955), 205-226; H. Wildberger, Jahwes Eigentumsvolk; P. Altmann, Erwählungstheologie und Universalismus im AT;
R.E. Clements, VT, 15 (1965), 300-312; H. Wildberger, in J. Stoebe,
FS W. Eichrodt, 307-324; H. Seebass, TDOT, II, 74-78; R. Rendtorff, in
J. Jeremias and L. Perlitt, FS H.W. Wolff, 75-86; J. Guillén Torralba,
La fuerza occulta de Dios, 1983.

8 To be sure, the term ʿam qādôš expresses some sort of relationship
with YHWH. But the basic meaning of qdš seems to include the idea of
separation so that there is in our text the idea of an "Aus- und

segullāh[9] (7:6; 18:9). This choice was YHWH's doing in total
fidelity to His oath to the patriarchs (7:8; cf. also 10:
15). Having chosen Israel, He initiated a covenant with her
whereby the God-people relationship was established. This
too was YHWH's honouring of the same oath of His (29:12; cf.
also 26:17-19[10] vis-à-vis 26:15). It is thus clear that the
divine oath lay completely at the foundation of YHWH's election[11] of and covenant with Israel.

2. The Land

There is no doubt that one of Deuteronomy's central concerns is the land[12]. Interest in the land springs from the

---

Absorderung von den Völkern" (L. Perlitt, Bundestheologie im AT, 57).

9 N. Lohfink, ZkTH, 91 (1969), 517-553, maintains that *ʿam sᵉgullāh* is
   practically untranslatable. However, there is the basic idea of pri-
   vate property which was later applied to a person's relationship of
   serfdom to his god or to a great king. L. Perlitt, Bundestheologie im
   AT, 57, sees in the expression "ein abgrenzender Verhältnisbegriff...
   Israel verdankt sich und gehort daher - Jahwe."

10 Taking the *hiphil* of 'mr to mean causing someone to declare something
   N. Lohfink, ZkTH, 91 (1969), 517-553, argues that in the passage under study, both Israel and YHWH make each other declare their relationship to each other as God-people and accept by oath to abide by
   this relationship. After comparing the text with Hittite and Egyptian
   treaty texts, N. Lohfink rejects any correspondence in form of our
   text to the vassal treaties in which "nur der Vassal einen Eid geleistet, der Oberherr dagegen nicht" (538). He has pointed out another form of vassal relationship which also demanded the suzerain to
   swear an oath - evidence of which is furnished by two Mari letters
   recording the treaty between Zimrilim of Mari and his vassal Talhayûm
   (cf. 539; also footnote 68 in the same article). On the basis of this
   evidence, Lohfink affirms, "Doch zeigen die vielen Belege dafür, dass
   auch bei Vassalitätsverhältnissen von beiden Seiten ein Eid geleistet
   wurde, in genügender Weise, dass Dt 26,17-19 keineswegs als Anspie-
   lung gerade auf das Element des Paritätischen in der gennanten Struk-
   tur verstanden muss" (540). This solves the problem as to how to re-
   concile the apparent parity between YHWH and Israel with the factual
   inequality between them.

11 A.D.H. Mayes, Deuteronomy, 185, affirms, "The three terms used for
   Israel's relationship with YHWH in this verse: holy, chosen, possession, together express the essence of deuteronomic election theology.
   Israel is set apart from the other nations to stand in a special
   relationship with God."

12 Cf. A.D.H. Mayes, Deuteronomy, 79-81.

sole fact that it was the land YHWH promised on oath to give
to the patriarchs (1:8,35; 6:10,18,23; 8:1; 9:4-5; 11:9,21;
19:8; 26:3,15; 27:3; 28:11; 30:20; 31:7,20,21,23; 34:4). In
fact it was in view of "going into and possessing this land"
that the Israelites' exodus from Egypt and journey through
the wilderness took place (1:7-8; 6:23; 26:3,5-10)[13]. In
other words the oath of land donation may be said to set the
orientation of Israel's history by determining its goal.

In view of the oath, Israel's history forged ahead towards
its goal regardless of her rebelliousness and unbelief
(1:35-39), YHWH's foreknowledge of her infidelity in the
land (31:20f) and the imminence of Moses' death (31:7,23;
34:4). In connection with this last point, the oath was the
reason for Joshua's appointment to succeed Moses as Israel's
leader (ch. 31). In other words, with the oath rested the
certitude of Israel's history to achieve its goal in her
final entry into and possession of the land.

3. Israel's Exclusive Fidelity To YHWH

YHWH's fulfillment of His oath was an expression of His
total fidelity to Israel (7:8-9[14]; 8:18; 9:5). YHWH's fidelity elicited Israel's exclusive fidelity to Him in the
land. Such fidelity had no place for idolatry or apostasy
(6:10-15; 7:25f; 8:17-20; 10:20-22; 13:18). In addition, it
demanded the faithful observance of all the laws established

---

13 G. von Rad, The Problem of the Hexateuch and Other Essays, 1-78, has
   argued for a "historical credo" in Dt. 26:5-10 from which the Hexateuch grew. N. Lohfink, Das Hauptgebot, 161-162, points out the juri-
   dical tone of the "historical credo": "Sklavenverhältnis, Pharao als
   der Herr, Ägypten also die örtliche Bindung. Die Tat Jahwes ist ein
   Rechtsakt." Accordingly, Israel's liberation from the Egyptian slavery was her entry into the servitude of YHWH her new master. The expression of this new service is the observance of the ʿēdōt, ḥuqqim
   and mišpāṭîm.
14 In 7:8,12-13, the verb ʾhb is used in apposition to references to the
   divine oath. As such it expresses YHWH's fidelity to the oath. For
   the equation of love with fidelity, cf. W.L. Moran, CBQ, 25 (1963),
   77-87; also A.O. Halder and G. Wallis, TDOT, I, 99-118, especially
   99-101; 114-116.

in the Sinai covenant (4:1; 6:1-3,16-18,20-25; 7:12-13; 8:1;
11:9,21; 30:15-20) to assure which the *tôrāh* was committed
to writing as a permanent document (27:3,8)[15]. In fact, in
the catechetical instruction given to children[16] in 6:20-25,
the history of Israel geared towards the fulfilment of the
oath provides "the meaning of the testimonies and the statutes and the ordinances" commanded by YHWH. Two specific
prescriptions backed up with a reference to the divine oath
concern the absolute prohibition of apostasy (13:18) and the
provision for cities of refuge (19:8)[17].

A difficulty concerning the relationship between Israel's
observance of the law and the divine oath needs some explanation. While the fulfilment of the oath in a great number
of texts founds Israel's obligations, there are texts that
present it as a consequence of the latter: thus, 4:1; 6:3,
18; 8:1; 11:21; 13:18; 30:16,20.

In an attempt to resolve the difficulty, it is noteworthy
that the texts listed above very likely belong to the stratum of a later addition - deuteronomistic - to the Book of
Deuteronomy[18]. Then there is the fact that of all these

---

15 The whole thrust of Dt. 27 seems to ensure Israel's faithful observance of YHWH's *tôrāh* in the land. It is completely in line with Dt's
   theology "tying Israel to YHWH and so people, land and law", so says
   D.J. McCarthy, Treaty and Covenant, 199.
16 Cf. J.A. Soggin, Old Testament and Oriental Studies, 72-77.
17 Opinions vary with regard to the origin of the establishment of these
   cities of refuge. J. L'Hour, Bib, 44 (1963), 17, maintains that the
   law concerning asylum was necessitated by the centralisation of the
   cult and thus first introduced by Deuteronomy. G. von Rad, Deuteronomy, 128f, calls this theory into question: "For what happened to
   those who sought protection at the altar (cf. 1 K. 1:50ff; 2:28ff)?
   It is difficult to imagine that they all remained for the rest of
   their lives in the confined area of the sacred precincts." Cf. also
   A.D.H. Mayes, Deuteronomy, 284f, for additional reasons to support
   this latter opinion. P.C. Craigie, Deuteronomy, 266f, maintains, "The
   city of refuge was not simply a place of safety, but a place in which
   the manslayer made atonement for the deed of which he was guilty."
   For a contrary opinion, cf. M. Weinfeld, Deuteronomy and the Deuteronomic School, 237. Two other important studies are: M. Greenberg,
   JBL, 78 (1959), 125-132; and A. Phillips, Ancient Israel's Criminal
   Law, 102-105.
18 Ch. 4 is commonly accepted as a late composition which brings together various deuteronomistic themes. Cf. A.D.H. Mayes, JBL, 100
   (1981), 23-51; also Id, Deuteronomy, 148-149; G. Braulik, Die Mittel
   deuteronomischer Rhetorik. Dt. 6:3 belongs to the unit Dt. 5:1-6:3;

texts, only 4:1; 6:8 and 8:1 present the oath as totally
dependent on Israel's observance of YHWH's commandments. The
rest presume that Israel was already in possession of the
land. What depended on her fidelity was YHWH's blessing on
her in the land in the form of a further numerical increase
(6:3; 13:18; 30:16), long life (11:21; 30:20) and expansion
of territorial boundaries (11:22-24).

With so close a connection between the divine oath and the
Sinai covenant, it is possible that for the author responsible for the addition of these texts, the distinction between
them was no longer of importance as he presented the fulfilment of the former as dependent on Israel's observance of
the laws of the latter!

4. YHWH's Forgiveness

We have already noted that Israel's history could never
come to a standstill in view of the oath. Even when it was
on the verge of a total breakdown on account of the people's
unbelief in YHWH, the oath was the saving factor. In his intercession, Moses fully realized that the oath was the un-
mistakable "trumpcard" to secure YHWH's forgiveness for the
people (9:27f). He was right. The granting of forgiveness
took the form of the writing of two tables of stone and the

---

thus, N. Lohfink, Das Hauptgebot, 165. In another study in BZ, 9
(1965), 17-23, Lohfink has tried to argue for a deuteronomistic reworking of an earlier decalogue in this unit. While Dt. 6:4-9,20-25,
by virtue of the association of sign (vv. 4-9) and question (vv. 20-
25) in catechetical instruction, form the basis of Dt. 6, vv. 10-18
constitute a later addition; cf. G. Seitz, Redaktionsgeschichtliche
Studien zum Deuteronomium, 70ff. A.D.H. Mayes points out that Dt. 8:1
is a "late summary designation for the whole law" (cf. Deuteronomy,
190) from the same hand as Dt. 4 (id, 208). The expression "multiply
you" in Dt. 13:18 seems to indicate its late character - cf. Dt. 1:10
and 7:13. In any case, Dt. 13:18 presumes that the land was in Israel's possession, since it is part of the covenantal law to be observed in the land - cf. Dt. 12:1. Finally, Dt. 30:15-20, bringing
together the themes of the whole book of Deuteronomy - commandments,
blessing and curse, witnesses - is a fitting conclusion to the book.
Its connections of language and thought are, however, with the deuteronomistic rather than the deuteronomic sections of the book. So
A.D.H. Mayes, Deuteronomy, 370.

command to resume the journey towards the land (10:1-11).
History thus continued.

On this ground, the oath remained a perpetual source of
hope for Israel. Even when her relationship with YHWH had so
badly broken down that there resulted in a reversal of the
oath - numerical reduction, dispossession from the land and
even a journey back to Egypt (4:27; 28:63,68) - the oath
could never be cancelled or annulled. On the contrary it
held out for Israel the possibility of a renewed numerical
increase as well as a return to the land (30:5). To honour
it, YHWH would be merciful (4:31).

5. Cultic Offering In One Central Sanctuary

The last two prescriptions of the Deuteronomic Code, viz.
the cultic offering of the first-fruit (26:1-11) and the
ceremony for the offering of the triennial tithe (26:12-15),
are brought into connection with the divine oath to the patriarchs. In the first prescription, the reference to the
oath forms an integral part of the offerer's declaration
which is an acknowledgement of YHWH's fidelity (v. 3).
Viewed from this perspective, the whole offering was intended to be a thanksgiving ceremony. Thus, the divine oath
constituted the reason for Israel's ritual.

The second ceremony consists of an oral declaration of
one's total honesty in fulfilling the tithe offering (vv.
13-14) and a prayer for blessing (v. 15). The prayer appeals
to YHWH's oath to the patriarchs. An implication of this
could be that while an Israelite who had honestly completed
his tithe offering deserved the desired blessing, he would
still need to count on YHWH's oath to be certain of the
blessing! YHWH's oath would thus serve to underline His
fidelity.

The two rites were to be carried out in the one central
sanctuary of YHWH's choice: "the place which YHWH would
choose" (v. 2). The expression "before YHWH your God" most

probably has the same significance as the above to mean a
central sanctuary[19]. The centralization of cult in one sanctuary - a fundamental concern in Dt - was motivated by a desire to purify Israel's worship. It was necessary in order
to ensure exclusive fidelity to YHWH as centralization would
facilitate control of cultic practices. Exclusive fidelity
to YHWH on Israel's part was called for by YHWH's fidelity
to His oath as clearly demonstrated by His leading the Israelites into the promised land (26:1). This fidelity is recalled in both rites through their references to the oath in
vv. 3 and 15, thereby indirectly supporting the idea of one
central sanctuary for the people.

   To sum up, it may be affirmed that for a book concerned
with one God, one people and one sanctuary in the land, the
patriarchal oath is appealing. Not only does it promise the
land and numerical increase as well as blessing in the land
but it also underscores YHWH's total fidelity to Israel
whereby He chose her and calls for Israel's exclusive fidelity to Him!

Appendix
Gen. 15: Not The Work Of The Deuteronomist

   In the opening chapter of Part Two of this work we traced
the simultaneous influence of P and the Deuteronomist on
Gen. 15. Due to an increasing acceptance of the Deuteronomist in an extensive area of the Pentateuch[20] and even of
other parts of the Old Testament[21], there is a need to take
a stand vis-à-vis the view held by some scholars[22] that that
literary school was the author of Gen. 15. Notwithstanding
the priority of the theologoumenon of the divine oath to the
law in the Book of Deuteronomy that we have argued for
above, the centrality of the *tôrāh* to the Deuteronomistic

---

19 Cf. A.D.H. Mayes, Deuteronomy, 61.
20 Cf. R. Rendtorff, The Old Testament, 162f.
21 R. Rendtorff, The Old Testament, 185.
22 Cf. table between pages 30 and 31 above.

theology remains an undeniable fact[23]. Israel's history is
assessed precisely on this criterion[24]. Thus, the exile is
viewed as a punishment for Israel's infidelity to this *tôrāh*
(Dt. 28:36,49f,64f). Therefore, the only way out of the
exile was for Israel to turn away from her sins and cleave
to YHWH. This, we have seen, was the point of emphasis in
the Deuteronomistic compendia[25].

Gen. 15 makes a clean break from this Deuteronomistic
theology of history as it emphasizes the unilateral *b^erît*.
The author was convinced that Israel's history would have
broken down long ago if it had to depend solely on Israel's
fidelity to the covenantal law. But it did not. This was
because of YHWH's utter fidelity to His oath to Israel's
patriarchs. It was this oath that set Israel's history as
narrated in the Pentateuch on its orbit. To the author's
mind, this oath was still valid for the Israelites of his
generation. The experience of their forefathers beginning
with the patriarchs and continuing through to the conquest
of the land was a type of the experience of the current
generation of Israelites. Just as the former were liberated
and brought into the promised land by YHWH, the latter could
now confidently expect to enjoy the same favourable intervention by YHWH. Their hope for it would surely be enkindled
if they could only be convinced of the vitality and validity
of this oath through a reflection on its working in the history of their forefathers. That precisely was the author's
aim in composing Gen. 15 as a theological compendium. And
that precisely also made him differ from the Dtr writings.

---

23 Cf. M. Weinfeld, Deuteronomy and the Deuteronomic School, 158ff.
24 Cf. L. Perlitt, Bundestheologie im AT, 7.
25 Cf. Jos. 23 and Jdg. 2:6-3:6.

CHAPTER 8

LITERARY POSITION OF GENESIS 15
IN THE PENTATEUCH

If Gen. 15 is a theological compendium of Pentateuchal
history, its present position in Genesis - after Gen. 14
rather than at the beginning of this history, i.e. before
Gen. 12 - requires some explanation. Obviously, such an
examination must necessarily involve a study of the literary function of the chapters preceding Gen. 15 and its
relationship with them in respect of the entire Pentateuchal
history. In this connection the position of Gen. 17 too deserves at least a brief analysis as it also contains God's
promises to Abraham.

I. Genesis 12-13

It has long been observed[1] that there exists a marked
parallelism between Abraham's itinerary in Gen. 12:4b-9 and
Jacob's in 33:18-35:27, although Abraham entered the land
presumably from the north while Jacob from the northeast.
The following outline may help to give a clearer picture of
the parallelism.

Abraham		Jacob	
12:5Bb-6:	Land of Canaan - Shechem Presence of the Canaanites Inability to settle.	33:18: 34:30:	Shechem in the land of Canaan "odious to the Canaanites" Inability to settle.
7a	: Promise of land donation to descendants.	33:19:	bought a piece of land (pos- session of land).
7b	: Altar to YHWH	20:	Altar to YHWH.
8	: Moved to mountain with Bethel in the west and Ai in the east. Altar to YHWH. Called on the name of YHWH	35:1-6:	Bethel. Altar. Called the place El-Bethel.
9	: Journeyed on towards the Negeb (= southwards).	16:	Journeyed on towards Ephra (Bethlehem) - thus, southwards.
13:18	: Abraham at Mamre.	27:	Jacob at Mamre.

Going right beyond Gen. 12:9 into Abraham's return from
Egypt, B. Vawter agrees with the view that "a certain standardization had been imposed on the narrative even in a pre-
literary stage[2] based on the three important Canaanite as
well as Israelite sanctuaries of Shechem, Bethel and Mamre.
A further precision of this view may be proposed. The parallel actions carried out by the two patriarchs seem to go
beyond a mere standardization and indicate a deliberate intention to present either Abraham's itinerary as a condensa-

---

1 Cf. e.g. U. Cassuto, A Commentary on the Book of Genesis, Part II,
  304.
2 B. Vawter, On Genesis, 175-176. The parallels he draws vary from
  mine.

tion of Jacob's or the latter as an expansion of the former.
Whichever way the relationship between the two itineraries
may have originally been intended, the present form of the
text seems to favour Gen. 12:4b-9 as a nutshell parallel to
Jacob's journey through the land.

If Gen. 12:4b-9 serves the above function, 12:10-13:18
seems intended "to present us... through the symbolic conquest of Abram, with a kind of forecast of what would happen
to his descendants later"[3]. For the section seems to bear a
parallel pattern with the history of Abraham's descendants
as is borne out by the following outline.

Abraham	Abraham's Descendants

Gen. 12:10aA:
  Famine drove Abraham down to
  Egypt
	Gen. 41:57-42:3; 43:1,15:
	  Famine forced Jacob to send his
	  sons to Egypt.

	Gen. 46:1:
	  Jacob and his family went down
	  to Egypt.

to sojourn (*lāgur*) there.	Gen. 47:4:
	  "We have come to sojourn (*lāgur*)
	  in the land.

Gen. 12:10bB:
  kî-kābēd hārā'āb bā'āreṣ
	Gen. 43:1:
	  wᵉhārā'āb kābēd bā'āreṣ

Gen. 12:11-13:
  Abraham's secret plan with Sarah
  before meeting Pharaoh –
  for good treatment in Egypt.
	Gen. 46:33-34:
	  Joseph's instruction to his family
	  so as to get the best land in
	  Egypt (cf. 47:6).

Gen. 12:16:
  Abraham's wealth on account of
  Sarah.
	Gen. 47:6:
	  Best land (Goshen).

Gen. 12:17:
  YHWH afflicted Pharaoh and his
  household with plagues:
  wayᵉnagga' ... *nᵉgā'îm gᵉdōlîm,*
	Ex. 7:14-11:30:
	  The plagues of Egypt - afflicting
	  all Egyptians.

Gen. 12:18:
  Pharaoh summoned Abraham:
  wayyiqrā' par'ōh lᵉ'abrām
	Ex. 12:31:
	  Pharaoh summoned Moses:
	  wayyiqrā' lᵉmōšeh ulᵉ'ahărōn

Gen. 12:19:
  qaḥ wālēk
	Ex. 12:32:
	  qᵉḥû ... wālēku

---

3 U. Cassuto, A Commentary on the Book of Genesis, Part II, 305f; cf.
  also H. Gunkel, Genesis, 173; and B. Jacob, Genesis, 354-357.

Gen. 12:20:	Ex. 12:33:
wayšall^{e}ḥû ōtô ...	Egyptians could not wait *l^{e}šall^{e}ḥām min-hā'āreṣ*
Gen. 13:2:	
Abraham's great wealth as he departed from Egypt: with cattle, silver and gold.	Israelites went off with great wealth: jewelry of silver and gold, clothing.
Gen. 13:1,3:	Num. 13:17:
Negeb to Bethel (between Bethel and Ai)	Moses sent evaluators to the Negeb. Conquest Tradition – after entering land by way of Gilgal and Jericho... Ai... east of Bethel (Jos. 7:2) Stationed between Bethel and Ai to the west of Ai (Jos. 8:9).
Built an altar and called on YHWH's name.	Built an altar on Mt. Ebal (Jos. 8:30).

A word needs to be said about the inclusion of Lot in Gen. 12-13. Does he have a role to play in the function of the two chapters as a prelude to the Israelites' journey and entry into the land? If so, what role?[4]

In the Lot episode in Gen. 12-13, it does seem "that all the land east of the Jordan is conceded to Lot, the father of the Transjordanian peoples"[5]. Gen. 18-19[6] which also contain a Lot-Sodom tradition constitute an aetiology whose primary focus is to explain Lot's position as father of the Transjordanian peoples. Thus, it would seem that the Lot episode in Gen. 12-13 serves as a prelude to Gen. 18-19. However, there is something more. The Israelites' non-hostile attitude towards these peoples during their encounter with them as they were entering the promised land (Num. 20-21) was determined by this tradition. Viewed in this

---

4 W. Vogels, SR, 4 (1974-75), 55, maintains that Gen. 13 highlights Abraham's readiness to sacrifice the land (to satisfy Lot's egoistic choice) just as he was ready to sacrifice his only son in Gen. 22. Recently, L.R. Heyler, JSOT, 26 (1983), 77-88, affirms that the leading theme of the Abraham cycle is the problem of an heir (82) and the "primary purpose" of Gen. 13 "is to draw attention to the crisis of faith which Lot precipitated by the choice of pasturage outside the land of Canaan. At stake is nothing less than Lot's elimination as heir to the covenant promise" (85).

5 J. Van Seters, Abraham in History and Tradition, 226.

6 For the literary and thematic unity of these two chapters, cf. J. Van Seters, Abraham in History and Tradition, 215-220.

perspective, the Lot episode in Gen. 12-13 goes beyond
being a prelude to Gen. 18-19. It also prepares the ground
for the Israelites' encounter with these peoples in later
history.

To sum up, it seems clear that Gen. 12:4b-13:18 is intended as a prelude to the rest of the Pentateuch. Its emphasis
is more geographical than historical, as it is marked by
itineraries and the circumstances either occasioning or surrounding them till Abraham finally settled down "by the oaks
of Mamre" in v. 18.

The entire journey is presented as being carried out under
YHWH's command: $lēk-l^eḵā$ (Gen. 12:1aB); $wayyēlek$ $'abrām$ (12:
4aA). It was not an empty journey but, as we have seen[7], one
essentially marked by divine promises of numerical increase,
blessing and land donation placed at the beginning (12:2-3)
and at the end (13:14-16) of the entire prelude, perhaps, to
form some sort of inclusion. 13:17 has YHWH commanding Abraham to take a symbolic possession of the land and, though
not said, one may surmise Abraham executing the order and at
the end of it he settled down by the "oaks of Mamre" (v.
18). If so, this settling down could well be a foretaste of
Abraham's possession of the land.

Thus, the divine promises that hold the entire prelude together provide it with its theological perspective!

---

7 Cf. pages 105-113 above.

II. Genesis 14

Gen. 14 is indeed a much-disputed chapter as regards its
composition, datation, sources and historicity[8]. It is beyond the scope of this thesis to review this debate or be
involved in it. For my purpose, it is enough to state my
concurrence with J. Van Seters' position[9] and support it
with my main reasons, and then draw the necessary conclusion
vis-à-vis Gen. 15.

J. Van Seters holds that Gen. 14 is a very late composition. Its deuteronomistic flavour would support this late
datation[10]. But there are also indicators against the chapter belonging to either of the two sources[11]. Its core event

---

8 Basically, scholars' opinions on Gen. 14 may be divided into two
groups: those arguing for Gen. 14 as an authentically historical document and those against. The former group hold an early datation
for the chapter. For a thorough review of these studies, cf. W. Schatz,
Genesis 14, 13-61. More recent studies include: M. Peter, VT, 29
(1979), 114-119; Id, in M. Carrez et alii, De la Torah au Messie, 97-
105; N.-E. Andreasen, in C.D. Evans et alii, Scripture in Context,
59-77; and Y. Muffs, JJS, 33 (1982), 83-107. The second group of
views generally agree on a later date for the chapter: e.g. H. Gunkel,
Genesis, 279-290; M.C. Astour, in A. Altmann, Biblical Motifs, 65-112;
W. Schatz, Genesis 14. More recently, T.L. Thompson, The Historicity
of the Patriarchal Narratives, 187-195, disproves all historicity of
Gen. 14.

9 J. Van Seters, Abraham in History and Tradition, 112-120; 296-308,
sees an archaizing tendency in Gen. 14. To my mind, he has successfully scraped off this archaic coat to reach the rather late - post-
exilic - character of the chapter. A very recent study by J. Doré, in
M. Carrez et alii, De la Torah au Messie, 75-95, attempts to demonstrate the literary unity of the chapter.

10 The deuteronomistic flavour has already been pointed out by M.C. Astour, in A. Altmann, Biblical Motifs, 69-74. Similarities with the P
source are in the vocabulary: *rekuš*, *yᵉlîd bayit* and *nepeš*.

11 An indication against Dt is the fact that the author of Gen. 14 "has
no qualms about making Abraham a treaty partner to three Amorite
chieftains of the Hebrew region". For, Dt. is against such a treaty
(7:2). It shows that what smacks of Dtr in the chapter is a convention "closely broader than its use by the Deuteronomist, although it
is unlikely that it is any earlier" - both quotations are taken from
J. Van Seters, Abraham in History and Tradition, 303f. An indication

is Abraham's rescue of Lot in vv. 13-16[12] which is given an
international setting: the invasion by four eastern kings
(vv. 1-12). This episode stemmed from the post-exilic period. The insertion of the Melchizedek episode (vv. 18-20)
came in even later as Melchizedek most probably represented
the priesthood of the second temple.

Of all the four eastern nations, only Shinar and Elam are
clearly identifiable[13]: Shinar being Babylonia and Elam
being clearly the state north-east of the Persian Gulf. Van
Seters postulates that "since virtually all the names and
countries are intended to be the archaic counterparts of
later entries it is clear that Elam must really stand for
Persia"[14]. Gen. 14 presents Persia heading a coalition of
which Babylonia was a member. Both facts would be unimagina-
ble except in the post-exilic period[15].

Granted the very late date of Gen. 14, it is altogether
possible and very likely that it was inserted into the Pentateuch only after Gen. 15. For, while Gen. 15 focuses on
the promise of land donation, thereby maintaining a certain
continuity with Gen. 12-13, Gen. 14 presumes Abraham already
in possession of the land of Canaan. The land was not at
stake[16]. Abraham's pursuit of the foreign invaders was for
no other purpose than to rescue his nephew Lot, as a secondary consequence of which the king of Sodom was saved.

It is most probably on account of this Lot-Sodom concern

---

against P is the use of *rwm yd* rather than P's usual *nś' yd* for the
taking of an oath. The expression used by Gen. 14 is also found in
Dan. 12:7 (cf. Van Seters, id, 304).

12 While J.A. Emerton, VT, 21 (1971), 403-439, maintains that the core
event is preserved in vv. 13-17 and 21-23, and probably in vv. 10-11,
he excludes all references to Lot from it on the ground that they are
a secondary addition. But, as J. Van Seters, Abraham in History and
Tradition, 298f, has pointed out, the inclusion of Lot "provides the
whole motivation for Abraham's subsequent action. If references to
Lot are to be removed, a radical emendation of the entire story - not
just of this text - would be necessary."

13 So J.A. Soggin, A History of Israel, 100.

14 J. Van Seters, Abraham in History and Tradition, 305.

15 Interestingly enough, H. Gunkel, Genesis, 189-190, has pointed out
that Gen. 14 reflects a style quite characteristic of Jewish popular
stories in the Persian and Hellenistic periods.

16 J. Van Seters, Abraham in History and Tradition, 306.

that "Gen. 14 is very skilfully included in the patriarchal
narrative precisely at the place where it belongs: after the
story of the separation of Abraham and Lot and the latter's
sojourn in Sodom, and before the story of the destruction of
Sodom and Gomorrah and Lot's salvation"[17]. Its position before Gen. 15 certainly preserves an immediate continuity
with Gen. 12-13 - an understandable concern in view of the
rather unique contents of the chapter. Moreover, its author
might have been struck by the military overtone of Gen. 15
and thought his work might provide a fitting setting to it.
All this, notwithstanding the contrary situation he posed to
Gen. 12-13 and Gen. 15 regarding the land.

---

17 So M.C. Astour, in A. Altmann, Biblical Motifs, 68.

III. Genesis 17

Gen. 17 is another chapter loaded with promises. In fact
most of the promises it contains are similar to those in
Gen. 15: posterity, land and son. An obvious question that
arises is: is there no redundancy between the two chapters?
If none, what is the position of one in respect of the
other?

For any attempt at a solution to have a chance of being
satisfactory, it ought to take into account the context of
Gen. 17. For, it is in relation to this context that the
chapter finds its role and therefore takes its meaning. "The
context for this unit is established by the Hagar-Ishmael
tradition in Gen. 16 and the Sarah-Isaac tradition in Gen.
21"[18]. The two traditions are linked through the notice in
16:1-4 about Sarai's barrenness and her proposal to beget a
son for Abraham. This link may indeed be said to set in motion the part of the Abraham cycle that comes after it as it
introduces its central theme: the promise of a son for the
patriarch made in Gen. 18:1-5 and fulfilled in 21:1-7[19].

Gen. 17 fuses the above two traditions together and provides a theological foundation for the special position of
Isaac as Abraham's heir vis-à-vis Ishmael: with Isaac YHWH
promised to establish an eternal covenant (cf. vv. 15-21).
This marks Gen. 17 off from the simple and probably the more
original promise of a son in Gen. 18:9-15[20]. However, it
cannot be denied that Gen. 17 touches the core of Gen. 16:1-
25:10. In this sense, it may be said that Gen. 17 is to the
Abraham cycle what Gen. 15 is to the entire Pentateuchal
history.

---

18 G.W. Coats, Genesis, 133.
19 Cf. R. de Vaux, The Early History of Israel, 168.
20 S.E. McEvenue, The Narrative Style of the Priestly Writer, 152f,
   says, "Gen. 17 is theologically reflected from beginning to end." Cf.
   also G. von Rad, Genesis, 193.

A difficulty arises from the apparent similarity in theme
as well as thematic sequence between Gen. 15 and Gen. 17.
For, on the basis of such a similarity, it has been suggested that Gen. 15 was one of the two sources[21] - Gen. 18
being the other[22] - of Gen. 17. If correct, such a position
casts some doubt on the hypothesis we have attempted to establish, that is, that the author of Gen. 15 knew almost
the entire Pentateuch.

We shall now re-examine the so-claimed parallelism between
Gen. 15 and 17:1-18. To be sure, the theophanies in 15:1 and
17:1-2 and the promises of numerous progeny and land in
15:4-5,7,18 and 17:4-8 may pass as parallels. But there are
also elements that upset the suspected parallelism. Firstly,
Abraham's reactions in 15:2-3 and 17:3a can scarcely be considered to constitute a parallelism. The first is a verbal
response that seeks a confirmatory sign; the second is an
act of obeissance. Secondly, "walk before Me, and be blame-
less" in 17:1 is a command and hardly corresponds to 15:6
which is a statement of Abraham's faith reckoned to him as
righteousness. Thirdly, Gen. 17 contains El Shaddai's repeated promise to be God: in v. 7 to Abraham and his descendants and in v. 8 to his descendants alone. This promise
echoes very much the formula of the Sinai covenant: "I shall
be your God and you will be My people"[23]. Not only is this
promise absent in Gen. 15 but there seems to be a clear intention in the chapter to transform radically the concept of
the Sinai covenant: *kārat berît* is now used for YHWH's oath
to Abraham. Finally, the central focus in Gen. 17 is on descendants and son who is very explicitly named[24] while that
in Gen. 15 is on descendants whose history is foretold and
on land[25]. On the ground of these "anti-parallel" elements,
it seems improbable that Gen. 17 drew on Gen. 15[26].

---

21 S.E. McEvenue, The Narrative Style of the Priestly Writer, 152;
   J. Van Seters, Abraham in History and Tradition, 284-285.
22 S.E. McEvenue, The Narrative Style of the Priestly Writer, 153-154.
   This is also the view of H. Gunkel, Genesis, 271, and C. Westermann,
   The Promises to the Fathers, 136.
23 Cf. J. Skinner, Genesis, 293. N. Lohfink, ZkTh, 91 (1969), 517-553,
   discusses this form in great detail.

IV. Smooth Sequence From Genesis 13 To 16

If Gen. 15 is a late addition to the Pentateuch and Gen.
14 even later, there should be signs of some interruption of
the sequence between what precedes and what follows them or
at least their removal should not disrupt such a sequence.
We think that such a sequence does exist.

Although Gen. 16:1 does not start off with a *wayyiqtol*
construction, it does bear a thematic continuity with Gen.
12-13. In Gen. 13:14-16 there are two promises of land and
numerous posterity. 13:17 has YHWH commanding Abraham to
take a symbolic possession of the land. It is perfectly imaginable that Abraham executed YHWH's command at the end of
which he settled down "by the oaks of Mamre" (v. 18). It is
quite natural after this to expect attention to be paid to
the second promise. Gen. 16:1-4 seems to satisfy this expectation since the first step to having numerous descendants
must necessarily be the modest possession of children. 16:1
states an obstacle to the fulfilment of this promise and
16:2-4 present Sarai's proposal for its realization.

Sarai's proposal involved Hagar, her Egyptian maid, whose
presence is certainly not out of place in the context of
Abraham's return from Egypt in 13:1. According to 12:16,

---

24 Cf. G. von Rad, Genesis, 192.
25 So G.W. Coats, Genesis, 133: "It is not surprising, then, that this
   unit in contrast to the parallel in Gen. 15 (JE) subordinates the
   promise for land to the promise for great posterity." J. Van Seters'
   view, "The promise of land does not have as prominent a place in Gen.
   17 as it does in chap. 15, but one cannot conclude from this that P
   plays down the promise theme" (Abraham in History and Tradition,
   289), seems to reflect his awareness of the weakness of this parallelism he has drawn between the two chapters.
26 J. Hoftijzer, Die Verheissungen an die drei Erzväter, does not accept any dependence between these two chapters. This view is apparent
   from his thesis that the two chapters were the two sources for all
   the promises to the patriarchs in the Pentateuch. On the ground that
   Gen. 15 is a late composition and addition to the Pentateuch, we do
   not agree with Hoftijzer's thesis.

Abraham had obtained in Egypt a whole horde of cattle and menservants as well as maid-servants. It is totally possible and quite probable that Hagar was one of these maid-servants given to Sarai.

Another point that merits some consideration has to do with the place of Abraham's residence. Gen. 13:18 locates it "by the oaks of Mamre". In 18:1 we are told that "the Lord appeared to him by the oaks of Mamre". Meanwhile no movement of the patriarch has been recorded except that in Gen. 14. While without this late addition there is consistency between 13:18 and 18:1 as regards place, this consistency is badly disrupted by the addition[27].

One such disruption is that Gen. 14 leaves Abraham in "the Valley of Shaveh" (14:17) without further information about Abraham's return to the "oaks of Mamre". Another is the redundance of the promises of land and progeny contained in Gen. 15 vis-à-vis 13:14-16.

Removal of Gen. 14 and 15 not only does not disrupt the sequence between Gen. 12-13 and Gen. 16 onwards but makes it more apparent.

---

27 Here, the king of Sodom met Abraham after his return from his victory over the four eastern kings. The patriarch was also met by Melchizedek, king of Salem (vv. 18-20). Wherever these two encounters might have taken place, it was certainly not "by the oaks of Mamre" - as chapter 14 applies the name "Mamre" to a person (v. 24b). Thus in Gen. 14 Abraham does not seem to settle "by the oaks of Mamre".

V. Probable Reason For The Composition
And Addition Of Genesis 15

The concern Gen. 15 shows for the land favours the exilic
period as the probable time for its composition. Its author's broad familiarity with the Deuteronomistic and Priestly traditions would seem to date it in a later part of the
exile.

By this time much theological thinking had already been
made about the fall of Jerusalem and the exile[28]. One theological trend that emerged interpreted the two related
events as the meting out of God's punishment on His unfaith-
ful people (cf. e.g. Ezk. 5:7-17; 7)[29]. In other words, what
proved to be operative in Israel's history was the Sinai
covenant of which blessings and curses constituted an essential part (cf. Dt. 28).

Attempts were made to raise the hope of the exiles for a
restoration. The Deuteronomistic school explained the entire
pattern of history as a working out of rebellion and forgiveness (cf. Dt. 30; Jos. 22-23; Jdg. 2-3; 2 Sam. 12; 2 K 17)[30].
This pattern offered hope of divine forgiveness. Jeremiah
asserted this hope in terms of a restoration (Jer. 30-33)[31]

---

28 There was so much theological thinking from this period that D.W.
   Thomas entitled his study of the period "The Sixth Century B.C.: A
   Creative Epoch in the History of Israel", JJS, 6 (1961), 33-46.
29 P.R. Ackroyd, Exile and Restoration, 39-61, presents four main types
   of reaction to the fall of Jerusalem and the exile: (a) a return to
   older cults, the theological reason behind it being that the two
   events resulted from a neglect of them; (b) acceptance of the religion of the conquerors, since their gods proved to be more powerful
   than YHWH; (c) recognition of divine judgement, since the people of
   Israel had failed to heed the warning given by their prophets; (d)
   recognition of the disaster as "historification" of the cultic Day
   of YHWH.
30 Cf. P.R. Ackroyd, Exile and Restoration, 75.
31 Cf. P.R. Ackroyd, Exile and Restoration, 58-61; B. Oded, in J.H.
   Hayes and J.M. Miller, Israelite and Judaean History, 484; J. Bright,
   Covenant and Promise, 191-196.

and in fact in terms of a new covenant (Jer. 31:31-34)[32].
"Ezekiel 40-48 is simply a large-scale and detailed pro-
gramme for the rebuilding of the temple, the restoration of
its worship and the reconstitution of the state"[33]. Deutero-
Isaiah portrayed Abraham as the ground for YHWH's restoration of His people (Is. 41:8; cf. also Is. 51:2) and even
announced that Cyrus, a pagan ruler, would be YHWH's agent
to bring about this restoration (Is. 45:1-7)[34].

Notwithstanding all these attempts, the shaken foundations
of Israel's faith had not been totally restored. What had
happened to YHWH's promise of the inviolability of Zion as
His chosen city (cf. 2 K. 18:13-20:11 = Is. 36-39; Jer. 7:4)
and the eternal Davidic dynasty (2 Sam. 7)? At best, there
was a good reason to call YHWH's fidelity to question, in
which case the exiles could not be sure of a restoration. At
worst, the current disaster only proved YHWH's weakness when
opposed by the Babylonian gods - in which case the exiles
were trapped in hopeless despair unless they turned to these
gods. In fact, many seemed to have decided to worship these
latter, as the strong polemics against idols in Is. 40-48
seem to indicate[35].

From the adverse response of the exiles, one basic question that might well have been asked by many was: what is
there to guarantee a return to the land and its inheritance?
That too was the question asked by the patriarch Abraham in
Gen. 15:8: "Adonay YHWH, how am I to know that I shall
possess it (i.e. the land)?"

It is likely that Abraham's question is intended to reflect the exiles'[36]. If so, the same response given to

---

32 A. Cholewiński, Bib, 66 (1985), 96-111, argues for the covenant in
   the land of Moab as a concrete presentation or, if not, a "prefigura-
   tion" of the "new covenant" announced by the prophets.
33 This is a citation from J.A. Soggin, A History of Israel, 254. Cf.
   also B. Oded, in J.H. Hayes and J.M. Miller, Israelite and Judaean
   History, 484.
34 Cf. J.A. Soggin, A History of Israel, 263; P.R. Ackroyd, Exile and
   Restoration, 118-137; B. Oded, in J.H. Hayes and J.M. Millers,
   Israelite and Judaean History, 516-519.
35 Cf. J. Bright, Covenant and Promise, 188.
36 J. Van Seters, Abraham in History and Tradition, 265.

Abraham - that is, the prophecy about the fate of his descendants followed by the unilateral and unconditional oath
of land donation to them (Gen. 15:13-16,18) - would also
seem to be the appropriate response for the exilic community. For, the experience of the patriarch's descendants was
essentially the same as that of his community and the unre-
voked oath of land donation would be efficacious for the
exiles as they were also descendants of the patriarch,
albeit belonging to another generation.

As presented in Gen. 15, the divine oath lay at the foundation of Israel's entire history. This means that even the
Sinai covenant was rooted in it. The theological significance of this for the exilic community was that whilst the
Sinai covenant was really operative in the double disaster
of the fall of Jerusalem and the exile, the ultimate force
behind history was still the divine oath. It was by virtue
of this that the exiles would return to the land.

What the exilic community would need was faith - the kind
of faith that their ancestor Abraham had. History itself
would provide the necessary sign to support it. More proxi-
mately, the fulfilment of the prophecies about the double
disaster as YHWH's punitive response to the people's breach
of the Sinai covenant should serve as a sign of YHWH's fidelity to His covenant and the genuineness of the prophecies.
In turn, it should leave no doubt in the exiles' minds that
prophecies about the restoration would come true because
YHWH was also faithful to His oath of land donation to
Abraham.

More remotely, the history of the exilic community's ancestors as recorded in the Pentateuch provided an unfailing
testimony to YHWH's fidelity to this oath of His. That was
probably why the author of Gen. 15 was keen to present this
important work, albeit in summary form, to the exilic community. By this, he hoped not only to lend credibility to
the various attempts to rekindle the exiles' hope of a return to the promised land but also to provide the real foundation for such a hope.

As a theological compendium of the Pentateuch, Gen. 15

would have an appropriate place in that corpus. The question is: where to insert it? We have briefly reviewed the observations of scholars who see in Gen. 12-13 a résumé of Jacob's itinerary in the land, the journey of his family down to Egypt and finally the experiences of the Israelites in Egypt as well as their journey back to the promised land[37]. As these observations are pretty striking, they would not have escaped the attention of the author of Gen. 15 who had undoubtedly been working very closely with the Pentateuch. Taken together, they seem to focus on the itineraries and their circumstances. The emphasis of Gen. 12-13 therefore seems to be more geographico-historical than anything else. Yet geography and history only constitute the stage in which YHWH's relationship with the Israelites, beginning with Abraham their ancestor, was lived out. This was quite likely the view of the author of Gen. 15 who then saw that his work, reflecting the theological thrust of the Pentateuch, would be a fitting complement to Gen. 12-13 as a "preface" to the entire Pentateuch.

----

37 Cf. pages 198-201 above.

CONCLUSION TO PART TWO

After tracing the recapitulation of the individual compo-
nents of the Pentateuchal history in Gen. 15, we are now in
a position to take into account an important study contributed by D.J.A. Clines[1]. His synchronic analysis of the Pentateuch treats it from the point of view of theme. Theme is
certainly a central concern of ours as well.

The entire thrust of Clines' study as regards the Pentateuchal history (that is, the Pentateuch minus Gen. 1-11) is
to demonstrate that its theme "is the partial fulfilment -
which implies also the partial non-fulfilment - of the promise to or blessing of the patriarchs"[2]. His treatment of
each of the five books of the Pentateuch is oriented towards
verifying the overall theme at the level of the individual
book[3]. In brief, his consistent conclusion at the end of his
analysis of each book is that the threefold promise of a
great posterity, divine relationship and land finds partial
fulfilment and this amidst a lot of threats that come from
both within and without the recipients of the promise. Not
every detail of Clines' work may stand up to serious objections. However, as a whole his thesis is well grounded in
the text of the Pentateuch and is of relevance to our work.

The tension Clines has pointed out between the promise and
its fulfilment in the Pentateuch is also reflected in Gen.
15[4]. Indeed, despite its optimistic tone, Gen. 15 is not
blind to the hazards encountered by the promises it presents
as they are launched off towards its fulfilment.

The first of such hazards is Abraham's childlessness ag-
gravated by the presence of a potential usurper. In the

---

1 D.J.A. Clines, The Theme of the Pentateuch.
2 Id, 29.
3 Id, 45-60.
4 Thus also R.P. Gordon, Themelios, 1 (1975), 19.

face of this double hazard there is no way in which the promise of a great reward is going to find its fulfilment.   An
impossible obstacle indeed, but not insurmountable to YHWH
who then promises a son. The promise of a son is a stepping
stone to that of innumerable descendants.

   Next, Abraham is presented as not being totally clear
about the workability of YHWH's promise of land to him (vv.
7f). Following upon this, both the promises of great posterity and land, as predicted in vv. 13-16, will be exposed to
powers of destruction. One such power is Egypt whose oppres-
sive thumb would threaten the very survival of Abraham's
descendants. How then will the promises of progeny and land
find their fulfilment? And even if the latter will take
place, its long delay casts a dark shadow: "four generations"
after Abraham's death (v. 16). To crown it all, Gen. 15 ends
on a note, optimistic no doubt, but still falling short of a
complete fulfilment of the promise of land.

GENERAL CONCLUSION

From this study we have undertaken, a few conclusions
about Gen. 15 may be highlighted.

1. The chapter was composed as a compendium of the Pentateuchal history. It presents this history from the viewpoint
of the theological thrust of the Pentateuch itself, strongly
directed by the theologoumena of the divine oath to the patriarchs and their response of faith to it.

2. The "theologization" of the Pentateuchal history in the
chapter to highlight the two theologoumena results in the
conversion of this history into a sign to support faith in
the divine oath declared in v. 6. The conversion itself is
drawn on the Pentateuch where Israel's faith is very much
supported by history as a sign.

3. Gen. 15 exhibits great liberty in reinterpreting the
technical understanding of *kārat* *b^erît* in order to align it
with the unilateral character of the divine oath.

4. The compositional unity of Gen. 15 - from the literary,
structural and thematic perspectives - marks it as the work
of one single author.

5. The author commands a broad familiarity with not only
the Pentateuchal traditions but also the prophetic literature. In addition to the prophetic flavour of his work, he
seems to betray his special liking for, if not his rooting
in, this literature.

a) He makes particular use of Is. 7:1-17 to present the
theologoumenon of faith supported by sign, which theologoumenon is a hallmark of the Isaian passage.

b) Jer. 34:18-20 provides him the rite by which to express
YHWH's self-obligation to free Abraham's descendants and
give them the land, thus underscoring the unilateral nature
of the oath. Since it would hardly be probable that YHWH's

self-obligation involved His self-imprecation especially in
terms of destruction, it is plausible that the author of
Gen. 15 altered the meaning of the rite. Rather than having
it to mean the destruction of the oath-maker as in Jer. 34,
he most probably intended it to express YHWH's oath to destroy the oppressors of Abraham's descendants.

6. Given the equally dominant Deuteronomistic, Priestly
as well as prophetic traits in Gen. 15, it is impossible to
identify its author with any of these schools. In fact, his
theology of Israel's history is essentially different from
that of the Deuteronomist. It may well be possible that he
did not belong to any of these schools but was just an official scribe or teacher who saw the need to compose his work.

7. The author's scriptural familiarity favours a late datation for his work. His concern for the land and, to some
extent, his concern for a great posterity point to the exilic period as the probable time in which he composed his
work.

8. Given this date for the composition, the author's intention would evidently be to strengthen the faith of the
exiles and provide them with a hope of a return to the land.
a) The Pentateuch was offered as the foundation of this
faith and hope because it recorded an almost similar experience made by Israel's forefathers in a foreign land and
their liberation by YHWH their God on the ground of His unilateral oath to their patriarchs.
b) This unilateral oath was valid for all generations of
Abraham's descendants. YHWH's destruction of the Egyptians
and the Assyrians had taken place. It should now serve to
guarantee the destruction of the Babylonians, the present
oppressors of Abraham's descendants, thereby securing the
latter's liberation and return to the promised land.

9. In respect of its canonical position in the Pentateuch,
Gen. 15 seems to bear the following relationship to the
chapters immediately before and after it:
a) It did not know Gen. 14 which was probably a later composition.
b) It was inserted after Gen. 12-13, despite the disruption

it caused to the smooth sequence from these two chapters to
Gen. 16, because Gen. 12-13 appeared to present a geographico-historical overview of the Pentateuch. Thus, Gen. 12-13
and 15 together would serve as a good "preface" to the entire Pentateuch.
c) It serves as a theological compendium to the entire Pentateuchal history as Gen. 17 does to the Abraham cycle.

ABBREVIATIONS

AfO	Archiv für Orientforschung
AJBI	Annual of the Japanese Biblical Institute
An. Bib.	Analecta Biblica, Rome
ANET	Ancient Near Eastern Texts Relating to the Old Testament, (Ed. J. PRITCHARD), Princeton, [3]1969
AOAT	Alter Orient und Altes Testament, Kevelaer/Neukirchen-Vluyn
ATD	Das Alte Testament Deutsch, Göttingen
AThANT	Abhandlungen zur Theologie des Alten und Neuen Testaments, Zürich
BA	Biblical Archaeologist
BASOR	Bulletin of the American Schools of Oriental Research
BBB	Bonner biblische Beiträge, Bonn
BDB	A Hebrew and English Lexicon of the OT, by F. BROWN, S.R. DRIVER, C.A. BRIGGS, Oxford, 1907 (Reprinted, 1966)
BEvt	Beiträge zur evangelischen Theologie, München
BHK	Biblia Hebraica, (Ed. R. KITTEL)
BHS	Biblia Hebraica Stuttgartensia
BhTh	Beiträge zur historischen Theologie, Tübingen
Bib	Biblica
Bib et Or	Biblica et Orientalia, Rome
BiR	Biblical Research
BKAT	Biblischer Kommentar: Altes Testament, Neukirchen
BN	Biblische Notizen
BS	Bibliotheca Sacra
BWANT	Beiträge zur Wissenschaft vom Alten und Neuen Testament, Stuttgart
BZ	Biblische Zietschrift
BZAW	Beihefte zur Zietschrift für die alttestamentliche Wissenschaft, Berlin
CBQ	Catholic Biblical Quarterly
CTM	Currents in Theology and Mission
Evt	Evangelische Theologie
FS	Festschrift
Ges-K	Gesenius' Hebrew Grammar (Ed. E. KAUTZSCH, Eng. Tr. A.E. COWLEY), Oxford, 1910
HorizBT	Horizons in Biblical Theology
HTR	Harvard Theological Review
ICC	International Critical Commentary, Edinburgh
IDB	Interpreter's Dictionary of the Bible (Ed. G.A. BUTTRICK)
IDB Suppl	Interpreter's Dictionary of the Bible, Supplementary Volume
JAOS	Journal of the American Oriental Society
JCS	Journal of Cuneiform Studies
JJS	Journal of Jewish Studies
JSOT	Journal for the Study of the Old Testament
JSOT Suppl	JSOT Supplement Series, Sheffield
JSS	Journal of Semitic Studies
JTC	Journal for Theology and the Church

NCB	New Century Bible Commentary, London/Grand Rapids
NICOT	New International Commentary of the Old Testament, Grand Rapids
OTL	Old Testament Library, London
PJ	Palästina-Jahrbuch
RHR	Revue de l'Histoire des Religions
RStOr	Rivista di Studi Orientali
SB	Sources Bibliques, Paris
SBS	Stuttgarter Bibel-Studien, Stuttgart
Sem	Semitica
SOTS Mon Ser	Society for Old Testament Study - Monograph Series, London
SR	Studies in Religion (= Sciences Religieuses)
St.Bib T	Studies in Biblical Theology, London
TDNT	Theological Dictionary of the New Testament (Ed. G. KITTEL, (G. FRIEDRICH)
TDOT	Theological Dictionary of the Old Testament (Ed. G.J. BOTTERWECK, H. RINGGREN)
THAT	Theologisches Handwörterbuch zum Alten Testament (Ed. E. JENNI, C. WESTERMANN)
ThB	Theologische Bücherei, München
ThBer	Theologische Berichte
ThLZ	Theologische Literaturzeitung
ThWAT	Theologisches Wörterbuch zum Alten Testament (Ed. G.J. BOTTERWECK, H. RINGGREN)
TynB	Tyndale Bulletin
TZ	Theologische Zeitschrift
VT	Vetus Testamentum
VT Suppl	Vetus Testamentum Supplements, Leiden
WB	Die Welt der Bibel, Düsseldorf
WMANT	Wissenschaftliche Monographien zum Alten und Neuen Testament, Neukirchen
WThJ	Westminster Theological Journal
WuD	Wort und Dienst
ZAW	Zeitschrift für die Alttestamentliche Wissenschaft
ZDMG	Zeitschrift des Deutschen Morgenländischen Gesellschaft
ZkTh	Zeitschrift für katholische Theologie
ZThK	Zeitschrift für Theologie und Kirche

BIBLIOGRAPHY

ACHTMEIER, E.R., "Righteousness in the OT", IDB, 4, 80-85.
ACKROYD, P.R., Exile and Restoration. A Study of Hebrew Thought of the
    Sixth Century BC, London, 1968.
ALT, A., "God of the Fathers", Essays on Old Testament History and
    Religion, Oxford, 1966, 1-77 (Trans. Der Gott der Väter, Stutt-
    gart, 1929).
ALTMANN, P., Erwählungstheologie und Universalismus im Alten Testament,
    (BZAW 92), Berlin, 1964.
ANBAR, M., "Genesis 15: A Conflation of Two Deuteronomic Narratives",
    JBL, 101 (1982), 39-55.
ANDREASEN, N.E.A., "Genesis 14 in its Near Eastern Context", Scripture
    in Context: Essays on the Comparative Method, (Ed. C.D. EVANS,
    W. HALLO, J.B. WHITE), (Pittsburgh Theological Monograph 34),
    Pittsburgh, 1980, 59-77.
ASTOUR, M.C. "Political and Cosmic Symbolism in Genesis 14 and in its
    Babylonian Sources", Biblical Motifs, Origins and Transformations,
    (Ed. A. ALTMANN), Cambridge (Massachusetts), 1966, 65-112.
BALTZER, K., The Covenant Formulary, Philadelphia, 1971 (Trans. Das
    Bundesformular (WMANT 4), Neukirchen, 1960).
BARTLETT, J.R., "Sihon and Og, Kings of the Amorites", VT, 20 (1970),
    257-277.
BEGRICH, J., "Das Priesterliche Heilsorakel", ZAW, 52 (1934), 81-92.
BEYERLIN, W., Origins and History of the Oldest Sinaitic Traditions,
    Oxford, 1965 (Trans. Der Ältesten Sinaitraditionen Herkunft und
    Geschichte, Tübingen, 1961).
BOOIJ, Th., "Mountain and Theophany in the Sinai Narrative", Bib,
    65 (1984), 1-26.
BRAULIK, G., Die Mittel deuteronomischer Rhetorik erhoben aus Dtn 4,1-40,
    (An. Bib. 68), Roma, 1978.
BRIGHT, J., A History of Israel, Philadelphia, [3]1981.
—, Covenant and Promise. The Future in the Preaching of the Pre-
    exilic Prophets, London, 1977.
CAQUOT, A., "L'alliance avec Abram (Genèse 15)", Sem, 12 (1962), 51-66.
CASSUTO, U., A Commentary on the Book of Genesis, II, Jerusalem, 1964
    (Trans. Hebrew original, 1949).
CAZELLES, H., "Connexions et Structure de Gen. xv", RB, 69 (1962),
    321-349.
CHILDS, B.S., "A Traditio-Historical Study of the Reed Sea Tradition",
    VT, 20 (1970), 406-418.
—, Exodus, (OTL), London, 1974.
—, Introduction to the Old Testament as Scripture, London, 1979.
CHOLEWIŃSKI, A., "Zur Theologischen Deutung des Moabbundes", Bib, 66
    (1985), 96-111.
CHRISTENSEN, D.L., "Two Stanzas of a Hymn in Deuteronomy 33", Bib, 66
    (1985), 382-389.
CLEMENTS, R.E., "Deuteronomy and Jerusalem Cult Tradition", VT, 15
    (1965), 300-312.
—, Abraham and David: Gen. 15 and its Meaning for Israelite Tradi-
    tion, (St. Bib T 2/5), London, 1967.

CLINES, D.J.A., The Theme of the Pentateuch, (JSOT Suppl 10), Sheffield, 1982.
COATS, G.W., "The Traditio-Historical Character of the Reed Sea Motif", VT, 17 (1967), 253-265.
—, Rebellion in the Wilderness, Nashville, 1968.
—, "Despoiling the Egyptians", VT, 18 (1968), 450-457.
—, "A Structural Transition in Exodus", VT, 22 (1972), 129-142.
—, "The Wilderness Itinerary", CBQ, 34 (1972), 135-152.
—, "Moses in Midian", JBL, 92 (1973), 3-10.
—, "The Joseph Story and Ancient Wisdom: A Reappraisal", CBQ, 34 (1973), 285-297.
—, "History and Theology in the Sea Tradition", Studia Theologica, 29 (1975), 53-62.
—, From Canaan to Egypt. Structural and Theological Context for the Joseph Story, (CBQ Monograph Series 4), Washington D.C., 1976.
—, "Conquest Traditions in the Wilderness Theme", JBL, 95 (1976).
—, "The King's Loyal Opposition: Obedience and Authority in Exodus 32-34", Canon and Authority, (Ed. G.W. COATS, B.O. LONG), Philadelphia, 1977, 91-109.
—, Genesis with an Introduction to Narrative Literature. (The Forms of the Old Testament Literature, 1), Grand Rapids, 1983.
COOKE, G.A., A Critical and Exegetical Commentary on the Book of Ezekiel, (ICC), Edinburgh, 1936.
CRAIGIE, P.C., The Book of Deuteronomy, (NICOT), Grand Rapids, 1976.
CROSS, G.M., "The Song of the Sea and Canaanite Myth", JTC, 5 (1968), 1-25.
—, Canaanite Myth and Hebrew Epic: Essays in the History of the Religion of Israel, Cambridge (Massachusetts), 1973.
DAALEN, D.H. van, "The 'emunah/pistis of Habakkuk 2.4 and Romans 1.17", Studia Evangelica, VII, (Papers presented to the Fifth International Congress on Biblical Studies at Oxford, 1973), (Ed. E.A. LIVINGSTONE), Berlin, 1983, 524.
DAHOOD, M., "Northwest Semitic Notes on Genesis", Bib, 55 (1974), 76-82.
DAVIES, G.I., "The Wilderness Itineraries: A Comparative Study", TynB, 25 (1974), 46-81.
—, The Way of the Wilderness, (SOTS Mon Ser 5), Cambridge, 1979.
—, "The Wilderness Itineraries and the Composition of the Pentateuch", VT, 33 (1983), 1-13.
DORÉ, J., "La recontre Abraham-Melchisédech et le problème de l'unité littéraire du Genèse 14", De la Torâh au Messie, études d'exégèse et d'herméneutique bibliques offertes à H. Cazelles, (Ed. M. CARREZ, J. DORÉ, P. GRELOT), PARIS, 1981, 75-95.
EMERTON, J.A., "The Riddle of Gen. 14", VT, 21 (1971), 403-439.
FALK, Z., "Hebrew Legal Term: III", JSS, 14 (1969), 39-44.
FISHBANE, M., "Composition and Structure in the Jacob Cycle (Gen. 25:19-35:22)", JJS, 26 (1975), 15-38.
—, "Exodus 1-4. The Prologue of the Exodus Cycle", Text and Texture. Close Readings of Selected Biblical Texts, New York, 1979, 63-76.
FOHRER, G., "Priesterliches Königtum", TZ, 19 (1963), 359-362.
FOKKELMAN, J.P., Narrative Art in Genesis: Specimen of Stylistic and Structural Analysis, Amsterdam, 1975.
FREEDMAN, D.N., "The Poetic Structure of the Framework of Deuteronomy 33" The Bible World. Essays in Honor of Cyrus H. Gordon, (Ed. G. RENDSBURG, R. ADLER, M. ARFA, N.H. WINTER), New York, 1980, 25-46.

FRITZ, V., Israel in der Wüste. Traditionsgeschichtliche Untersuchung
    der Wüstenüberlieferung des Jahwisten, Marbürg, 1970.
FUHS, H.F., Sehen und Schauen. Die Wurzel ḥzh im Alten Orient und im
    Alten Testament. Ein Beitrag zum prophetischen Offenbarungsemp-
    fang, Würzburg, 1978.
GAMMIE, J.G., "Theological Interpretation by Way of Literary and Tradi-
    tion Analysis: Genesis 25-36", Encounter with the Text. Form and
    History in the Hebrew Bible, (Ed. M. BUSS), Philadelphia and
    Missoula, 1979, 117-132.
GASTON, L., "Abraham and the Righteousness of God", HorizBT, 2 (1980),
    39-68.
GERLEMAN, G., Zephanja. Textkritisch und Literarisch Untersucht, Lund,
    1942.
GESENIUS, W. - KAUTZSCH, E., Genenius' Hebrew Grammar, Oxford, [2]1910
    (Trans. in accordance with 28th German edition, 1909).
GINSBERG, H.L., "Abram's 'Damascene' Steward", BASOR, 200 (1970), 31.
GOLDMAN, S., From Slavery to Freedom, London/New York, 1958.
GORDON, C.H., Ugaritic Textbook, (Analecta Orientalia 38), Rome, 1965.
GORDON, R.P., "Preaching from the Patriarchs: Background to the Exposi-
    tion to Gen. 15", Themelios, 1 (1975), 19-23.
GRAY, G.B., Numbers, (ICC), Edinburgh, 1903.
GREENBERG, M., "The Biblical Concept of Asylum", JBL, 78 (1959), 125-132.
—, "The Thematic Unity of Exodus III-XI", Fourth World Congress of
    Jewish Studies, I, Jerusalem, 1967, 151-154.
—, "The Redaction in the Plagues Narrative in Exodus", Near Eastern
    Studies in Honor of W.F. Albright, (Ed. H. GOEDICKE), Baltimore/
    London, 1971, 243-252.
GREENFIELD, J.C.. "A Hapax Legomenon mmšq ḥrwl", Studies in Judaica,
    Karaitica and Islamica. FS Leon Nemoy, (Ed. S.R. BRUNSWICK),
    Ramat-Gan, 1982, 79-82.
GROSS, H., "Glaube und Bund. Theologische Bemerkungen zu Genesis 15",
    Studien zum Pentateuch. FS Walter Kornfeld, (Ed. G. BRAULIK),
    Wien/Frankfurt, 1977, 25-37.
GUILLÉN TORRALBA, J., La fuerza occulta de Dios. La elección en el
    Antiguo Testamento, (Institución San Jerónomio, 15), Valencia-
    Córdeba, 1983.
GUNKEL, H., Genesis: übersetzt und erklärt, Göttingen, [3]1910.
GUNN, D.M., "The 'Battle Report': Oral or Scribal Convention?", JBL, 93
    (1974), 513-518.
—, "The 'Hardening of Pharaoh's Heart': Plot Character and Theology
    in Exodus 1-14", Art and Meaning: Rhetoric in Biblical Literature,
    (Ed. D.J.A. CLINES, D.M. GUNN, A.J. HAUSER), (JSOT Suppl 19),
    Sheffield, 1982, 72-96.
HASEL, G.F., "The Meaning of the Animal Rite in Gen. 15", JSOT, 19
    (1981), 61-78.
HAMP, V., BOTTERWECK, G.J., "dîn". TDOT, III, 187-194.
HAY, L.S., "What really happened at the Sea of Reeds?", JBL, 83 (1964),
    397-401.
HEINISCH,P., Das Buch Genesis. Übersetzt und erklärt, Bonn, 1930.
HENNINGER, J., "Was bedeutet die rituelle Teilung eines Tieres in zwei
    Hälften?", Bib, 34 (1953), 344-353.
HEYLER, L.R., "The Separation of Abraham and Lot. Its significance in
    the Patriarchal Narratives", JSOT, 26 (1983), 77-88.
HILLERS, D.R., "Declarative Verbs in Biblical Hebrew", JBL, 86 (1967),
    320-324.
—, Covenant: The History of a Biblical Idea, Baltimore, 1969.

HOFTIJZER, J., Die Verheissungen an die drei Erzväter, Leiden, 1956.

HÖLSCHER, G., Geschichtsschreibung in Israel. Untersuchungen zum Jah-
    wisten und Elohisten, (Revised and expanded edition), Lund, 1952,
    278-280.

HORT, G., "The Plagues of Egypt", ZAW, 69 (1957), 84-103; 70 (1958),
    45-59.

HUBMANN, F.D., "Randbemerkungen zu Jes 7,1-17", BN, 26 (1985), 27-46.

IRSIGLER, H., "Zeichen und Bezeichnetes in Jes 7,1-17. Notizen zum Imma-
    nueltext", BN, 26 (1985), 75-114.

ISBELL, C., "Exodus 1-2 in the Context of Exodus 1-14: Story Lines and
    Key Words", Art and Meaning: Rhetoric in Biblical Literature, (Ed.
    D.J.A. CLINES, D.M. GUNN, A.J. HAUSER), (JSOT Suppl 19), Sheffield,
    1982, 37-61.

ISHIDA, T., "The Structure and Historical Implications of the Lists of
    Pre-Israelite Nations", Bib, 60 (1979), 461-490.

JANZEN, J.G., "Habakkuk 2:2-4 in the Light of Recent Philological Ad-
    vances", HTR, 73 (1980), 53-78.

JEPSEN, A., "'āman", TDOT, I, 292-323.

—, "Zur Überlieferungsgeschichte der Vätergestalten", Wissenschaft-
    liche Zeitschrift der Karl-Marx-Universität, 3 (1953), 139-153.

JOHNSON, B., "Who reckoned righteousness to whom?", Svensk Exegetisk
    Årsbok, 51-52 (1986-87), 108-115.

JOÜON, P., Grammaire de L'Hebreu Biblique, Rome, 1923.

KAISER, O., "Traditionsgeschichtliche Untersuchung von Genesis 15", ZAW,
    70 (1958), 107-126.

—, Isaiah 1-12, (OTL) London, 1983 (Trans. Das Buch des Propheten
    Jesaja, Kepitel 1-12, (ATD 17), Göttingen, 5 1981).

KALLUVEETIL, P., Declaration and Covenant, (An. Bib. 88), Rome, 1982, 14.

KALLAI, Z., "The Wandering Traditions from Kadesh Barnea to Canaan: A
    Study in Biblical Historiography", JJS, 33 (1982), 175-184.

KAPELRUD, A.S., "The Interpretation of Jeremiah 34:18ff", JSOT, 22
    (1982), 138-140.

KAUFMANN, Y., The Religion of Israel, Chicago, 4 1969 (Trans. (abridged
    edition) of Hebrew original, Tel Aviv, 1937-1956).

KEIL, C.F., DELITZSCH, F., Commentary on the Old Testament in Ten
    Volumes. The Pentateuch I-III, Grand Rapids, 1980 (Trans.
    Biblischer Kommentar über das AT, Leipzig, 1878).

KESSLER, M., "The 'Shield' of Abraham?", VT, 14 (1964), 494-497.

KILIAN, R., Die vorpriesterlichen Abrahamsüberlieferungen literatur-
    kritisch und traditionsgeschichtlich untersucht, (BBB 24), Bonn,
    1966.

KIKAWADA, I.M., "Unity in Genesis 12:1-9", Proceedings of the Sixth
    World Congress of Jewish Studies, I, Jerusalem, 1977, 229-235.

KITCHEN, K.A., "D'Égypte au Jourdain", Hokhma, 2 (1976), 45-76.

KLINE, M.G., "Abram's Amen", WThJ, 31 (1968), 1-11.

KOCH, K., "Zur Geschichte der Erwählungsvorstellung in Israel", ZAW, 67
    (1955), 205-226.

KRAMER, S.N., The Sumerians. Their History, Culture and Character,
    Chicago, 1964.

KUTSCH, E., "Gesetz und Gnade. Probleme des alttestamentlichen Bundes-
    begriffs", ZAW, 79 (1967), 18-35.

—, "kārat berît, eine Verpflichtung festsetzen", Wort und Geschichte.
    FS K. Elliger, (Ed. H. GESE, H.P. RÜGER), (AOAT 18), Kevelaer und
    Neukirchen-Vluyn, 1973, 121-127.

—, Verheissung und Gesetz. Untersuchungen zum sogennanten Bund im
    Alten Testament, (BZAW 131), Berlin 1973.

LAMBDIN, T.O., Introduction to Biblical Hebrew, New York, 1971.

L'HOUR, J., "L'alliance de Sichem", RB, 69 (1962), 5-36, 161-184, 350-368.

—, "Une legislation criminelle dans le Deutéronome", Bib, 44 (1963), 1-28.

LIEDKE, G., Gestalt und Bezeichung alttestamentlicher Rechtssätze. Eine formgeschichtlichterminologische Studie, (WMANT 39), Neukirchen-Vluyn, 1971.

—, "*dīn*, richten", THAT, I, Col. 446f.

LINDBLOM, J., "Theophanies in Holy Places in Hebrew Religion", HUCA, 32 (1961), 95.

LOEWENSTAMM, S.E., "Zur Traditionsgeschichte des Bundes zwischen den Stücken", VT, 18 (1968), 500-506.

LOHFINK, N., "Darstellungskunst und Theologie in Dtn 1,6-3,29", Bib, 41 (1960), 105-134.

—, "Der Bundesschluss im Land Moab. Redaktionsgeschichtliches zu Dt. 28,69-32,47", BZ, 6 (1962), 32-56.

—, Das Hauptgebot. Eine Untersuchung literarischer Einleitungsfragen zu Dtn. 5-11, (An. Bib. 20), Rome, 1963.

—, "Zur Dekalogfassung von Dt. 5", BZ, 9 (1965), 17-32.

—, Höre, Israel. Auslegung von Texten aus dem Buch Deuteronomium, (WB 18), Düsseldorf, 1965.

—, Die Landverheissung als Eid. Eine Studie zu Gen. 15, (Stuttgarter Bibelstudien 28), Stuttgart, 1967.

—, "Dt. 26,17-19 und die 'Bundesformel'", ZkTh, 91 (1969), 517-553.

—, "*yrš*", THAT, III, Col. 953-985.

LORETZ, O., "*mgn* - 'Geschenk' in Gen. 15:1", UF, 6 (1973), 492.

LUCK, U., "Gerechtigkeit in der Welt - Gerechtigkeit Gottes", WuD, 12 (1973), 71-89.

McCARTHY, D.J., "Moses' Dealings with Pharaoh: Ex. 7:8-10:27", CBQ, 27 (1965), 336-347.

—, "Plagues and the Sea of Reeds: Exodus 5-14", JBL, 85 (1966), 137-158.

—, "*Berīt* and Covenant in the Deuteronomistic History", Studies in the Religion of Ancient Israel, (Ed. P.A.H. de BOER), (VT Suppl 23), Leiden, 1972, 65-85.

—, Old Testament Covenant, Oxford, 1973.

—, Treaty and Covenant. A Study in Form in the Ancient Oriental Documents and in the Old Testament, (An. Bib. 21A), (Rev. Edition), Rome, 1978.

McEVENUE, S.E., "A Source-Critical Problem in Num. 14,26-38", Bib, 60 (1969), 453-465.

—, The Narrative Style of the Priestly Writer, (An. Bib. 50), Rome, 1971.

MASSON, O., "A propos d'un rituelle hittite pour la purification divine armée", RHR, 137 (1950), 5-25.

MAYES, A.D.H., Deuteronomy, (New Century Bible), Grand Rapids/London, 1979.

—, "Deuteronomy 4 and the Literary Criticism of Deuteronomy", JBL, 100 (1981), 23-51.

MENDENHALL, G.E., Law and Covenant in Israel and the Ancient Near East, Pittsburgh, 1955 = BA, 17 (1954), 26-46 and 49-76.

MOBERLY, R.W.L., At the Mountain of God. Story and Theophany in Exodus 32-34, (JSOT Suppl 22), Sheffield, 1983.

MOOR, J.C. de, "Cloud", IDB Suppl, 168.

MORGENSTERN, J., "The Despoiling of the Egyptians", JBL, 68 (1949), 1-28.

MORIARTY, F.L., "Numbers", The Jerome Biblical Commentary, I, (Ed.
    R.E. BROWN, J. FITZMYER, R.E. MURPHY), Englewood Cliffs, 1968.
MUFFS, Y., "Abraham the Noble Warrior", JJS, 33 (1982), 83-107.
MÜLLER, H.P., "Glauben und Bleiben", VTS, 26 (1974), 25-54.
NICHOLSON, E.W., "The Interpretation of Exodus xxiv 9-11", VT, 24
    (1974), 77-97.
—, "The Antiquity of the Tradition in Exodus xxiv 9-11", VT, 25
    (1975), 69-79.
—, "The Origin of the Tradition in Exodus xxiv 9-11", VT, 26 (1976),
    148-160.
—, "The Decalogue as the Direct Address of God", VT, 27 (1977),
    422-433.
—, "The Covenant Ritual in Exodus xxiv 3-8", VT, 32 (1982), 74-86.
NOTH, M., "Der Wallfahrtsweg zum Sinai", PJ, 36 (1940), 5-28.
—, A History of Pentateuchal Traditions, Englewood Cliffs, 1972
    (Trans. Uberlieferungsgeschichte des Pentateuch, Stuttgart, 1948).
—, The History of Israel, London, 1960 (Rev. Trans. Geschichte Is-
    raels, Göttingen, [2]1954).
—, "Old Testament Covenant-Making in the Light of a Text from Mari",
    The Laws in the Pentateuch and Other Studies, Edinburgh and London,
    1966, 108-177 (Trans. Gesammelte Studien zum AT, (ThB 6), München,
    [2]1960, 142-154).
—, Exodus, (OTL), London, 1962 (Trans. Das zweite Buch Mose. Exodus,
    (ATD 5). Göttingen, [2]1961.
—, Numbers; A Commentary, (OTL), London, 1968 (Trans. Das vierte Buch
    Mose, Numeri, (ATD 7), Göttingen, 1966).
ODED, B., "Judah and the Exile", Israelite and Judaean History, (Ed.
    J.H. HAYES and J.M. MILLER), London, 1977, 435-488.
OEMING, M., "Ist Genesis 15 ein Beleg für die Anrechnung des Glaubens
    zur Gerechtigkeit?", ZAW, 95 (1983), 182-197.
PANKNIN, B., "Zu JBL LXXI S. 212", ZAW, 70 (1958), 256.
PECKHAM, J.B., "The Composition of Dt. 9:1-10:11", Word and Spirit.
    Essays in Honor of D.M. Stanley SJ, (Ed. J. PLEVNIK), Willowdale,
    1975, 3-59.
PERLITT, L., Bundestheologie im Alten Testament, (WMANT 36), Neukirchen-
    Vluyn, 1969.
PETER M., "Wer sprach den Sagen nach Genesis XIV über Abraham aus?",
    VT, 29 (1979), 114-119.
—, "Die historische Wahrheit in Genesis 14", De la Tôrah au Messie,
    études d'exégèse et d'herméneutique bibliques offertes a H.
    Cazelles, (ED. M. CARREZ, J. DORÉ, P. GRELOT), Paris, 1981, 97-
    105.
PETERSEN, D.L., "Covenant Ritual. A Traditio-Historical Perspective",
    BiR, 22 (1977), 7-18.
PHILLIPS, A., Ancient Israel's Criminal Law, Oxford, 1972.
—, "A Fresh Look at the Sinai Pericope", VT, 34 (1984), 39-62;
    282-294.
POLZIN, R.M., Biblical Structuralism: Method and Subjectivity in the
    Study of Ancient Texts, Philadelphia/Missoula, 1977, 174-201.
PROCKSCH, O., Die Genesis übersetzt und erklärt, Leipzig, [2,3]1924.
PURY, A. de, Promesse divine et Légende cultuelle dans le Cycle de
    Jacob, Paris, 1975.
QUELL, G., SCRHENK, G., "dikē, dikaios, dikaiosynē, etc", TDNT, II
    174-178; 185-187; 195-198; 212-224.
RAD, G. von. "The Form-Critical Problem of the Hexateuch", The Problem
    of the Hexateuch and Other Essays, Edinburgh and London, 1966.

1-78 (Trans. Das formgeschichtliche Problem des Hexateuch, (BWANT 4/26), Stuttgart, 1938 = Gesammelte Studien zum Alten Testament, I, München, 1958, 9-86).

—, "'Righteousness' and 'Life' in the Cultic Language of the Psalms", Id, 243-266 (Trans. "'Gerechtigkeit' und 'Leben' in der Kultsprache der Psalmen", FS A. Bertholet, (Ed. W. BAUMGARTNER, O. EISSFELDT, K. ELLIGER, L. ROST), Tübingen, 1950, 418-437 = Gesammelte Studien zum Alten Testament, I, München, 1958, 225-247).

—, "Faith Reckoned as Righteousness", Id, 125-130 (Trans. "Die Anrechnung des Glaubens zur Gerechtigkeit", ThLZ, 76 (1951), 129-132 = Gesammelte Studien zum Alten Testament, I, München, 1958, 130-135).

—, Genesis; A Commentary, (OTL), London, [3]1972 (Trans. Das erste Buch Mose, Genesis, (ATD 2/4), Göttingen, [9]1972.

—, "Israel before Jahweh", Old Testament Theology, I, Edinburgh and London, 1962, 376-380 (Trans. Theologie des Alten Testaments, I, München, 1957, 376-380.

—, Deuteronomy, London, 1966 (Trans. Das fünfte Buch Mose: Deuteronomium, (ATD 8), Göttingen, 1964.

RAST, W.E., "Habakkuk and Justification by Faith", CTM, 10 (1983), 169-175.

REINER, E., "Šurpu. A Collection of Sumerian and Akkadian Incantations", AFO Beiheft, 11 (1958).

RENDTORFF, R., "The 'Yahwist' as Theologian? The Dilemma of Pentateuchal Criticism", JSOT, 3 (1977), 2-10.

—, Das überlieferungsgeschichtliche Problem des Pentateuch, (BZAW 147) Berlin/New York, 1977.

—, "Genesis 15 im Rahmen der theologischen Bearbeitung der Vätergeschichten", Werden und Wirken des Alten Testaments: FS. C. Westermann, (Ed. R. ALBERTZ, H.P. MÜLLER, H.W. WOLFF, W. ZIMMERLI), Göttingen, 1980, 74-81.

—, "Die Erwählung Israels als Thema der deuteronomischen Theologie", Die Botschaft und die Boten. FS H.W. Wolff (Ed. J. JEREMIAS, L. PERLITT), Neukirchen-Vluyn, 1981, 75-86.

—, The Old Testament. An Introduction, London, 1985 (Trans. Das Alte Testament: Eine Einführung, Neukirchen, 1983).

—, "The Future of Pentateuchal Criticism", Henoch, 6 (1984), 1-14.

REUMANN, J., Righteousness in the New Testament, Philadelphia, 1982. 12-22.

REVENTLOW, H.G. "Rechtfertigung im Horizont des Alten Testaments", BEvT, 58 (1971), 10.

RICHTER, W., Traditionsgeschichtliche Untersuchung zum Richterbuch, (BBB 18), Bonn, [2]1966.

—, Die Bearbeitungen "Retterbuches" in der deuteronomistischen Epoche, (BBB 21), Bonn, 1964.

ROULLIARD, H., La Péricope de Balaam, Paris, 1985, 347-350.

ROWLEY, H.H., The Biblical Doctrine of Election, London, 1950.

SAKENFELD, K.D., "The Problem of Divine Forgiveness in Num. 14", CBQ, 37 (1975), 317-330.

SCHARBERT, J., "'B[e]rît' im Pentateuch", De la Tôrah au Messie. Études d'exégèse et d'herméneutique bibliques offertes à H. Cazelles, (Ed. M. CARREZ, J. DORÉ, P. GRELOT), Paris, 1981, 161-170.

SCHATZ, W., Genesis 14. Eine Untersuchung, Bern/Frankfurt, 1972.

SCHMID, H.H., Gerechtigkeit als Weltordnung, (BhTh 40), Tübingen, 1968.

—, "Rechtfertigung als Schopfungsgeschehen: Notizen zur alttestamentlichen Vorgeschichte neutestamentlichen Themas", Rechtfertigung.

FS E Käsemann, (Ed. J. FRIEDRICH, W. PÖHLMANN, P. STUHLMACHER), Tübingen, 1976, 403-414.

—, Der sogennante Jahwist. Beobachtungen und Fragen zur Pentateuchforschung, Zürich, 1976.

—, "Gerechtigkeit und Glaube: Genesis 15:1-6 und sein biblisch-theologischer Kontext", EvT, 40 (1980), 396-420.

SCHMITT, H.C., "Redaktion des Pentateuch im Geiste der Prophetie", VT, 32 (1982), 170-189.

SCHULZ, A., "Eli\^cezer?", ZAW, 52 (1934), 274-279.

SEEBASS, H., "Gen. 15:2b", ZAW, 75 (1963), 317-319.

—, "bāchar", TDOT, II, 74-87.

SEITZ, C., Redaktionsgeschichtliche Studien zum Deuteronomium, (BWANT 93) Stuttgart, 1971.

SIEVI, J., "Wunder und Zeichen in der Exodus-Tradition", ThBer, 5 (1976), 13-35.

SIMIAN-YOFRE, H., Messianic Hope in the Prophets, I, (Mimeographed Class Notes for Students of the Pontifical Biblical Institute, Rome), Rome, 1984.

SIMPSON, C.A., The Early Traditions of Israel. A Critical Analysis of the Pre-deuteronomistic Narrative of the Hexateuch, Oxford, 1948, 73-75.

SKA, J.L., "Le plaies d'Égypte dans le récit sacerdotal (p^g)", Bib, 60 (1979), 23-35.

—, "La sortie d'Égypte (Ex 7-14) dans le récit sacerdotal (p^g) et la tradition prophétique", Bib, 60 (1979), 191-215.

—, "La place d'Ex 6,2-8 dans la narration de l'exode", ZAW, 94 (1982), 530-548.

SKINNER, J., A Critical and Exegetical Commentary on Genesis, (ICC), Edinburgh, ^{2}1930.

SKWERES, D.E., Die Rückverweise im Buch Deuteronomium, (An. Bib. 79), Rome, 1979.

SMALTZ, W.B., "Did Peter die in Jerusalem?" JBL, 71 (1952), 211-226.

SMEND, R., Die Erzählung des Hexateuch auf ihre Quellen untersucht, Berlin, 1912.

—, "Zur Geschichte von h'myn", FS Baumgartner, (VT Suppl 16 (1967)), 288-290.

SNIJDERS, L.A., "Genesis xv. The Covenant with Abram", Studies on the Book of Genesis, (Ed. B. GEMSER, J. HOFTIJZER), (OTS 12), Leiden, 1958, 261-279.

SOGGIN, J.A., "Cultic-Aetiological Legends and Catechesis in the Hexateuch". Old Testament and Oriental Studies, (Bib et Or 29), Rome, 1975, 72-77 (Trans. "Kultätiologische Sagen und Katechese im Hexateuch", VT, 10 (1960), 341-347).

—, Joshua, (OTL), London, 1978 (Trans. Le Livre de Josué, Neuchâtel, 1970).

—, Judges, (OTL), London, 1981.

—, A History of Israel, London, 1984 (Trans. La Storia d'Israele dalle origini alla rivolta di Bar-Kochba, 135 d.C., Brescia, 1984).

—, "Das Wunder am Meer und in der Wüste, Exodus cc. 14-15", D'Ugarit à Qumran. Mélanges bibliques et orientaux an l'honneur de M. Mathias Delcor. (Ed. A. CAQUOT, S. LÉGASSE, M. TARDIEU), (AOAT 215) Kevelaer/Neukirchen-Vluyn, 1985, 379-385.

SUMNER, W.A., "Israel's Encounters with Edom, Moab, Amnon. Sihon and Og according to the Deuteronomist", VT, 18 (1968), 216-228.

SUTHERLAND, D., "The Organization of the Abraham Narratives", ZAW, 95 (1983), 337-343.

THOMAS, D.W., "The Sixth Century BC: A Creative Epoch in the History of Israel", JSS, 6 (1961), 33-46.

THOMPSON, T.L., The Historicity of the Patriarchal Narratives. The Quest for the Historical Abraham, Berlin/New York, 1974.

—, "The Joseph and Moses Narratives", Israelite and Judaean History, (Ed. J.H. HAYES, J.M. MILLER), London, 1977, 210.

UNGER, M.F., "Some Comments on the Text of Gen. xv 2.3", JBL, 72 (1952), 49f.

VAN SETERS, J., "The Conquest of Sihon's Kingdom: A Literary Examination" JBL, 91 (1972), 182-197.

—, Abraham in History and Tradition, New Haven/London, 1975.

VATTIONI, F., "Ancora su ben-mešeq di Gen. 15:2", RStOr, 40 (1965), 9-12.

—, "Genesi 15:9-11", Biblos-Press, 6 (1965), 53-61.

VAULX, J. de, Les Nombres, (Sources Bibliques), Paris, 1972.

VAUX, R. de, "L'itinéraire des Israélites de Cadès aux plaines de Moab", Hommages à André Dupont-Sommer, (Ed. A. CAQUOT, M. PHILONENKO), Paris, 1971, 331-342.

—, The Early History of Israel, Philadelphia, 1978 (Trans. Histoire ancienne d'Israël: Des Origines à l'Installation en Canaan, Paris, 1971; and Histoire ancienne d'Israël: La Période des Juges, Paris, 1973.

VAWTER, B., On Genesis: A New Reading, Garden City, 1977.

VERMÈS, G., Scripture and Tradition in Judaism, Haggadic Studies, (Studia Post-biblica 6), Leiden, 1961.

VOGELS, W., "Abraham et l'offrande de la Terre (Gn 13)", SR, 4 (1974-75), 51-57.

VOLZ, P., RUDOLPH, W., Der Elohist als Erzähler, ein Irrweg der Pentateuchkritik? An der Genesis erläutert, (BZAW 63), Berlin, 1933.

VRIES, S.J. de, "The Origin of the Murmuring Tradition", JBL, 87 (1968), 51-58.

VRIEZEN, Th. C., Die Erwählung Israels nach dem Alten Testament, (AThANT 24), Zürich, 1953.

—, "Exodusstudien. Exodus I", VT, 17 (1967), 334-353.

WAGENAR, S., "Die Kundschaftergeschichten im Alten Testament", ZAW, 76 (1964), 255-269.

WALSH, J.T., "From Egypt to Moab. A Source Critical Analysis of the Wilderness Itinerary", CBQ, 39 (1977), 20-33.

WEIDNER, E., "Der Staatsvertrag Aššurnirâsis VI. von Assyrien mit Mati'-'ilu von Bit-Agusi", AfO Beiheft, 8 (1932), 17-34.

WEINFELD, M., "The Covenant of Grant in the Old Testament and in the Ancient Near East", JAOS, 90 (1970), 184-203.

—, "Addenda to JAOS 90 (1970), 184", JAOS, 90 (1970), 468-469.

—, Deuteronomy and the Deuteronomic School, Oxford, 1972.

—, "berît", TDOT, II, 253-279.

WEISMAN, Z., "National Consciousness in the Patriarchal Narratives", JSOT, 31 (1985), 55-73.

WELLHAUSEN, J., Die Composition des Hexateuchs und der historischen Bücher des Alten Testaments, Berlin, [4]1963.

WENHAM, G.J., "The Symbolism of the Animal Rite in Gen. 15: A Response to G.F. Hasel. JSOT 19 (1981), 61-78", JSOT, 22 (1982), 134-137.

WESTERMANN, C., "Types of Narrative in Genesis", The Promises to the Fathers, Philadelphia, 1980, 1-94 (Trans. "Arten der Erzählung in der Genesis", Forschung am Alten Testament. Gesammelte Studien, (ThB 24), München, 1964, 9-91 = Die Verheissungen an die Väter, Göttingen, 1976).

—, "The Promises to the Fathers", Id, 95-186 (Trans. Die Verheissungen an die Väter, Göttingen, 1976).

WESTERMANN,C., Genesis 12-36, (BKAT I/2), Neukirchen-Vluyn, 1981.

—, Genesis 37-50, (BKAT I/3), Neukirchen-Vluyn, 1982.

WHITE, H.C., "The Joseph Story: A Narrative which consumes its Content",
Semeia, 31 (1985), 49-69.

WILDBERGER, H., Jahwes Eigentumsvolk, (AThANT 37), Zürich, 1960.

—, "'Glauben', Erwägungen zu h'myn", Hebräische Wortforschung.
FS W. Baumgartner, (VT Suppl 16 (1967) Leiden, 372-386).

—, "'Glauben' im Alten Testament", ZThK, 65 (1968), 129-159.

—, "Die Neuinterpretation des Erwählungsglaubens Israels in der Krise
der Exilszeit", Wort-Gebot-Glaube. FS W. Eichrodt, (Ed. J.STOEBE),
(AThANT 59), Zürich, 1970, 307-324.

—, Jesaja 1-12, Neukirchen-Vluyn, ^{2}1980.

WISEMAN, D.J., "Abban and Alalaḫ", JCS, 12 (1958), 124-129.

WÜRTHWEIN, E., "Jesaja 7:1-9. Ein Beitrag zu dem Thema: Prophetie und
Politik", Theologie als Glaubenswagnis. FS K. Heim, (Ed.
E. WÜRTHWEIN), Hamburg, 1954, 47-63 = E. WÜRTHWEIN, Wort und
Existenz, Göttingen, 1970, 127-143.

ZIMMERLI, W., "Ich bin Yahweh", Geschichte und Altes Testament. FS A. Alt,
(Ed. G. EBELING), Tübingen, 1953, 179-209 = W. ZIMMERLI, Gottes Of-
fenbarung. Gesammelte Aufsätze zum Alten Testament, (ThB 19),
München, 1963, 11-40.

—, "Alttestamentliche Prophetie und Apokalyptic auf dem Wege zur
Rechtfertigung des Gottlosen", Rechfertigung. FS E. Käsemann,
(Ed. J. FRIEDRICH, W. PÖHLMANN, P. STUHLMACHER), Tübingen, 1976,
572-592.

—, 1 Mose 12-25. Abraham, (Zürcher Bibelkommentare, 1.2), Zürich,
1976.

NB. T = Table between pages 30 and 31.